COLLECTED WRITINGS OF W. D. GANN

VOLUME 1

COLLECTED MARKETING BROCHURES

INTERVIEWS & ARTICLES

ANNUAL FORECASTS & TRADING RECORDS

BY

WILLIAM D. GANN

COSMOLOGICAL ECONOMICS
WWW.COSMOECONOMICS.COM

THIS SERIES IS PUBLISHED BY THE:

INSTITUTE OF COSMOLOGICAL ECONOMICS

COSMOLOGICAL ECONOMICS
IS AN IMPRINT OF:

SACRED SCIENCE INSTITUTE

WWW.SACREDSCIENCE.COM

INSTITUTE@SACREDSCIENCE.COM

US: 800-756-6141 ϴ INTL: 951-659-8181

COSMOLOGICAL ECONOMICS

THE MASTERS OF TECHNICAL ANALYSIS SERIES

The Masters of Technical Analysis Series brings together a collection of the most important classical and modern works on technical analysis and financial market forecasting. These classic works from the Golden Age of Technical Analysis were carefully selected by the late Dr. Jerome Baumring of the Investment Centre Bookstore in the 1980's, as representing the most valuable and important works in technical analysis ever written. They were included as the foundational source texts for his program in advanced financial market analysis and forecasting, and serve as the ideal foundation for any analyst seeking a thorough education in market theory and technical trading.

The Golden Age of technical analysis was a period from the early 1900's through the 1960's where the foundational theories of modern financial analysis were initially developed. The ideas and technologies developed during this fruitful period have formed the basis for most modern technical market theory, which is considered to be mostly a repetition or reworking of these past ideas and techniques developed by the Old Masters of the Golden Age. In these historical works can be found the timeless trading wisdom which has laid the foundation for all modern investment theory and literature. These techniques are as useful in today's markets as they were in the past, providing rare and valuable insights, tools and strategies that give the modern trader an edge over traders and investors that are unaware of these time honored tools.

Each quality reprint of these classical texts has been reproduced as an exact facsimile of the original text, maintaining the original layout, typeset, charts, and style of the author and time period, helping to preserve and communicate a sense of the feeling of the original work that a reproduction in modern format does not capture. Many of these rare works and courses were originally printed in only very small private editions or as correspondence courses, so that the originals were easily lost or destroyed over time. Our reproductions of these important source works have been printed on acid free paper and bound in a quality hardcover format that will compliment any trading library and help to preserve this important resource for generations to come.

The series is also currently being digitized and archived for permanent digital preservation by the Institute of Cosmological Economics, creating a searchable reference library of market wisdom accessible globally and available in new digital formats to keep the knowledge fresh and accessible through new devices and technology as we advance further into the information revolution. To see our full catalog of hardcover reprints, new publications, and digital editions please visit our website at www.CosmoEconomics.com.

Market Brochures
Interviews And Articles
Annual Forecasts
Trading Records
W. D. Gann

This collection of writings contains an assortment of marketing brochures which were used by Gann to market his courses and services, annual forecasts for a year in advance, interviews with Gann and articles about him, and a selection of his trading records. These writings are very enlightening, explaining in clearer words than in his books and courses, Gann's methodology and vision of the markets. There are important clues in these writings to Gann's background research and to the importance and purpose of each of his courses. They also help to draw a personal portrait of the Master himself. Included is a smattering of rare Master Charts to titillate the imagination.

MARKETING BROCHURES

- Science and Stock
- Supply and Demand Letter
- Mathematical Formula for Market Predictions
- How I Forecast Stock, Cotton, and Grain Markets
- Scientific Stock Forecasting or Large Profits on Small Risks
- Satisfied Clients Tell You the Story of My Successful Service
- Investors! Up-To-Date Practical Complete Wall Street Education
- Learn Before You Lose or Why You Lose Money on Stocks and How to Make Profits
- Comparison of Dow Theory and W. D. Gann's Method in Dow Jones Industrial Averages

INTERVIEWS AND ARTICLES

- The Ticker and Investment Digest, 1909
- A Brighter Outlook for the Stock Market and General Business Conditions, 1921
- Gann Foretold Run of Stocks, 1922
- Poor Business, Damaged Crops, Strikes and Bank Failures in 1923 Predicted by Profit.
- Gann to Tour Country by Plane For Broad business Survey, 1933

ANNUAL FORECASTS

- Annual Forecast for 1919
- Annual Forecast for 1920
- Annual Forecast for 1921
- Annual Forecast for 1922
- Annual Forecast for 1929
- Annual Forecast for 1933
- Annual Forecast for 1934
- Annual Forecast for 1935

TRADING RECORDS

- Trading Records for 1933
- Trading Records for 1934
- Trading Records for 1935
- Trading Records for DJIA 1897-1939
- Trading Recrods for DJIA 1897-1914

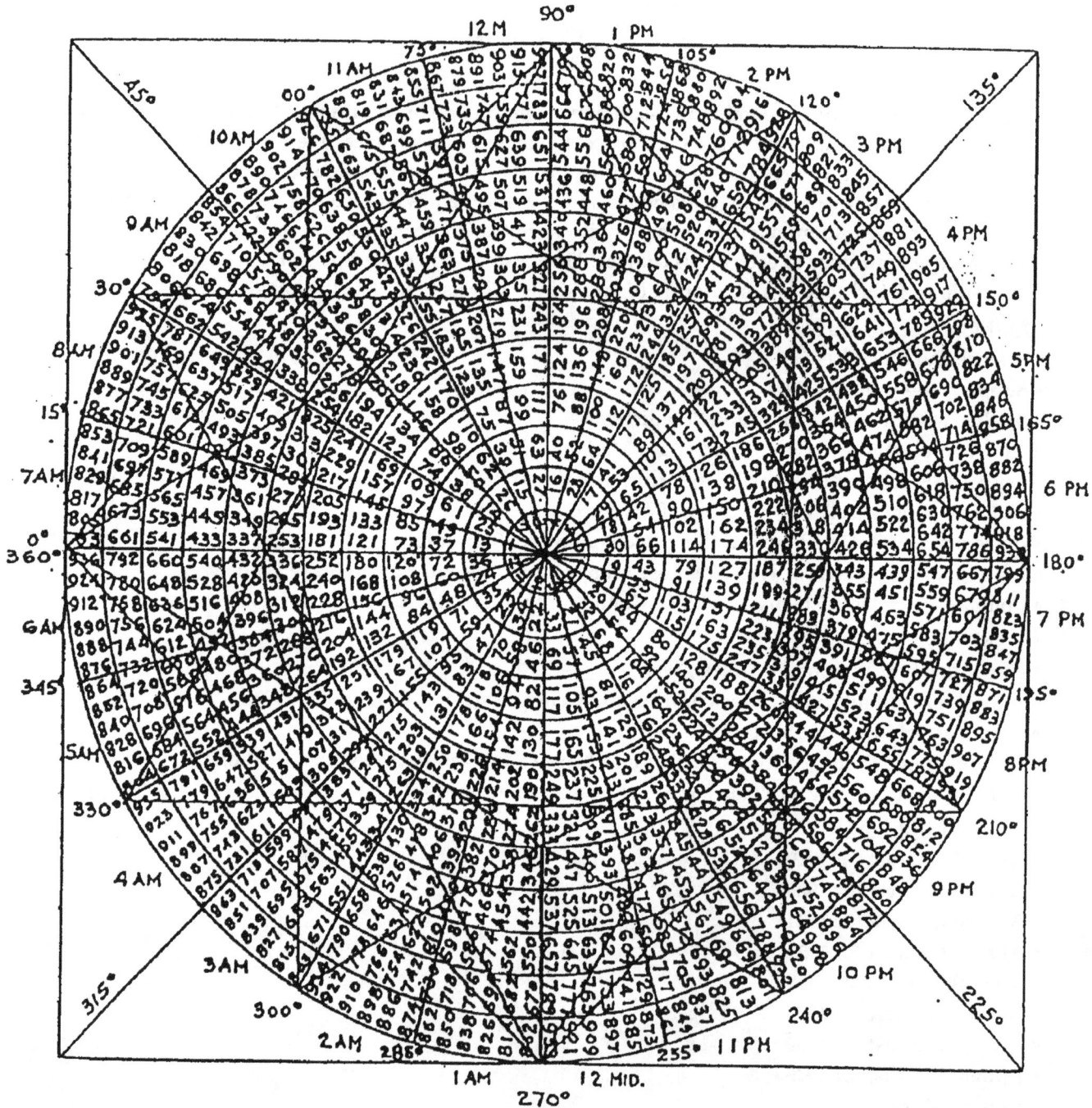

SCIENTIFIC STOCK FORECASTING

or

LARGE PROFITS ON SMALL RISKS

"Prove all things and hold fast to that which is good."

The man who guesses and gambles on hope is sure to lose, while the man who follows Science and buys when insiders buy and sells when insiders sell makes profits. The proof of the pudding is in the eating. Time proves all things, even when stocks and commodities make tops and bottoms. With our Master Time Factor we are able to tell long before important events take place when stocks and commodities will reach high or low, because we know by mathematical science when time cycles repeat. These valuable rules are all in the Bible if you know where to find them.

●

W. D. GANN'S RECORD

We publish the record of W. D. Gann's achievement in Wall Street and what others have said and written about him in order that you may judge for yourself the value of Mr. Gann's Service to you. The Bible says that we should judge the future by the past. W. D. Gann has made a record for accuracy that warrants you in following his advice in the future.

●

35 Years in Wall Street

W. D. Gann has devoted over 35 years to study and research and has spent over $300,000 to develop a dependable method based on mathematical science that will determine the trend of stocks and commodities. Let us review his record:

Mr. Gann came to New York in 1908. He has been established in New York for 28 years, doing business under his own name, and has issued Stock Forecasts to the public for 19 years. These Forecasts have proved remarkably accurate and investors and traders have profited by his advice.

In 1909 he forecast the exact day and almost the exact price at which the Dow-Jones railroad and industrial stock averages would sell in the month of August. This record was published in the Ticker Magazine in December, 1909. This magazine and other magazines and newspapers throughout the country commented on Mr. Gann's remarkable forecasts and trading record.

We reproduce on the opposite page an article that appeared in the "Ticker Magazine" (now the "Magazine of Wall Street") in December, 1909. The article was written by the editor, the late R. D. Wyckoff.

THE
TICKER
INVESTMENT AND DIGEST

| Investment: The placing of capital in a more or less permanent way, mainly for the income to be derived therefrom. | Speculation: Operations wherein intelligent foresight is employed for the purpose of deriving a profit from price changes. |

| Vol 5 | DECEMBER, 1909 | No. 2 |

WILLIAM D. GANN

An Operator Whose Science and Ability Place Him in the Front Rank—
His Remarkable Predictions and Trading Record.

SOMETIME ago the attention of this magazine was attracted by certain long pull stock market predictions which were being made by William D. Gann. In a large number of cases Mr. Gann gave us in advance the exact points at which certain stocks and commodities would sell, together with prices close to the then prevailing figures which would not be touched.

For instance, when New York Central was 131 he predicted that it would sell at 145 before 129.

So repeatedly did his figures prove to be accurate, and so different did his work appear from that of any expert whose methods we had examined, that we set about to investigate Mr. Gann and his way of figuring out these predictions, as well as the particular use which he was making of them in the market.

The results of this investigation are remarkable in many ways.

It appears to be a fact that Mr. Gann has developed an entirely new idea as to the principles governing stock market movements. He bases his operations upon certain natural laws, which, though existing since the world began, have only in recent years been subjected to the will of man, and added to the list of so-called modern discoveries.

We have asked Mr. Gann for an outline of his work and have secured some remarkable evidence as to the results obtained therefrom. We submit this in full recognition of the fact that in Wall Street a man with a new idea—an idea which violates the traditions and encourages a scientific view of the proposition—is not usually welcomed by the majority, for the reason that he stimulates thought and research. These activities said majority abhors.

Mr. Gann's description of his experience and methods is given herewith. It should be read with a recognition of the established fact that Mr. Gann's predictions have proved correct in a large majority of instances.

"For the past ten years I have devoted my entire time and attention to the speculative markets. Like many others, I lost thousands of dollars and experienced the usual ups and downs incidental to the novice who enters the market without preparatory knowledge of the subject.

"I soon began to realize that all successful men, whether lawyers, doctors, or scientists, devoted years of time to the study and investigation of their particular pursuit or profession before attempting to make any money out of it.

"Being in the brokerage business myself and handling large accounts, I had opportunities seldom afforded the ordinary man for studying the cause of success and failure in the speculations of others. I found that over ninety per cent of the traders who go into the market without knowledge or study usually lose in the end.

"I soon began to note the periodical

3

recurrence of the rise and fall in stocks and commodities. This led me to conclude that natural law was the basis of market movements. I then decided to devote ten years of my life to the study of natural law as applicable to the speculative markets and to devote my best energies toward making speculation a profitable profession. After exhaustive researches and investigations of the known sciences, I discovered that the Law of Vibration enabled me to accurately determine the exact points to which stocks or commodities should rise and fall within a given time. The working out of this law determines the cause and predicts the effect long before the Street is aware of either. Most speculators can testify to the fact that it is looking at the effect and ignoring the cause that has produced their losses.

"It is impossible here to give an adequate idea of the Law of Vibration as I apply it to the markets, however, the layman may be able to grasp some of the principles when I state that the Law of Vibration is the fundamental law upon which wireless telegraphy, wireless telephones and phonographs are based. Without the existence of this law the above inventions would have been impossible.

"In order to test out the efficiency of my idea I have not only put in years of labor in the regular way, but I spent nine months working night and day in the Astor Library of New York and in the British Museum of London, going over the records of stock transactions as far back at 1820. I have incidentally examined the manipulations of Jay Gould, Daniel Drew, Commodore Vanderbilt and all the other important Wall Street manipulators from that time to the present day. I have examined every quotation of Union Pacific prior to and from the time of E. H. Harriman's securing control, and can say that of all the manipulations in the history of Wall Street, Mr. Harriman's was the most masterly. The figures show that, whether unconsciously or not, Mr. Harriman worked strictly in accordance with natural law.

"In going over the history of markets and the great mass of related statistics, it soon becomes apparent that certain laws govern the changes and variations in the value of stocks and there exists a periodic or cyclic law, which is at the back of all these movements. Observation has shown that there are regular periods of intense activity on the Exchange followed by periods of inactivity. Mr. Henry Hall, in his recent book devoted much space to 'Cycles of Prosperity and Depression' which he found recurring at regular intervals of time. The law which I have applied will not only give these long cycles or swings, but the daily and even hourly movements of stocks. By knowing the exact vibration of each individual stock I am able to determine at what point each will receive support and at what point the greatest resistance is to be met.

"Those in close touch with the markets have noticed the phenomena of ebb and flow, or rise and fall in the value of stocks. At certain times a stock will become intensely active, large transactions being made in it; at other times this same stock will become practically stationary or inactive with a very small volume of sales. I have found that the Law of Vibration governs and controls these conditions. I have also found that certain phases of this law govern the rise in a stock and an entirely different rule operates on the decline.

"While Union Pacific and other railroad stocks which made their high prices in August were declining, United States Steel common was steadily advancing. The Law of Vibration was at work, sending a particular stock on the upward trend, whilst others were trending downward.

"I have found that in the stock itself exists its harmonic or inharmonic relationship to the driving power or force behind it. The secret of all its activity is therefore apparent. By my method I can determine the vibration of each stock and by also taking certain time values into consideration I can in the majority of cases tell exactly what the stock will do under given conditions.

"The power to determine the trend of the market is due to my knowledge of the characteristics of each individual stock and a certain grouping of different stocks under their proper rates of vibration. Stocks are like electrons, atoms, and molecules, which hold persistently to their own individuality in response to the fundamental Law of Vibration. Science teaches 'that an original impulse of any kind finally resolves itself into periodic or rhythmical motion,' also 'just as the pendulum returns again in its swing, just as the moon returns in its orbit, just as the advancing year ever brings the rose of spring, so do the properties of the elements periodically recur as the weight of the atoms rises.'

"From my extensive investigations, studies and applied tests, I find that not only do the various stocks vibrate, but that the driving forces controlling the stocks are also in a state of vibration. These vibratory forces can only be known by the movements they generate on the stocks and their values in the market. Since all great swings or movements of the market are cyclic they act in accordance with the periodic law.

"Science has laid down the principle that 'the properties of an element are a periodic function of its atomic weight.' A famous scientist has stated that 'we are brought to the conviction that diversity in phenomenal nature in its different kingdoms, is most intimately associated with numerical relationship. The numbers are not intermixed, chaotically and accidentally, but are subject to regular periodicity. The changes and developments are also seen to be in many cases undulatory.'

"Thus, I affirm, every class of phenomena, whether in nature or in the stock market, must be subject to the universal law of causation and harmony. Every effect must have an adequate cause.

"If we wish to avert failure in speculation we must deal with causes. Everything in existence is based on exact proportion and perfect relationship. There is no chance in nature, because mathematical principles of the highest order lie at the foundation of all things. Faraday said: 'There is nothing in the Universe but mathematical points of force.'

"Vibration is fundamental; nothing is exempt from this law; it is universal, therefore applicable to every class of phenomena on the globe.

"Through the Law of Vibration every stock in the market moves in its own distinctive sphere of activities, as to intensity, volume and direction; all the essential qualities of its evolution are characterized in its own rate of vibration. Stocks, like atoms, are really centers of energies, therefore they are controlled mathematically. Stocks create their own field of action and power; power to attract and repel, which principle explains why certain stocks at times lead the market and

'turn dead' at other times. Thus to speculate scientifically it is absolutely necessary to follow natural law.

"After years of patient study I have proven to my entire satisfaction as well as demonstrated to others that vibration explains every possible phase and condition of the market."

In order to substantiate Mr. Gann's claims as to what he has been able to do under this method, we called upon Mr. William E. Gilley, an Inspector of Imports, 16 Beaver street, New York. Mr. Gilley is well-known in the down-town district. He himself has studied stock market movements for twenty-five years, during which time he has examined every piece of market literature that has been issued and procurable in Wall Street. It was he who encouraged Mr. Gann to study out the scientific and mathematical possibilities of the subject. When asked what had been the most impressive of Mr. Gann's work and predictions, he replied as follows:

"It is very difficult for me to remember all the predictions and operations of Mr. Gann which may be classed as phenomenal, but the following are a few: In 1908 when Union Pacific was 168⅛ he told me that it would not touch 169 before it had a good break. We sold it short all the way down to 152⅝, covering on the weak spots and putting it out again on the rallies, securing twenty-three points profit out of an eighteen-point move.

"He came to me when United States Steel was selling around 50 and said 'This Steel will run up to 58 but it will not sell at 59. From there it should break 16¾ points. We sold it short around 58⅜ with a stop at 59. The highest it went was 58¾. From there it declined to 41¼—17½ points.

"At another time wheat was selling at about 89c. He predicted that the May option would sell at $1.35. We bought it and made large profits on the way up. It actually touched $1.35½.

"When Union Pacific was 172, he said it would go to 184⅞ but not an eighth higher until it had had a good break. It went to 184⅞ and came back from there eight or nine times. We sold it short repeatedly with a stop at 185 and were never caught. It eventually came back to 172½.

"Mr. Gann's calculations are based on natural law. I have followed his work closely for years. I know that he has a firm grasp of the basic principles which govern stock market movements, and I do not believe any other man on earth can duplicate the idea or his method at the present time.

"Early this year he figured that the top of the advance would fall on a certain day in August and calculated the prices at which the Dow-Jones averages would then stand. The market culminated on the exact day and within four-tenths of one per cent. of the figures predicted."

"You and Mr. Gann must have cleaned up considerable money on all these operations," was suggested.

"Yes, we have made a great deal of money. He has taken half a million dollars out of the market in the past few years. I once saw him take $130, and in less than one month run it up to cover $12,000. He can compound money faster than any man I ever met."

"One of the most astonishing calculations made by Mr. Gann was during last summer (1909) when he predicted that September wheat would sell at $1.20. This meant that it must touch that figure before the end of the month of September. At twelve o'clock, Chicago time, on September 30th (the last day) the option was selling below $1.08, and it looked as though his prediction would not be fulfilled. Mr. Gann said 'If it does not touch $1.20 by the close of the market it will prove that there is something wrong with my whole method of calculation. I do not care what the price is now, it must go there.' It is common history that September wheat surprised the whole country by selling at $1.20 and no higher in the very last hour of the trading, closing at that figure.

So much for what Mr. Gann has said and done as evidenced by himself and others. Now as to what demonstrations have taken place before our representative:

During the month of October, 1909, in twenty-five market days, Mr. Gann made, in the presence of our representative, two hundred and eighty-six transactions in various stocks, on both the long and short side of the market. Two hundred and sixty-four of these transactions resulted in profits; twenty-two in losses.

The capital with which he operated was doubled ten times, so that at the end of the month he had one thousand per cent. of his original margin.

In our presence Mr. Gann sold Steel common short at 94⅞, saying that it would not go to 95. It did not.

On a drive which occurred during the week ending October 29th, Mr. Gann bought Steel common at 86¼, saying that it would not go to 86. The lowest it sold was 86⅛.

We have seen him give in one day sixteen successive orders in the same stock, eight of which turned out to be either the top or the bottom eighth of that particular swing. The above we can positively verify.

Such performances as these, coupled with the foregoing, are probably unparalleled in the history of the Street.

James R. Keene has said, "The man who is right six times out of ten will make his fortune." Here is a trader, who, without any attempt to make a showing (for he did not know the results were to be published), establishes a record of over ninety-two per cent profitable trades.

Mr. Gann has refused to disclose his method at any price, but to those scientifically inclined he has unquestionably added to the stock of Wall Street knowledge and pointed out infinite possibilities.

We have requested Mr. Gann to figure out for the readers of The Ticker a few of the most striking indications which appear in his calculations. In presenting these we wish it understood that no man, in or out of Wall Street, is infallible.

Mr. Gann's figures at present indicate that the trend of the stock market should, barring the usual rallies, be toward lower prices until March or April, 1910.

He calculates that May wheat, which is now selling at $1.02, should not sell below 99c. and should sell at $1.45 next spring.

On cotton, which is now at about the 15c. level, he estimates that, after a good reaction from these prices, the commodity should reach 18c. in the spring of 1910. He looks for a corner in the March or May option.

Whether these figures prove correct or not, will in no sense detract from the record which Mr. Gann has already established.

Mr. Gann was born in Lufkin, Texas, and is thirty-one years of age. He is a gifted mathematician, has an extraordinary memory for figures, and is an expert Tape Reader. Take away his science and he would beat the market on his intuitive tape reading alone.

Endowed as he is with such qualities, we have no hesitation in predicting that within a comparatively few years Wm. D. Gann will receive full recognition as one of Wall Street's leading operators.   R. D. W.

Note—Since the above forecast was made, Cotton has suffered the expected decline, the extreme break having been 120 points. The lowest on May wheat thus far has been $1.01⅛. It is now selling at $1.06¼.

•

In 1912 Mr. Gann forecast the election of Woodrow Wilson and has been correct in forecasting the election of every President since that time. Many of these forecasts have been published in newspapers throughout the country.

In the spring of 1918 Mr. Gann forecast the end of the World War. This forecast was sent out to newspapers throughout the country, and in January, 1919, the New York Herald and other papers gave Mr. Gann credit for forecasting the end of the war and the Kaiser's abdication.

In his 1919 Annual Stock Forecast, issued late in 1918, he forecast a big bull market for 1919 and especially referred to a boom in oil stocks.

His Stock Forecasts for 1920 and 1921 indicated a bear market with sharp declines. The 1921 Forecast called the exact date for bottom on stocks in August, 1921.

In 1923 Mr. Gann wrote "Truth of the Stock Tape" and forecast a big advance in chemical and airplane stocks, which followed during the Coolidge bull campaign. This book has been reviewed by newspapers and magazines throughout the country and favorably commented on by college professors, business men, investors and traders, all of whom agree that it is the best book ever written on the subject.

His Stock Forecasts for 1924 and 1925 outlined the bull market which followed.

In the spring of 1927, Mr. Gann wrote "The Tunnel Thru the Air, or Looking back From 1940," which contained many remarkable forecasts in regard to stocks and commodities and world events which have been fulfilled. In this book Mr. Gann said that from 1929 to 1932 there would be the worst panic in the world's history. Writing under date of "October 3, 1931" on page 323, he said, "The New York Stock Exchange closed to prevent complete panic because the people were panic-strcken and selling stocks regardless of price." It is a matter of history that the New York Stock Exchange did consider closing on October 3 to 5, but decided to stop short selling. The low of that panicky decline was reached on October 5 and a rally of 33 points in industrial stock averages followed to November 9, 1931.

His 1929 Stock Forecast, issued on November 23, 1928, and based on his Master Time Factor, indicated the end of the full market in August and early September, 1929. He stated in no uncertain terms that the panic would start in September, 1929, and that it would be a great deluge with a Black Friday. We quote from the Forecast:

"AUGUST—A few of the late movers will advance this month and reach final high. * * * Unfavorable news will develop which will start declines and the long bull campaign will come to a sudden end. Money rates will be high and final top will be reached for a big bear campaign. Stand from under! Don't get caught in the great deluge! Remember it is too late to sell when everyone is trying to sell. * * *

"SEPTEMBER—One of the sharpest declines of the year is indicated. There will be loss of confidence by investors, and the public will try to get out after it is too late. Storms will damage crops and the general business outlook will become cloudy. War news will upset the market and unfavorable developments in foreign countries. A 'Black Friday' is indicated and a panicky decline in stocks with only small rallies. The short side will prove the most profitable. You should sell short and pyramid on the way down."

In the spring of 1930, Mr. Gann wrote "Wall Street Stock Selector," which was published in June, 1930. In this book he had a chapter headed, "Investors' Panic," which described conditions just as they occurred during 1931, 1932 and 1933. We quote from the book, pages 203-04:

"The coming investors' panic will be the greatest in history, because there are at least 15 to 25 million investors in the United States who hold stocks in the leading corporations, and when once they get scared, which they will after years of decline, then the selling will be so terrific that no buying power can withstand it. Stocks are so well distributed in the hands of the public that since the 1929 panic many people think that the market is panic-proof, but this seeming strength is really the weakest feature of the market. * * *

"Love of money has been the cause of all financial troubles and depressions in the past, and the coming panic will be the greatest the world has ever known, because there is more money in the United States than ever before, therefore more to fight for."

Thousands of people have bought this book and profited by reading and studying it. The book has been favorably commented on by such papers as The Financial Times of London, England, Wall Street Journal, New York Daily Investment News, Coast Investor, and many other newspapers and magazines throughout the world.

On February 10, 1932, Mr. Gann said that stocks were bottom for a big rally. His 1932 Stock Forecast, issued October 21, 1931, called March 8 for last top for another big decline. During the latter part of June, 1932, and early July he strongly advised buying stocks, stating that final bottom had been reached, as shown by his market letter issued July 8, the day that most stocks reached final bottom. We quote from page 6 of the 1932 Forecast:

"The latter part of June, July, August and September are the most active and bullish months of the year, when sharp advances will be recorded. First extreme high is indicated around September 20 to 21, when stocks should make extreme high for the year. Then follows a decline, reaching bottom around October 4 to 5."

Between July 8 and September 8 many stocks advanced 20 to 60 points. The market reached high of a secondary rally on September 23, from which a big decline followed, making low in the latter part of November and early December, as indicated in the Forecast.

On March 1, 1933, by the use of his Master Time Factor Mr. Gann forecast bottom for stocks and commodities and advised buying for a big advance, as shown by the market letters issued March 1 and 3 given below. This is another proof of the great value of Mr. Gann's discovery of a Master Time Factor.

•

MARKET LETTERS AT A CRITICAL TIME

STOCK LETTER
Advice for Thursday and Friday's Markets
March 1, 1933.

The stock market received good support on Tuesday despite unfavorable news of bank failures and bank holidays. Today there were more bank holidays and suspension of payment of deposits, but the market gave a wonderful demonstration of strength, rallying several points and closing at the top of the day.

The bad news is out and the market has been discounting it since the middle of January. It is the old, old story: When news is out and everybody knows it, it is too late to act on it. It always pays to buy when things look the worst and to sell when they look the best. Very few people would believe me if I told them now how high stocks would sell a few months later, just as they would not believe in the early part of last July that stocks would go up 40 to 50 points in as many days. Now is the time to have faith in America and to buy stocks to hold for the long pull! We are at the turning point and the stock market always blazes the trail for business to follow.

STOCK LETTER
Advice for Week Beginning
March 6, 1933

March 3, 1933.

The stock market gave an excellent account of itself the past week, standing up against the worst banking news that we have had since 1907, which indicates—as I have told you for some time—that the big people hold the stocks and are not going to be frightened into selling them. They know that the worst is over and that better times are ahead. President Roosevelt will speedily inaugurate a constructive program which will restore confidence and start a buying wave throughout the country. Most stocks are selling far below their intrinsic value. This was demonstrated today when shorts, who had pounded the market all the week started to cover, bringing about a sharp rally of 3 to 7 points.

The Dow-Jones 30 Industrial averages failed to break 49 and rallied above 54. We are confident that they have seen the final bottom and expect these averages to advance above 70 before declining below 50. Crossing 56 will indicate 65 and crossing 66 will indicate much higher. The railroad averages have held remarkably strong throughout the decline, failing to break 23. We do not expect this level to be reached. Crossing 26 will be the signal for higher prices and crossing 28 will indicate much higher.

The Public Utility averages indicate final bottom and crossing 24 will indicate much higher.

The Herald Tribune averages on 100 stocks failed to break 79. We don't expect this level to be reached. Crossing 83 will indicate higher prices.

We strongly advise holding all long stocks or buying some of the best stocks on the list without waiting for much reaction.

Expect some very bullish news next Monday or Tuesday which will cause increased activity and higher prices. The extreme high for the week should be reached on Friday afternoon or Saturday morning.

SPECIAL LETTER
The Spirit That Made America
Still Lives

March 4, 1933.

The banks in New York City, Chicago and the greater part of the United States will be closed Saturday, March 4, and Monday, March 6, and some of them probably longer, but this need not worry anyone. The action now taken by financial leaders and the action that will be taken by President Roosevelt after he takes office at noon today will mark the end of this depression, in my opinion. This opinion is based upon a scientific study of time cycles, which indicate that a crisis always marks the end of a depression and then the turn comes quickly, just as in September, 1929, stocks were skyrocketing and suddenly out of a clear blue sky the crash developed. We are now at the other extreme, all unfavorable factors discounted.

America is the greatest country in the world and the spirit that made it the greatest country in the world still lives. The spirit of the Americans that won the Revolution in 1776 and made this the greatest independent country in the world was the same spirit and the same indomitable courage that united this country after the Civil War, when men went back to their homes hungry and barefoot and began to reconstruct and build the new South. This country has passed through many crises and has always emerged stronger and better. This will be no exception. America is going to lead the world out of the depression, and this seeming dark cloud has a silver lining.

It is the duty of every one of us to cooperate with President Roosevelt and his Administration; have the same faith, the same confidence that we would if America was surrounded on the east, on the north, on the west, and on the south by foreign foes. Under those conditions, we would leave every cent of our money in the banks; we would sacrifice everything we had to save the country. That is what we should do now—leave our money in the banks. Those who have withdrawn should put their money back in the bank, because it is going to be safe there. No one man or group of men can do everything to restore prosperity. We must all do our part and President Roosevelt will steer the Ship of State to safety.

I believe that before the Exchange opens next Tuesday some very constructive measures will be taken and that public confidence will be restored and that stocks will go very much higher. The shorts are trapped. The bears will be taught the old saying that he who sells what isn't his'n must buy one day or go to prison, and "A good thing to remember, and a better thing to do, is to work with the constructive forces and not with the wrecking crew." Money is not everything, and the man who sacrifices his country's interest and is so unpatriotic as to sell stocks short in a crisis and try to wreck the country, is the man who must pay for his selfishness.

Should the United States through any government action, go off the gold standard, it will be bullish and start a wave of prosperity throughout this country, because foreign countries can then buy our goods. Going off the gold standard would produce inflation in commodities and wheat and cotton would go sky-rocketing.

I believe that the news between now and next Tuesday will be constructive and bullish. I advise you to hold your stocks or your commodities and not try to withdraw your money from the banks, for in doing so you will only make bad matters worse for yourself and others. In a few months you will look back on March 4th as the day when the tide turned and America started back on the royal road to prosperity!

W. D. GANN.

●

KEEPING UP TO DATE

Mr. Gann has always been progressive and believes in keeping up to date. In April, 1933, he bought a specially equipped airplane for making crop surveys. Many of the newspapers throughout the country commented on this progressive step. The following article appeared in the. New York Daily Investment News, May 26, 1933:

NEW YORK DAILY INVESTMENT NEWS

GANN TO TOUR COUNTRY BY PLANE FOR BROAD BUSINESS SURVEY

Wayne, Mich., May 25.—W. D. Gann, stock market analyst, of 99 Wall St., today left here for New York with the first 1933 model Stinson Reliant plane, piloted by Elinor Smith, woman aviator.

Mr. Gann will use the plane for an extensive tour of the country during which he will study cotton, wheat and tobacco crop and business conditions. He will leave on this tour early in June.

The forecaster expects to make speed in the gathering of first hand information on business conditions by use of the airplane.

The plane is equipped with blind-flying apparatus, extra-large fuel tanks to afford a flying range of 750 miles and with radio receiving equipment. The plane is powered with a Lycoming engine and is capable of 135 miles per hour.

By receiving radio advices on market conditions, Mr. Gann calculates that he will be able at all times to gauge his operations in the markets and send up-to-the-minute advise to his clients, even though he is many miles away from his Wall Street office.

As far as is known, Mr. Gann will be the first Wall Street adviser to use a plane as part of his equipment in studying market conditions.

The recent burst of activity in the markets, following the closing of the banks and leading stock and commodity exchanges, prompted the analyst to buy the plane.

He decided that rapid-changing conditions made it necessary for him to gather his data on crops and business at first hand.

Mr. Gann is a member of the Commodity Exchange, Inc., and also of the New Orleans Cotton Exchange. During his tour of the country he will visit the cotton belt in the south and southwest, the tobacco fields in the south, and the wheat stand in the middle west.

At all times during the trip he will communicate regularly with his office by wire and by radio. He expects to make talks in various cities to Kiwanis and Rotary Clubs, chambers of commerce and other business organizations.

His itinerary will include the following cities:

Washington, D. C.; Richmond, Va.; Raleigh, N. C.; Atlanta, Ga.; Birmingham, Ala.; Memphis, Tenn.; New Orleans, La.; Little Rock, Ark.; Houston and Dallas, Texas; St. Louis, Detroit and Chicago.

•

1933 STOCK FORECAST:

Mr. Gann's 1933 Stock Forecast called for top July 17 and a sharp decline to July 21. Stocks reached high on July 17 and a wide-open break followed, with the average down 25 points in 4 days.

1934 STOCK FORECAST:

His 1934 Forecast indicated top for February 13th and the high was reached on averages February 5th and 15th. The next low was indicated for May 11th to 12th, and the market made low on May 14th. The next top was indicated for June 22nd; stocks reached high on June 19th. The last low for 1934 was forecast for July 21st to 23rd and the extreme low of the year was reached on July 26th. The Forecast called for the last top for September 8th to 10th, and stocks reached top of the rally on September 6th. A reaction followed to September 17th, the exact date indicated in the Forecast for low. The next top was forecast for October 5th and 6th and the industrial averages reached top October 11th. The next bottom was called for October 23rd to 24th and the lows were reached October 26th. The next top was indicated, according to the Forecast, for December 4th to 5th. The averages reached top on December 6th and a reaction followed. The Forecast indicated high for the end of December and the averages reached high for the month on December 31st.

•

A CROP SURVEY IN SOUTH AMERICA

In the early part of March, 1935, Mr. Gann made a trip to South America to study crop conditions and get first hand information on the increase in production of cotton in Peru, Chile, Argentine, and Brazil. On this trip he covered about 18,000 miles by airplane and more than 1,000 miles by automobile, driving into the country to see the conditions of soil and the possibilities for increased production of Wheat, Corn and Cotton, which will influence prices in the United States market by underselling, due to lower cost of labor in Argentine and Brazil. While in South America, Mr. Gann was interviewed by many newspapers.

11

We reproduce part of an article which appeared in the Beunos Aires Herald, March 21, 1935.

BUENOS AIRES HERALD

Thursday, March 21, 1935

SCIENCE AND STOCK

An Astonishing Claims

Records of 1,000 Years

THE man who guesses and gambles on hope is sure to lose, while the man who follows science makes profits. There is cause and effect for everything and by time element and the cycle theory everything can be mathematically determined.

Mr. W. D. Gann, member of the New Orleans Cotton Exchange and the Rubber Exchange of New York, who stated that he has devoted over 30 years to study of time cycles and spent $300,000 (U.S.) to develop a dependable method based on mathematical science that will determine the trend of stocks and commodities. The success attending his methods he asserts, are borne out by his own good fortune on the American markets, and his accuracy in forecasting the futures markets for the past twenty years has been very widely commented upon in the Press in all parts of the United States.

Mr. Gann told a HERALD reporter yesterday that he has carried his records of grain back over 1,000 years and cotton records nearly 400 years. The former he was able to gather the most accurate information about from old British records, while in his search for cotton cycles he visited Egypt and India. More recently he has used his own aeroplane extensively in America for getting round the country quickly to make forecasts on the cotton crops.

●

1935 STOCK FORECAST:

His 1935 Forecast indicated first top for January 9th to 10th and the high was reached on January 7th. The next top was forecast for February 13th. The actual highs were reached February 18th, from which a sharp decline followed, making low for the year on March 18th. The Forecast called for the last low on March 28th, and the averages made a second low on March 25th. From the low in March, the Forecast indicated a big advance of at least 32 points in the Dow-Jones Industrial averages.

August 28th and 29th indicated top for a reaction. The averages reached top on August 27th and then reacted. The Forecast called for the next top September 12th to 15th. High on the averages was reached September 11th. The Forecast indicated the next bottom for September 24th to 25th; the last low was made September 20th and 26th.

The Forecast called for top October 26th to 28th, and the averages reached high on October 28th, which was the high of the year up to that time. The Forecast indicated November 15th to 16th as the last high of the year. The actual high of the Dow-Jones 30 Industrial averages was reached on November 20th, from which a reaction of 10 points on averages followed. The Forecast called for low December 9-10th and 23rd. The low of the reaction was made on December 16th and 19th. The Forecast called for a rally to December 31st, and this rally took place.

Mr. Gann has also been issuing Annual Forecasts on Cotton, Wheat and other commodities for many years. These Forecasts have shown the same percentage of accuracy that the Stock Forecasts have.

These Annual, Forecasts on Stocks, Cotton, and Grain are issued in October and November each year for the following year.

W. D. GANN MAKES PROFITS TRADING ACCORDING TO HIS OWN METHODS

Many ask the question, "If Mr. Gann can forecast the market accurately, why does he sell service or write market letters?" He has answered that question before, that he finds pleasure in giving his knowledge to help others who need help; money is not everything in life.

Below we publish a record taken from brokers' statements, showing the trades made by Mr. Gann during the past 3 years. This is proof that he can and does make money by following his own rules and methods. Before you buy a Market Letter Service or a course of instructions, get the record of actual trading by the man who is behind it, if he has not made money following his own advice, why should you pay money for it and follow it and risk your money?

W. D. GANN'S TRADING RECORD FOR 1933

From August 1 to December 31:
    Total number of trades—135—of which 112 showed profits and 23 losses.
    Percentage of accuracy on the total number of trades........................ 83%
    Percentage of profits to losses.. 89.9%
Total number of trades for the entire year of 1933: 479 trades, of which 422
    were profits and 57 showed losses.
    Percentage of accuracy.. 88.1%
    Percentage of profits on capital used........................ 4000% or 40 for 1

TRADING RECORD FOR 1934

From January 1 to December 31: Total number of trades—362.

	Trades			Profits				Losses
Cotton	147 trades,	of which		135	showed profits	and		12 losses
Grain	170 "	"	"	161	"	"	"	9 "
Rubber	23 "	"	"	21	"	"	"	2 "
Silver	7 "	"	"	7	"	"	"	0 "
Silk	4 "	"	"	3	"	"	"	1 "
Stocks	11 "	"	"	10	"	"	"	1 "

Total for yr. 362 trades, of which 337 showed profits and 25 losses.
    Percentage of accuracy on the total number of trades...................... 93.09%
    Percentage of profits to losses.. 93.10%
    Percentage of profits on capital used.................................... 800% or 8 for 1.

TRADING RECORD FOR 1935

Commodities:
    Total trades in Cotton, Grain and Rubber—98—of which 83 showed profits
        and 15 showed losses.
    Percentage of accuracy on total number of trades.................................. 85%
    Percentage of profits to losses.. 82%
    Percentage of profits on capital used.. 336%
Stocks:
    Total number of trades—34—of which 29 showed profits and 5 losses.
    Percentage of accuracy on total number of trades.............................. 85.5%
    Percentage of profits to losses.. 83%
    Percentage of profits on capital used 100%
    Such a record of accuracy proves that W. D. Gann has discovered a Master
Time Factor and Cycle Theory that works and can be depended upon in future.

NEW STOCK TREND DETECTOR

In December 1935, Mr. Gann wrote a new book, NEW STOCK TREND DETECTOR, bringing "Wall Street Stock Selector" up-to-date, with new rules never before published and a method of trading that formerly sold for $1000.00. This book covers changed conditions caused by the new Securities Exchange laws. It gives an example of trading in Chrysler Motors from 1925 to the end of 1935 and new rules on Volume of Sales. This book with the two former books will give you a valuable stock market education.

A SET OF TEXT BOOKS

TRUTH OF THE STOCK TAPE, alone, price $3.00. We have a few single copies on hand.

NEW STOCK TREND DETECTOR, alone, price $3.00. Contains 14 Charts.

TRUTH OF THE STOCK TAPE, WALL STREET STOCK SELECTOR and NEW STOCK TREND DETECTOR, together price, $8.00. The three books contain 55 valuable charts, proving the rules.

THE TUNNEL THRU THE AIR, free with order for the 3 books at $8.00, or TUNNEL THRU THE AIR, alone, $1.00.

With these books and rules you can learn how to select the best stocks to buy and detect the trend of new active leaders.

COURSES OF INSTRUCTION

Some readers of Mr. Gann's books want to take up his advanced courses after they have learned all they can from his books.

1936 MASTER FORECASTING METHOD: This course includes his Master Time Factor and Cycle Theory, enabling one to make up annual forecasts one year or more in advance on the general market or on individual stocks. It contains all his new discoveries made from 1933 to 1936. For the first time this method is in shape so that it can be taught by correspondence.

NEW MECHANICAL METHOD AND TREND INDICATOR: This Method is simple and based on fixed rules which can be learned in a very short time thru correspondence and the time required to keep it up is only 15 to 30 minutes each day. With this Method your trading indications are determined by fixed rules which tell you whether the trend is up or down; give you definite buying and selling points; tell you where to place a stop loss order to protect your principal and profits. This is the best method for a busy man.

If interested in these Courses, write for details.

PERSONAL SERVICE

Personal Service consists of a general supervision of your account. First, you advise us the amount of money you have to use for trading purposes; then we tell you the amount of stocks and commodities you should trade in; give you specific buying and selling instructions; advise you where to place stop loss orders and when to pyramid. We send you telegrams as often as necessary and write you personal letters.

This is not a market letter service. We never advise you to buy or sell more than one to three stocks at the same time. You report when you buy or sell anything. We keep a list of your holdings and watch them constantly and advise you by wire or letter just what to do. This Service entitles you to advice on Cotton, Grain or other commodities, if you wish to trade in them.

Price of this Service is $50 per month
$150 for three months
$275 for six months
$500 per year.

PART-OF-PROFITS PLAN: Instead of paying the full price of the subscription, you may pay $25 per month for Personal Service and agree to pay 5% of the net profits on the trades you make. With this proposition you must trade in not less than 100 shares and report promptly when you make trades according to our instructions.

When the markets are active, you should take this Service if the size of your account warrants it.

SUBSCRIPTION RATES

SUPPLY AND DEMAND LETTER:

Tri-weekly Stock Letter $15.00 per month, three months $40.00, six months $75.00, or $150.00 per year. Issued on Monday, Wednesday and Friday. Covers list of active and best stocks to trade in.

Weekly Stock Letter $6.00 per month, six months $33.00, or $60.00 per year. Issued every Friday. Contains outlook for the following week and trading recommendations on active stocks.

Tri-weekly Commodity Letter $15.00 per month, three months $40.00, six months $75.00, or $150.00 per year. Issued on Monday, Wednesday and Friday. Gives advice on Cotton, Wheat, Corn, Oats, Rye, Lard, Coffee and Sugar.

Weekly Commodity Letter $6.00 per month, six months $33.00, or $60.00 per year. Issued every Friday. Covers same commodities as the Tri-weekly Letter and contains forecast for the following week.

Combination rates:
Tri-weekly Stock and Commodity Letters $25.00 per month.
Weekly Stock and Commodity Letters $10.00 per month.

TELEGRAPH SERVICE:

Daily Telegraph Service on Stocks $30.00 per month, which includes the Tri-weekly Stock Letter. All messages sent collect in Private Code, which is furnishd free.

Daily Telegraph Service on Cotton $30.00 per month, including the Tri-weekly Commodity Letter.

Daily Telegraph Service on Grain $30.00 per month, including Letter.

Combined rate for telegrams on all commodities desired and stocks $45.00 per month.

Telegrams on important changes only, on stocks or commodities, $7.50 per month in addition to the price of the Tri-weekly or Weekly Letters.

Telegrams on important changes without Weekly or Tri-weekly Letter, $15.00 per month.

ANNUAL FORECASTS:

Annual Stock Forecast $100.00 per year.
Annual Cotton Forecast $100.00 per year.
Annual Grain Forecast $100.00 per year.
Annual Rubber Forecast, $100.00 per year.
Annual Coffee, Sugar and Cocoa Forecast $100.00 per year.

Supplements to all Forecasts are issued and mailed on the first of each month.

Prices of Annual Forecasts reduced on the first of each month.

Special Forecasst on Stocks or other Commodities made up on request.

All subscriptions payable in advance.

Mr. Gann is a member of the New Orleans Cotton Exchange and The Rubber Exchange of New York; member of the Royal Economic Society of London, and American Economic Society. He is a Christian and a member of the Masonic fraternity.

When you do business with W. D. Gann Scientific Service, Inc., you are dealing with an old-established reliable concern, with a record for accuracy that is excelled by none. Your interest is our interest. It has been well said: "He who serves best, prospers most." Our aim is to give you good service based on scientific knowledge and years of experience. Give our Service a trial and be convinced that we can help you to make profits.

W. D. GANN SCIENTIFIC SERVICE, INC.

88 Wall Street   New York, N. Y.

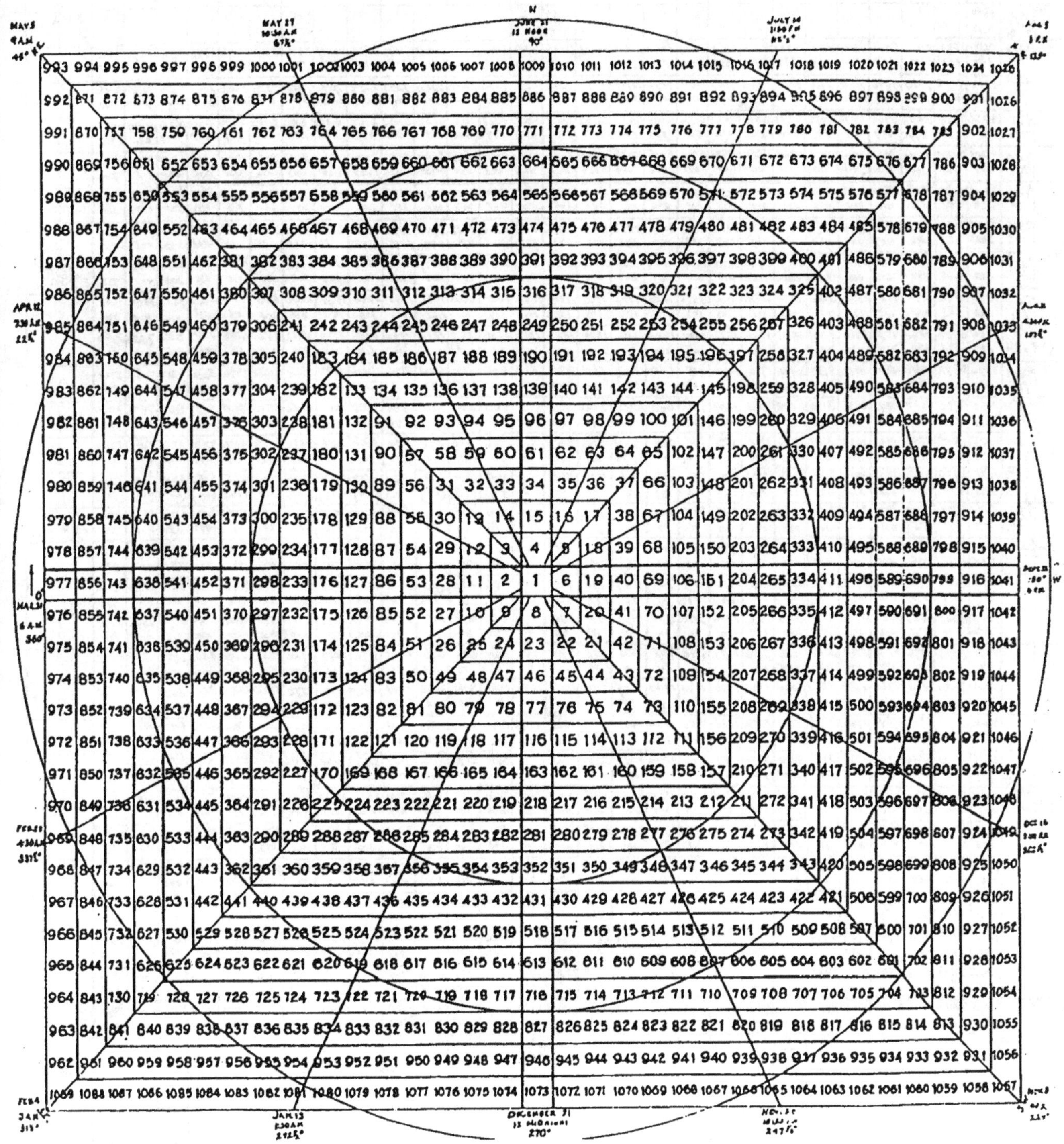

N

JUNE 21
12 NOON
90°

MAY 21
10:30 A.M.
67½°

JULY 24
1:30 P.M.
112½°

MAY 5
4 A.M.
45°

AUG 8
135°

APRIL 12
3 A.M.
112½°

MAR 21
6 A.M.
360°

FEB 21
4 A.M.
315°

SEPT 22
180°
W

OCT 16
10:30 A.M.
202½°

NOV 22
10:30
247½°

DECEMBER 21
12 MIDNIGHT
270°

JAN 13
8:30 A.M.
225°

FEB 4
JAN 5
315°

Master Price & Time Chart
for
Cotton, Coffee, Cocoa, Wool,
and Grains

HOW I FORECAST STOCK, COTTON, AND GRAIN MARKETS

Many people want to know what method I use to determine future indications on the markets. I keep charts of the various active stocks and also a set of averages. My charts are different from the charts kept by the average statistician because they are based on a discovery of my own. I have discovered a "time" factor that enables me to determine important tops and bottoms one year or more in advance. My Annual Forecasts on stocks, issued in December for ten years past, have proved remarkably correct.

I also keep special Time and Volume charts on stocks. My Volume charts enable me to tell when accumulation or distribution in stocks is taking place. By the "time" factor I determine in advance tops and bottoms of minor swings. I study each stock separately, as in all Bull markets some stocks are in a bearish position, while in Bear markets some few stocks are in a bullish position. To be correct one must study individual stocks, not averages. I also study each group of stocks separately, such as, Motors, Oils, Steels, Rails, and Coppers, as different groups are leaders in Bull or Bear cycles under different conditions. I determine the leading group by applying the "time" factor and study of Volume.

I am considered an expert tape reader and watch the ticker daily for indications of quick changes. The "Ticker Magazine" in 1909 said: "He is a gifted mathematician, has an extraordinary memory for figures, and is an expert Tape Reader. Take away his science and he would beat the market on his intuitive tape reading alone."

The Cotton and Grain markets can also be forecasted by this "time" factor, which enables me to tell when extreme highs and lows will be made, as well as the minor moves. I keep Time charts on commodities as no Volume of sales is published. After all the important thing for every trader to know is the day approximate high and low prices will be made. The price makes little difference so long as you know about when bottom or top prices will be reached.

ANSWERS TO INQUIRIES

Hundreds of people write in from time to time asking for different kinds of information. In order to avoid having to answer a lot of unnecessary correspondence, we are answering frequent inquiries below.

MAGAZINES

Many people write and ask what magazines we consider best for an investor or a trader to read. We consider the *Magazine of Wall Street* one of the best magazines for information pertaining to the stock market. *B. C. Forbes' Magazine* is also good. It contains many valuable articles on financial affairs. The *Annalist* published weekly by the *New York Times* specializes on financial affairs and contains information valuable to traders and investors.

NEWSPAPERS

Investors and traders often want to know what newspapers we consider best for them to read.

The Wall Street Journal.—This is the best financial newspaper published. It specializes in presenting all facts and information pertaining to corporations throughout the country, as well as major foreign corporations. Pertinent national news, especially agricultural and political, is equally stressed. This was one of the first papers to publish a set of Averages on railroad and industrial stocks. These Averages go back to 1896. Since 1914, it has published an average of bond prices, and since 1928, a public utility stock average. All of these averages are published daily and are very valuable to investors and traders who want to keep up charts on these various groups. Another feature of the *Wall Street Journal* is that it publishes each day a list of stocks which make a new high for the year and a list that make a new low for the year. The *Wall Street Journal* does not publish any tips, rumors or misleading information. It publishes only reliable facts which are helpful to investors and traders. From time to time the *Wall Street Journal* publishes various charts on stocks, which are very helpful to traders and would cost them a lot of money if they had to secure the records and make up the charts themselves.

New York Daily Investment News.—This paper is specially good for active traders. It specializes in up-to-the-minute news on stocks and bonds, and publishes charts from time to time which are interesting and valuable to investors and traders.

The New York Evening Post.—This is also a good financial paper and contains many valuable special articles from time to time.

The New York Herald Tribune.—This paper carries averages on various groups of stocks as well as other information which is helpful to traders.

The New York Times.—This also has a special set of averages and is a good paper for investors and traders to read.

What investors and traders want is the facts about the different companies and reports and not tips or rumors. The above papers, all of which are published in New York City, strive to give facts and reliable information.

COMMODITIES

Traders who are interested in the different commodity markets often inquire what is the best paper to read on commodities.

The *Journal of Commerce* of New York City makes a specialty of commodities and covers everything in the field. *Commerce and Finance* of New York City, is another very valuable publication, which specializes in cotton, but covers other commodities and has interesting articles from time to time on stocks and other general financial affairs.

BROKERS

People write and ask if we consider such and such a firm of brokers reliable. We consider all members of the New York Stock Exchange, the New York Cotton Exchange, and the Chicago Board of Trade reliable, and advise traders to always keep their accounts with members of these responsible Exchanges. If in doubt about your broker, get a report through Bradstreet, R. G. Dun, or Bishop Service. For brokers not members of one of the leading Exchanges, you should get a private report through your banker or some commercial agency, before placing your account with them. You might be trading with a bucket shop and not know it.

WHERE TO OBTAIN PRICES

Frequent inquiries come in as to where traders can obtain high and low prices on different stocks and commodities. The *Financial Chronicle* and *Standard Statistics* give records of high and low prices and people interested can write these publications and obtain prices which they want.

For commodities.—*Cotton Facts*, published in New York City, specializes in statistical information on cotton. Records on high and low prices on grain can be secured from the Chicago Board of Trade or from brokers who are Members of the Chicago Board of Trade. The same with sugar, coffee, cocoa, rubber, silk, and other commodities. The brokers who are members of these various Exchanges are always glad to furnish records of past high and low prices and other statistical information to people who are interested and there is usually no charge by the broker for this kind of service.

ODD LOT TRADES IN STOCKS AND JOB LOTS IN GRAIN

Traders often inquire whether they can buy and sell odd lots of stocks. Most of the brokers who are Members of the New York Stock Exchange, accept orders for odd lots. Most all of them will buy stocks outright or for cash in any amount from one share on up. Job lots or 1000 bushels of grain are traded in on the Chicago Board of Trade. Some of the brokers handle job lots and some do not. You can inquire from any broker who is a Member of the Chicago Board of Trade and find out about trading in job lots or less than 5000 bushels, which is a round lot or a contract. The Chicago Board of Trade and New Orleans Cotton Exchange trade in 50 bales of cotton. No other reliable exchange will trade in less than 50-bale lots of cotton. Those that are trading in or soliciting business for odd lots of cotton in 10 bales or more, are as a rule bucket shops. Traders should be careful about placing their accounts with firms of this kind.

Coffee Riv. Jan 3000 Oct 2 1936

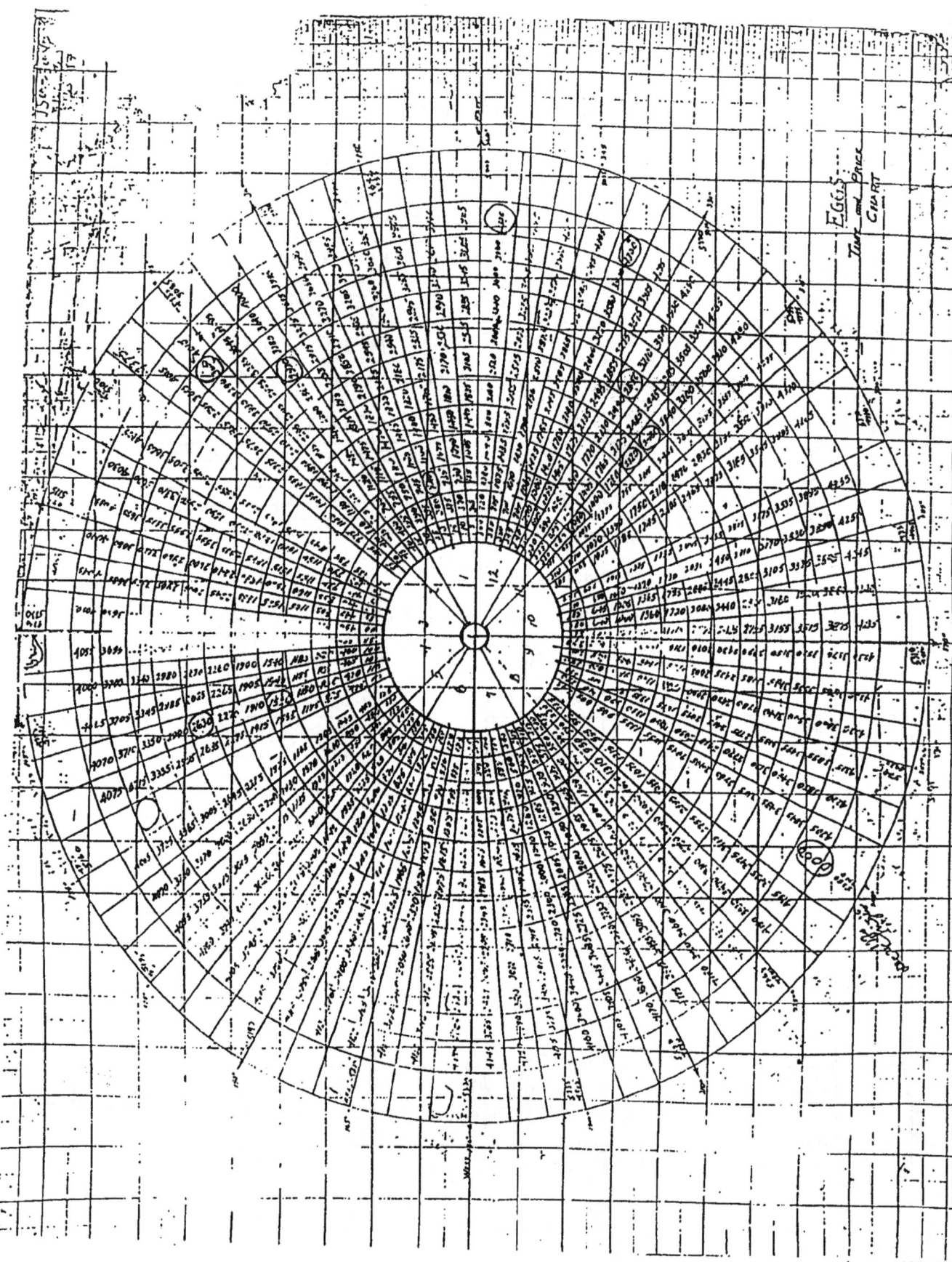

Egos
Time and Price Chart

A BRIGHTER OUTLOOK FOR THE STOCK MARKET AND GENERAL BUSINESS CONDITIONS

W. D. Gann, Who Is Regarded as an Authority on Predictions as to the Rise and Fall of Securities, Sees Better Times Ahead This Year for the Investing Public.

The closing months or days of the year 1920 became noted for the general depression of securities listed on stock exchanges. Complaints were heard on every side over the dull market and stocks then hit lower levels than they had in many a day during past years. The result was that very little was done in the way of investments and business in general was comparatively "dead," as the term goes in the financial world. Few investments were made and although the real opportunity for buying was at hand, when the stocks were down to rock bottom prices the public as a rule did not take advantage of this opportunity and hence pessimism was the talk of the day.

However, the tide seems now to be turning and the indications are that better times are ahead. Some may hazard this opinion on a mere guess while others base their optimistic predictions on past performances and on inevitable laws that govern the fluctuations of the stock market. Among the latter class of forecasters of financial events can be mentioned Mr. W. D. Gann, editor of the Supply and Demand Letter and senior member of the firm of W. D. Gann & Company, stock brokers, with offices at 18 Broadway, New York City. Mr. Gann has given technical advice and guidance for investors during the past twenty years and he is regarded as one of the best authorities in the country on predicting the trend of the market and the rise and fall of securities.

It is a well-known fact that fortunes are made and lost by those who trade in the securities listed on our various stock exchanges. However, some are more fortunate than others, and those who generally are successful are those who let expert guidance determine what stocks to sell or buy and when to do so. Business conditions and trade in general, both domestic and foreign, determine to a great extent what may be expected in the financial market. And a person who has made a serious and careful study of the causes of stock fluctuations is in a position to know where possible losses and profits may take place.

Mr. Gann has made noteworthy prognostications of the markets which proved to be true in course of time. His calculations are based on the Science of Letters, Numbers and Astrology. In 1909 his record in speculation created a sensation. The "Ticker Magazine" and many newspapers throughout the country commented on his accurate forecasts and trading record. And since that year his predictions on the movements of stocks have been just as remarkable. He sends out forecasts twelve months in advance and at the beginning of 1919 he predicted the bull market that year and the big decline in November of the same year. He foretold the advance in stocks last April and the severe decline in November and December last year. On the general run of stocks for last year, all his predictions, which were made at the beginning of 1920, came true. He spoke with emphasis of the declining market which could be expected at the end of last year. Happenings proved that his predictions were correct.

During an interview with the correspondent of the Journal of Commerce the other day Mr. Gann said that brighter times are ahead for stock market operators this year. There will be a gradual rise in stocks the present winter months and the beginning of the Harding administration will mark a notable rise in securities. Investments in securities will be quite active throughout the year. Mr. Gann finds that business conditions in general will improve this year and the old-time confidence will be restored to the investing public.

This gentleman has made some important predictions in his day. He foretold about nine months in advance the exact day of the Kaiser's abdication and the end of the World War. Mr. Gann also predicted the elections of both President Wilson and that of Harding. He has forecasted events in the lives of persons who are prominent in the political and business affairs of this nation, and these men testify to the accuracy of Mr. Gann's predictions. He showed the writer numerous letters from men high in the army and navy. State executives, banking officials, well-known clergymen, and hosts of others whose signatures to letters mean that the truth has been spoken. They are all men whose position and standing could not afford them to write or say anything unless they knew the true facts about which they were writing. This is a great credit to Mr. Gann and it proves that he knows whereof he speaks.

MASTER CHART
MAY SOY BEANS
PRICE & TIMING

444	443	442	441	440	439	438	437	436	435	434	433	432	431	430	429	428	427	426	425	424
368	367	366	365	364	363	362	361	360	359	358	357	356	355	354	353	352	351	350		423
369	300	299	298	297	296	295	294	293	292	291	290	289	288	287	286	285	284	349		422
370	301	240	239	238	237	236	235	234	233	232	231	230	229	228	227	226	283	348		421
371	302	241	188	187	186	185	184	183	182	181	180	179	178	177	176	225	282	347		420
372	303	242	189	144	143	142	141	140	139	138	137	136	135	134	175	224	281	346		419
373	304	243	190	145	108	107	106	105	104	103	102	101	100	133	174	223	280	345		418
374	305	244	191	146	109	80	79	78	77	76	75	74	99	132	173	222	279	344		417
375	306	245	192	147	110	81	60	59	58	57	56	73	98	131	172	221	278	343		416
376	307	246	193	148	111	82	61	48	47	46	55	72	97	130	171	220	277	342		415
377	308	247	194	149	112	83	62	49	44	45	54	71	96	129	170	219	276	341		414
378	309	248	195	150	113	84	63	50	51	52	53	70	95	128	169	218	275	340		413
379	310	249	196	151	114	85	64	65	66	67	68	69	94	127	168	217	274	339		412
380	311	250	197	152	115	86	87	88	89	90	91	92	93	126	167	216	273	338		411
381	310	251	198	153	116	117	118	119	120	121	122	123	124	125	166	215	272	337		410
382	313	252	199	154	155	156	157	158	159	160	161	162	163	164	165	214	271	336		409
383	314	253	200	201	202	203	204	205	206	207	208	209	210	211	212	213	270	335		408
384	315	254	255	256	257	258	259	260	261	262	263	264	265	266	267	268	269	334		407
385	316	317	318	319	320	321	322	323	324	325	326	327	328	329	330	331	332	333		406
386	387	388	389	390	391	392	393	394	395	396	397	398	399	400	401	402	403	404		405

GANN FORETOLD RUN OF STOCKS

Wall Street Scientist Forecasted Top of Bull Market Year in Advance.

HIS INDICATIONS UNCANNY

By ARTHUR ANGY,

(Financial Editor, The North Side News)

W. D. Gann has scored another astounding hit in his 1922 stock forecast issued in December, 1921. That forecast called for first top of the bull wave in April, second top in August, and the final top and culmination of the bull market October 8 to 15, and strange as it may seem, the average prices of twenty industrial stocks reached the highest point on October 14 and declined 10 points in thirty days after that date.

Mr. Gann predicted a big decline for the month of November. He said in the 1922 forecast: "November 10-14 panicky break." During this period stocks suffered a severe decline, many falling 10 points or more in four days, and on November 14 lowest average prices were made with 1,500,000 shares traded in on the New York Stock Exchange.

I found his 1921 forecast so remarkable that I secured a copy of his 1922 stock forecast in order to prove his claims for myself. And now, at the closing of the current year of 1922, it is but justice to say I am more than amazed by the result of Mr. Gann's remarkable predictions based on pure science and mathematical calculations.

The North Side News stands for a clean Wall Street and has rendered a great public service in helping to rid Wall Street of the bucket shop evil by publishing a series of articles in conjunction with the Magazine of Wall Street. We believe in branding a fake, and we believe in giving credit where due.

GANN NO TIPSTER.

Mr. Gann is no "Wall Street tipster" sending out market letters and so-called "inside information." Mr. Gann's results are obtained by profound study of supply and demand, a mathematical chart of money, business and commodities. He determines when certain cycles are due, and the order and the time when market movements will follow.

During the past thirty years many men have proclaimed discoveries and theories to "beat the Wall Street game," most of which resulted in loss to their followers. They could always tell by the chart just why the market did it after it happened. Mr. Gann's theory differs from the others in that he tells months in advance what stocks are going to do.

His forecast stated that some stocks would make high this year in April, some in August and others in October—the month when he predicted the bull movement would culminate. Of a list of a hundred stocks; thirty made highest prices in April and many declined, while others continued higher; twenty made high during August, and fifty made high of the year in October, from which the largest decline of the year has taken place.

His 1922 forecast indicated final tops on railroad stocks for August 14. The Dow Jones's averages on rails made high August 21 and reached the same average levels on September 11 and October 16, but did not exceed the high made in August, which was made seven days later than the exact date called for in the forecast.

HIS CHART A FACT.

Such accurate long range forecasting as Mr. Gann is doing sounds almost unbelievable, and how he does it I do not know, but the writer does know that he does it. My attention was first called to his 1921 forecast in which he predicted that stocks would be bottom in August, 1921, and advance to December, 1921. They did so. His chart or graph of the market one year in advance is a fact, and that the course of the stock market follows it astoundingly close is equally a fact.

Mr. Gann says the trouble with most chart makers is that they work with only one factor—space movements, or charts that record one to two points up or down—whereas there are three or more factors to be considered, space, volume and time. The most vital is time, and back of that is the cause of recurrence of high or low prices at certain intervals.

I asked Mr. Gann: "What is the cause behind the time factor?"

He smiled and said: "It has taken me twenty years of exhaustive study to learn the cause that produces effects according to time. That is my secret and too valuable to be spread broadcast. Besides, the public is not yet ready for it.

"Water seeks its level," continued Mr. Gann. "You can force it higher with a pump, but when you stop pumping it requires no force to cause it to return to its former level. Stocks are the same. They can be forced above their natural level of values to where lambs lose all fear, become charged with hope and buy at the top. Then stocks are permitted to sink to a level where hope gives way to despair and the most rampant bull becomes a bear and sells out with a loss. My discovery of the time factor enables me to tell in advance when these extremes must, by the law of supply and demand, occur in stocks and commodities."

Poor Business, Damaged Crops, Strikes and Bank Failures in 1923 Predicted by Prophet

William D. Gann Is 85 Per Cent Right in His Forecasts, His Followers Declare.

IS A MATHEMATICAL SEER

Foresaw Date of End of War and Election of Harding and Wilson.

"I knew you would be coming in to-day," was the greeting the unheralded reporter received on entering the office of William D. Gann at No. 49 Broadway. "When I looked at the calendar this morning and saw it was the third day of the third month of the year 1923 I knew I would receive callers from newspaper and publicity people."

Mr. Gann predicts other and more important things, such as stock quotations, end of wars and elections of Presidents, with an accuracy that has made him a recognized authority in Wall Street. He predicted the election of Wilson and of Harding, and he told of the abdication of the Kaiser and the end of the war to the exact date six months beforehand.

85 PER CENT CORRECT.

His daily Supply and Demand letter gives to his clients scientific forecasts on stocks, cotton and grain. And the clients who have followed his advice for twenty years testify that eighty-five per cent of his predictions are correct.

"I figure things by mathematics," Mr. Gann explained. "There is nothing mysterious about any of my predictions. If I have the data I can use algebra and geometry and tell exactly by the theory of cycles when a certain thing is going to occur again.

"If we wish to avert failure in speculation we must deal with causes. Everything in existence is based on exact proportion and perfect relationship. There is no chance in nature, because mathematical principles of the highest order lie at the foundation of all things. Faraday said:—'There is

William D. Gann, mathematical seer, whose forecasts are followed by thousands, sees poor year ahead.

nothing in the universe but mathematical points of force.'"

Mr. Gann's business outlook for 1923 forecasts a generally low average caused by strikes and threats of war in foreign lands and poor crop conditions.

OUTLOOK NOT ENCOURAGING.

"While there will be spurts of activity and some fairly good business during the spring and late summer, the general outlook is not encouraging and there is no indication of any boom in business this year.

"The foreign situation will play an important part in our business affairs as our government will have a lot of trouble on account of secret enemies in foreign countries.

"From April to June a serious falling off in business and financial troubles and bank failures are indicated. During April the laboring classes will be very much dissatisfied and strikes are threatened.

"During the fall a serious business depression will set in and the general outlook becomes cloudy.

Storms to Hurt Crops.

"The summer will see storms that will damage crops and by October business conditions will be bordering on a panic.

"In December loss of confidence on the part of the public and dissatisfaction with the administration at Washington will cause a serious wave of pessimism to fall over the entire country."

In 1921 Mr. Gann predicted that President Harding would be a war President, and he still holds to that prediction.

"I hope I am wrong," he said, "but the forecast still stands and has until 1924 to be fulfilled and mathematics do not lie."

Mr. Gann predicted the election of Woodrow Wilson because the cycle had come back again to a man with a name beginning with W and ending with N, Washington having been the first and last President with those two letters placed in that way.

The forecast which told of Harding's election has been explained by Mr. Gann as follows :—

Senator Warren G. Harding was born November 2, 1865. His name contains some of the most powerful fame and wealth-producing letters. The name Warren, beginning with W and ending with N, is very fortunate and gives him power to overcome obstacles and opponents. His name and numbers show that he will be conservative and act only after due consideration. His foreign policy will help him to win.

"His fortunate numbers are 2, 4, 6, 8 and 11. Note that the Declaration of Independence on July 4 and inauguration day on March 4 both fall on one of his fortunate numbers. The election takes place on the second day of the eleventh month, both fortunate numbers for him."

How He Works It Out.

On the other hand Mr. Gann predicted the defeat of Governor Cox because his name contained only one fortunate letter. There has never been but one President with the initial C. That was Cleveland. But the letter H recurs every tenth cycle. William H. Harrison was the ninth President. R. B. Hayes was the nineteenth President, so there was nothing left but for Warren G. Harding to be the twenty-ninth.

It might be well for the political parties to consult Mr. Gann before the nominations are made in 1924 to find out what letter is due to win in this election. They could then choose a man with the right kind of letters in his name.

Mr. Gann gets calls every day from men and women prominent in all walks of life asking him to cast their horoscope. He tells politicians whether or not they will be elected and solves other problems for clergymen, bankers and statesmen.

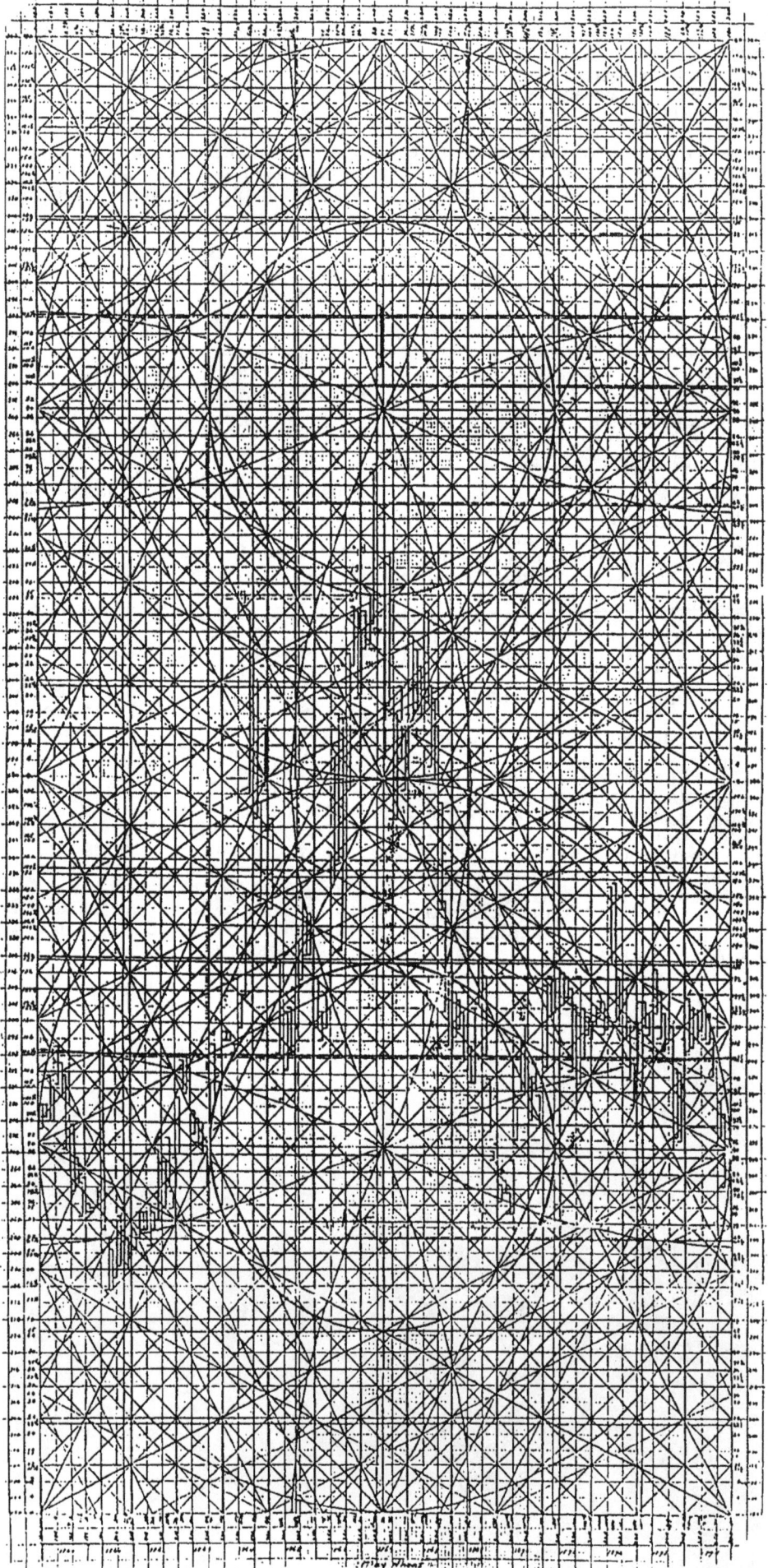

SATISFIED CLIENTS TELL YOU THE STORY
OF MY SUCCESSFUL SERVICE

I always prefer to have prospective clients read what others say about my Service rather than tell them about it myself.

The best references I can offer are satisfied subscribers who have made money following my advice. These letters and numbers of others from Banks, Lawyers, Doctors, Merchants and Brokers are on file in my office.

"The proof of the pudding is in the eating." Give the SUPPLY AND DEMAND LETTER and my ANNUAL FORECASTS a trial. You will be well pleased and become a booster for them.

Remember that Science always beats Guesswork. When you invest or speculate, follow expert scientific advice.

What Satisfied Subscribers Say:

CONSIDERS MY BOOK OF GREAT VALUE

INDIANAPOLIS, IND., December 13, 1920: "Concerning 'Speculation a Profitable Profession,' I think so much of this book I will never let anyone see it, and consider it so valuable that if I could not get another one, would not sell it at any price. It truly is the greatest gift ever bestowed on me by man." A. J.

THINKS SERVICE WONDERFUL; RECOMMENDS IT TO FRIENDS

COLUMBIA, S. C., January 22, 1921: "Your 1920 predictions were as near accurate as is humanly possible to foresee. I only regret that I did not know of your service sooner. While in Augusta, Ga., last week I told some friends of your wonderful service." W. C. A.

LIKES WAY I DO BUSINESS

ST. PAUL, MINN., March 10, 1921: "I must admit, Mr. Gann, I like the way you do business. Your Service is real service." A. J. D.

WILL SUBSCRIBE FOR NEXT YEAR'S FORECAST

DETROIT, MICH., July 19, 1921: "In the Fall I will subscribe for your next year's Letter as you seem to have made a very close prediction on the market condition of this year to date." J. W. K.

SERVICE WOULD HAVE SAVED HIM THOUSANDS OF DOLLARS

TYRONE, PA., August 29, 1921: "I sincerely regret not having your Service last May. It would have saved me thousands of dollars." T. P. D.

MAKING MONEY WHERE HE FORMERLY LOST

PITTSBURGH, PA., October 13, 1921: "I would like your 1922 prognostications when ready. Your readings and everything concerned are marvelous. Have made money where I formerly lost." C. D. A.

SAYS ANNUAL FORECASTS ARE GREAT

CHICAGO, ILL., October 29, 1921: "Your Forecasts on the market are great." R. A.

SAYS I AM A WIZARD

BUFFALO, N. Y., October 31, 1921: "You're a wizard of the first rank; how you do it I don't know." W. G. B.

THREE TIMES A SUBSCRIBER AND MAKES PROFITS

NEW YORK, N. Y., November 13, 1921: "I can't resist the impulse to write you and compliment you on the excellent service rendered me by your market letter. This is the third time that I have been a subscriber; in fact, each time that I come to New York I send in my subscription, and each time without an exception I have profited financially quite handsomely by following to the letter your advice." V. V. W.

FORECASTS ON COTTON CORRECT

DURHAM, N. C., November 15, 1921: "You have been very correct regarding the last big move in Cotton." M. R. V.

MADE MONEY; APPRECIATES SERVICE

CHICAGO, ILL., November 17, 1921: "Giving people their flowers while they are living is my motto. So I thought I could best express my appreciation of your service by telling you of the money I have made since I first began with it." H. N. A.

"HELPFUL HINTS" WORTH $15.00

KNOXVILLE, TENN., November 19, 1921: "Your Daily Letters are very satisfactory. The little book 'Helpful Hints for Stock Traders' is well worth the $15.00 I sent you." H. A. B.

COULD GET RICH ON MY FORECASTS

DETROIT, MICH., November 28, 1921: "You are wonderful. You know your business all right. If I had $5,000.00 I would be a rich man with your plan."
G. K. V.

LOOKS TO MY VALUABLE LETTER FOR ADVICE

EMAUS, PA., November 28, 1921: "I am being urged to sell my stocks by a boardroom man as I have a little profit in each, but will not do so until I am informed through your wonderful and very valuable Letter."
H. L. K.

CONSIDERS FORECASTS REMARKABLE

NEWPORT NEWS, VA., November 29, 1921: "I wish to commend you on the valuable service you are giving your subscribers. After looking back over the month's letters I have, it seems remarkable how you have forecasted in advance what has actually come to pass."
F. C. W.

LIKES COTTON PREDICTIONS

DURHAM, N. C., December 2, 1921: "That's some kind of cotton predictions you have been handing out. All good wishes."
M. R. V.

SAYS "YOU DESERVE MORE CREDIT THAN WEBSTER HAS WORDS TO EXPRESS THE THOUGHT"

KANSAS CITY, MO., December 3, 1921: "I want to take this opportunity to extend to you my appreciation for your splendid service on forecasting market movements. I have acted upon your advice as authority and so far have never had reason to regret my moves. It gives one a certain assurance and stimulates as a father's advice would to his son. You deserve more credit than Webster has words in which to express the thought."
F. M. W.

A DOUBTER HAS "BEEN SHOWN"

BOSTON, MASS., December 9, 1921: "I wish to compliment you on the accuracy of your advice and its great value to every investor or trader. I will admit quite frankly that I had never placed any credence in the many advice letters which are in existence, but I appreciate fully the value of your Letter. I certainly have 'been shown.'"
E. M. J.

SAYS ADVICE IS EXCELLENT; SENDS $200.00

TORONTO, CAN., December 16, 1921: "I enclose herewith $200.00 subscription for Daily Letter and Annual Forecast. Your advice is excellent."
R. J. M.

FORECAST SO GOOD WANTS IT ANOTHER YEAR

DETROIT, MICH., December 17, 1921: "I had your Forecast for the past year and it has proven so accurate that I want it for the coming year."

B. F.

LETTERS GIVE HIM FOUNDATION TO WORK ON

CLEVELAND, OHIO, December 27, 1921: "With your Letter before me every day, I feel like I had a good foundation to work on, whereas before I was working in the dark and had to guess which way stocks were going, and I certainly was way off the track most of the time during 1921 before I was getting your Letters, as I was bucking the downward trend and did not know any better, and now I feel quite safe in trading in stocks with your Letters before me every day."

W. A. O.

SUPPLY AND DEMAND LETTER SHOWED HIM THE LIGHT

INDIANAPOLIS, IND., January 1, 1922: "After floundering in the dark for several months, our subscription to the Supply and Demand Letter was surely a move in the right—profitable—direction and you may depend upon a renewal."

B. B.

MY SYSTEM ALMOST EXACT SCIENCE

HAVANA, CUBA, January 12, 1922: "Your Forecast is coming wonderfully true. Your system is almost an exact science."

A. E. K.

SAYS I AM THE ONLY MAN WHO CAN FURNISH NECESSARY INFORMATION

JACKSONVILLE, FLA., February 2, 1922: "You are the only man in this or any other country who is in a position to furnish the necessary information, that I know of. Some of the other wise financiers may have it, but they are not putting it out at any price. As a matter of fact, they are probably too selfish to enlighten the other fellow at any price. With every assurance of my deep appreciation of your efforts."

J. W. E.

REGARDS LETTER AS VALUABLE ASSET

BOSTON, MASS., March 31, 1922: "I would welcome exceedingly any special service which you might prepare. In fact, as I have already written you, I think I have found your Service to be very accurate and I am always willing to accept its advice for either quick turnovers or for long pull speculation. I can assure you that I regard your letter as a very valuable asset and just as much a private affair as my money."

M. J.

HAS $9,000.00 PROFIT ON MY SPECIALS

KANSAS CITY, MO., April 7, 1922: "I wish to thank you very much for information contained in your Service. At the present time I have nearly Nine Thousand Dollars profit and in all of your Specials."

W. C. F.

MADE BIG PROFITS ON WHEAT

KANSAS CITY, MO., April 15, 1922: "I wish to compliment you on your accuracy in your instructions on the grain market. It is the best I have known. Some market today, Saturday. I rode May Wheat from $1.30."

S. J. M.

MY LETTERS ARE THE BEST

PHILADELPHIA, PA., May 29, 1922: "Your Letters are interesting and we think are the best that we read. We got some information from some other quarters but not equal to yours."

C. J. R.

LOST $3,000.00 BY NOT FOLLOWING MY ADVICE

CINCINNATI, OHIO, June 2, 1922: "I know your Letter is good as I saw a man buy Crucible each time you said sell at 85 for a decline to 65. He bought; so took his loss not long ago, when you said trend up on Crucible. He lost $3,000.00 and these men will not pay for advice and try to discourage me. But I will not trade at all without your Letter or paid advice."

K. K.

WILL NOT TRADE WITHOUT IT

FORT WORTH, TEXAS, June 21, 1922: "Just feel complete loss of confidence to commit either way without your valued suggestions."

J. G. W.

MADE 30 TRADES WITH PROFIT

TOPEKA, KANSAS, October 15, 1922: "It has come to me through a friend that you have a specially effective trading system or a service. A certain customer of yours was said to have made some 30 or more deals following your Service all but one of which was successful."

B. H. P.

WIRE SERVICE EXCELLENT

LONG BEACH, CALIF., November 26, 1922: "Your wires have been excellent."

C. E. L.

MADE PROFITS ON PREDICTED BREAK

CHICAGO, ILL., November 26, 1922: "I acted on your Forecast that stocks would break in October, so went short and took my profits November 25."

R. W. K.

GANN'S DOPE THE BEST

DECATUR, GA., December 11, 1922: "I induced my brother-in-law to take your Letter. He is an old cotton and stock man and in a recent letter he said 'Gann's dope is the best I have ever seen.'"

EVERY TRADE SHOWS A PROFIT

WENONAH, N. J., December 12, 1922: "I have been getting your Supply and Demand Letter nearly three months and find it the best on the market. Since I have been taking your letter I have been making some of my money back which I lost some years back. Every transaction I have made since taking your Letter have made a profit out of it."   R. E.

CONGRATULATES ME ON ACCURATE FORECASTS

PAOLA, KANSAS, December 13, 1922: "As a subscriber to your 1920-22 Forecasts, wish to tell you I have been well pleased and especially with the monthly supplements and want to congratulate you on your remarkable talent."   P. M.

MISSED MARKET FOLLOWING ANOTHER LETTER

COLUMBUS, OHIO, December 16, 1922: "I am sorry to say that I missed the big decline this fall, owing to the fact that I was trying to follow some daily letter sent out from another city. Had I followed your Annual I would have come out very nicely."   F. B. M.

COULD HAVE SAVED $130,000.00

ROCHESTER, N. Y., January 12, 1923: "In cleaning up my files today I came across your 1922 yearly Forecast. You foretold exactly the big reaction starting in October and lasting for balance of year. I had $130,000.00 profit had I sold out in October."   A. F. N.

Master Price & Time Chart
for
Cotton, Coffee, Cocoa, Wool,
and Grain

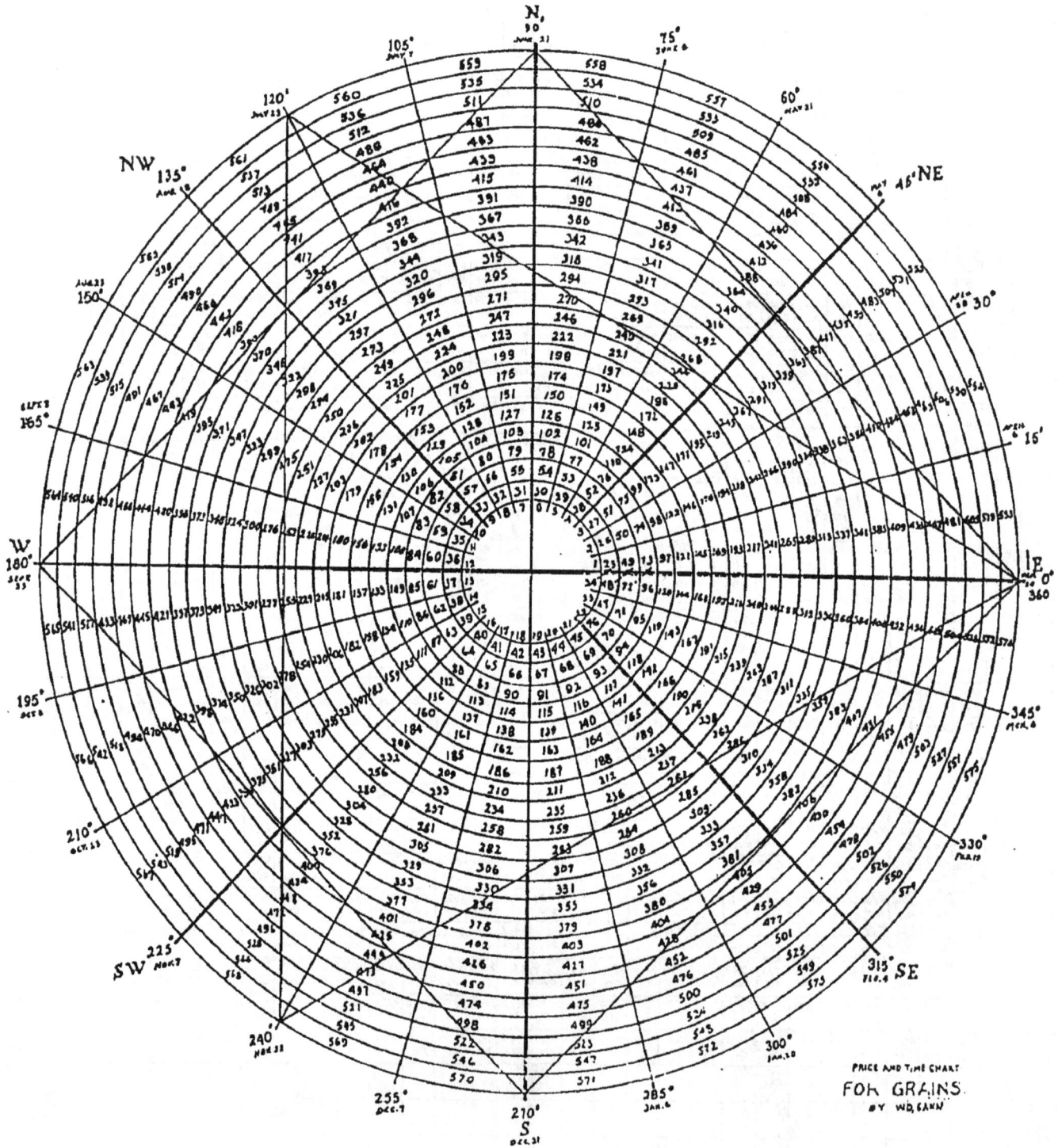

PRICE AND TIME CHART
FOR GRAINS
BY W.D. GANN

ANNUAL FORECASTS

In the following pages I am reproducing my Annual Forecasts issued since 1918. They appear exactly as when they were sent out one year in advance.

1919 A BULL YEAR FOR STOCKS

History repeats itself in the stock market as well as in the lives of men. My study of the measurement of time cycles indicates that 1919 falls in the cycle of advancing prices. This year will go down in history as one of a boom in oil stocks. Railroad issues will also have great advances. Steel stocks will be benefited by large increase in foreign business from March until August.

While the general aspects are for a more peaceful period, there is danger that the United States will have disputes with foreign powers during April, August and September, which will cause erratic fluctuations of stocks during these months. However, it is my judgment that all differences will be amicably adjusted and this country will not become involved in war. The Mexican problem will come up for settlement during this year and will cause some anxiety.

The year opens under a wave of slightly bullish influence which culminates between January 4th to 10th. Around the 20th to 25th a very depressing influence is indicated for stocks, when some marked declines may be expected. There will be talk of reduction in dividends and cut in prices of steel and copper. However, a Bull campaign always begins in gloom and ends in glory.

An accumulation of stocks will take place between January 20th and February 14th. Stocks bought during this period will show handsome profits on the advance in April and May.

The rise will start about the end of February and a strong upward tendency will be manifest during March when much optimistic talk will be in evidence.

The Bull wave continues, subject to minor reactions, until about May 10th, after which time a sharp reaction may be expected.

JUNE: During the first half of June the markets in London will be very strong and the buying from the other side will make its influence felt in our markets. From June 22nd to July 10th a depressing influence is shown and there is likely to be some marked depreciation in stocks.

JULY: After the 10th of July the Bull campaign will be resumed. There will be a boom in railroad stocks; also a large increase in foreign business.

AUGUST: Many stocks will reach the top of the boom between the 12th to 15th and have a quick decline to around August 23rd.

SEPTEMBER: A depressing influence is indicated from September 2nd to 8th. After that the Bull market will be resumed and stocks will advance until around September 23rd. If they are very strong around this time, it will be advisable to sell out all long stocks.

OCTOBER: During this month we will witness some marked decline in marine stocks. The general market should be strong up to the 6th or 7th and the bottom of the decline should be reached about October 24th.

NOVEMBER: This will be a very mixed month and a decline may be expected from the 10th to the 20th.

DECEMBER: The indications are that stocks will be weak and decline during the early part of the month and close at the end of the year very strong.

December 16th, 1918.

W. D. GANN.
81 New St., N. Y.

Note how the 1919 Forecast foretold the big boom in Oil stocks and called the exact date for the starting of the Bull campaign. It stated that the rise would begin the end of February.—Bottom on stocks was made February 10 and the big advance started February 14.—It also foretold the big decline November 10 to 20.—At this time many stocks declined 30 to 50 points in three weeks.

My mathematical calculations, based upon a Cycle Theory which I discovered, indicate two Bull and two Bear campaigns for this year. In looking ahead the important points to watch are:

A minor top of the first Bull wave about March 9. April will show much greater advances than March and the Spring Bull campaign will culminate around 22-24.

Distribution will take place during the early part of May. Railroad stocks are likely to reach high prices around May 12-17. The last half of May shows a downward tendency. The panicky decline continues during June, stocks reaching bottom around 10-16. The market will then be slow while accumulation is going on.

The second Bull campaign should start between July 15 and 20. Stocks should be very strong and rapid advances take place in August. Rails should have good advances; steels and coppers also show great activity. Many new issues will be floated during April and August. All stocks should be sold out in August as we will then see top of the great Bull cycle.

The last four months of 1920 all indicate declines and sales are advisable on rallies. A sharp, if not panicky decline will occur in September. Last half of November and first part of December will produce panicky conditions and great liquidation will be under way.

JANUARY: Great progress will be made on the Peace Treaty and there are strong indications that it will be ratified. This will cause rapid advances in stocks. Oils, steels, equipments, and rails all indicate higher prices. Markets should be top around 5-6; decline 13-14; rally to 20-21; decline 25-26; and close the month quite strong.

FEBRUARY: Quite bearish period. There will be war rumors, danger of trouble with Mexico, and probability of complications on account of financial depression in foreign countries. 2-3 slight rally; severe decline around 8-10, where bottom should be made and stocks bought; rally to around 14; decline to 20; and rally to 27.

MARCH: Some trouble is likely to develop in connection with the railroads being turned back to private ownership, which will cause declines. Disturbing conditions on account of war in Europe threatened. Top should be made around 9-10; decline 10-14; slight rally 15-16; decline 18-21, where bottom should be made for quite a rally to around 25; slight reaction around 27; then advance to 31. During last ten days of the month an improved condition in the rails.

APRIL: Indications very bullish and there will be some sensational advances. Grave danger of war with Mexico is threatened. However, it is not likely to disturb the Bull market to any great extent. The advances should start about the 3rd and continue with increasing volume and activity to around 24-25, where top of campaign should be reached and sharp decline start, running to end of the month.

MAY: England will face some grave financial troubles, but their affairs will probably be settled in a satisfactory way. Our trade and commerce will increase. Be careful about buying stocks as distribution will be taking place and you might not have a chance to sell before the big decline sets in. May 3rd should be top, decline to 6th; rally to 12th, when a slight decline should start. Rails are likely to be high between 12-17. Danger of marked decline in stocks 17-26; then rally to end of the month.

JUNE: This month falls in a cycle of very depressing influences. Serious danger of war, labor unrest, and strikes threatened. Something in connection with foreign countries will cause anxiety and help depress securities. The railroad situation will be far from satisfactory and their shares will decline. 2nd to 3rd slight rally. Sell out all long stocks and go short as balance of month is very bearish. A rapid decline should occur 7-16, where bottom should be made for a rally. Change in trend denoted around 23rd; 25-30 strong rally.

JULY: Stocks will be affected by strikes and labor troubles. Crop news will be bad and political uncertainties cloud the general outlook. However, accumulation will take place and a Bull wave start. 1st to 3rd slight advance; decline 7-9; rally to 16; sudden decline 20-22; balance of month tendency very strong. Something liable to happen to benefit rails and electrical stocks. Between July 20 and 28 trouble threatened to the United States on account of war, possibly with Mexico or Japan. If it comes, it might cause a sudden decline in stocks, followed by a sharp rally.

AUGUST: We will witness very wild and exciting fluctuations, but remember this is the last great boom in stocks. Conditions in France and Belgium will improve and enormous orders from foreign countries will make the situation here look rosy. The public will buy stocks regardless of price. August 1-5 slight decline; then big advance starts. 10-12, a sudden unexpected event may bring about a quick decline in some rails and steels, but they will rally sharply from any depression. Some stocks will be top around 14-15; but rails, steels, and equipments will continue the excited advance to around 23-25, when final top is indicated. Distribution will then start. Sell out and go short. 21-30: danger of break in oil and paper stocks.

SEPTEMBER: Financial conditions in London and Paris will be very unsettled and help to depress our markets. Strikes and labor troubles will be in evidence everywhere. The political outlook will be very disturbing. The worst decline of the year is signified. Do not be fooled into buying stocks as we are on the eve of a long depression. Rails may have slight advances but should be sold on all rallies. 1st to 3rd markets will be made to appear quite strong; 5-12 rapid decline; followed by slight recovery to 18th; 19-22 very depressing influence—stocks will decline rapidly, followed by slight rally to 27.

OCTOBER: Bad crop news, disturbing labor conditions, political uncertainties, and war or complications with foreign governments will cause declines. The cycle is very malefic from 7th to 31st and sales on rallies will prove more profitable than purchases. 1st to 5th, sharp decline; rally to 12th, decline to 18; slight rally to 21; then severe decline between 21 and 27.

NOVEMBER: While excited buying period will follow first few days after election, stocks should be sold on rallies. 5th to 8th strong tendency; slight rally 16-17—sell; panicky decline 20-23; followed by slight rise to 27; month closes under very depressing conditions. If stocks start to break after 11th, expect bad decline.

DECEMBER: Culmination of very malefic bearish cycle. Declines will be rapid and drastic. Frightened investors and speculators will liquidate regardless of price. General business outlook will become very gloomy and uncertain. The depressing cycle which began around November 18 will extend to December 19, when stocks should reach at least temporary bottom. 1st to 10th a severe decline; followed by a slight rally to the 12th; bad news about 14-15 will start another drastic decline extending to the 19th; very unsettled period 20-22; slight rally to the 25th; decline 26-28; final days of the year show advancing tendency.

December 10, 1919.

W. D. GANN.

This is an exact copy of my forecast sent out December 10th, 1919.

Note how accurately the 1920 market was forecasted and how the panicky decline of November and December was exactly foretold.—Low prices were made on December 22, 1920, in a panicky decline with a three-million share day. —The Forecast called for temporary bottom around this time.

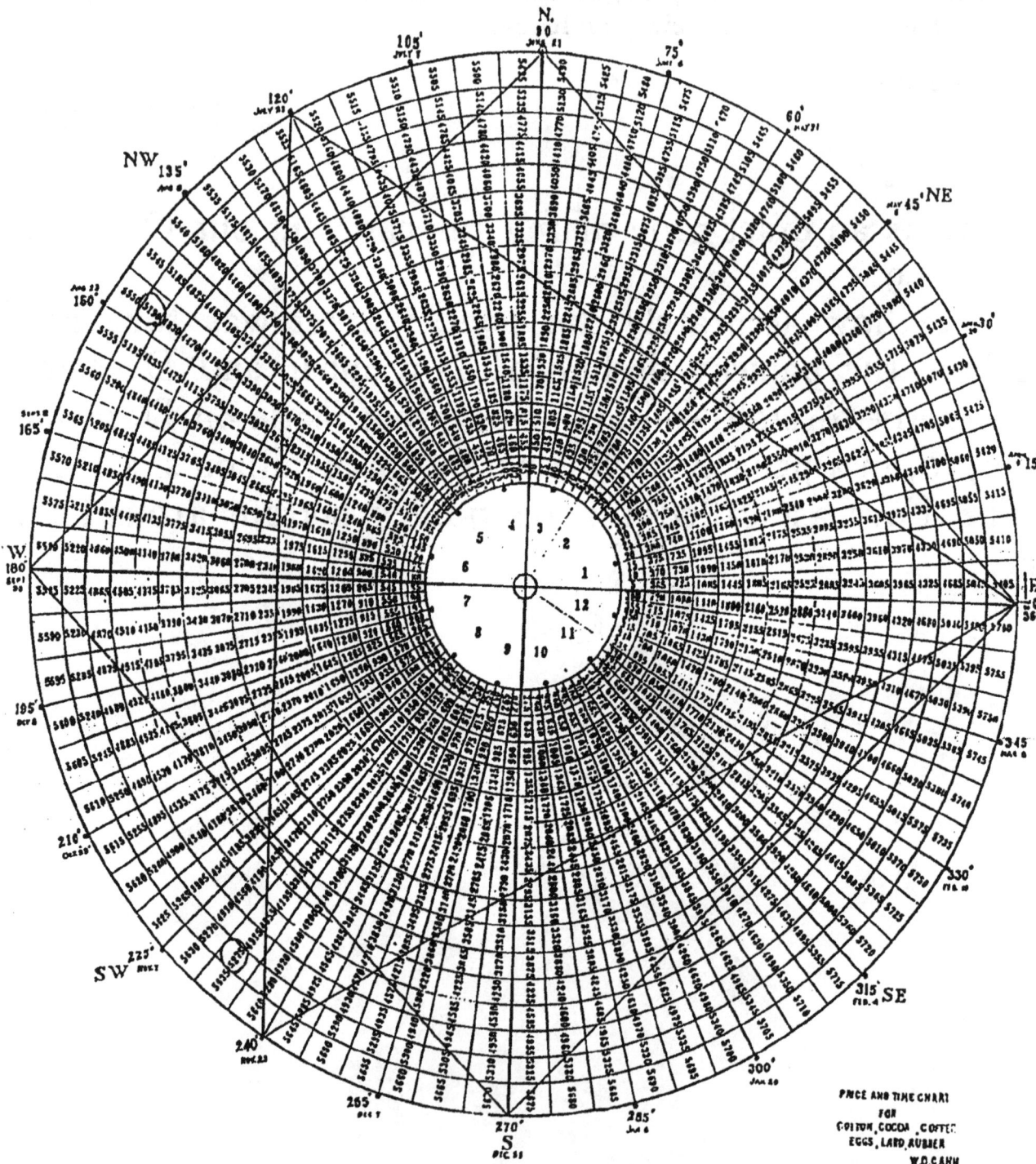

PRICE AND TIME CHART
FOR
COTTON, COCOA, COFFEE
EGGS, LARD, RUBBER
W.D. GANN

FORECAST OF THE STOCK MARKET FOR 1921

This year the markets will not have as wide fluctuations as we have witnessed during the past two years. Stocks will fluctuate in a narrow range, becoming dull and inactive after advances and holding for some time around the tops before starting a decline, also remaining dull and inactive around the bottoms after culmination of declines.

Railroad stocks will have much better advances and in many cases wider range of fluctuations than Industrials. The trend on Railroad stocks is much more bullish than on Industrials. On account of the time factor in this cycle at times indicating advances in Railroad stocks while Industrials are declining, it has been necessary for me to give you a separate forecast for the high and low days on Rails during the different months.

My forecast on general business conditions, enclosed, should be carefully read and taken into consideration with the calculations hereinafter given.

IMPORTANT POINTS OF THE YEAR

The low point for the general market will be reached between the 5th and 10th of February, although some stocks will make low around the 12th to 14th.

The Spring Bull campaign will start in February and will culminate between April 28th and May 3rd. You should certainly sell out long stocks on this advance, as the month of May indicates serious declines.

The markets will not be very active during June and July, having small advances and becoming dull and remaining in a narrow range.

August is a bearish month and quite a decline will take place. In fact, one bottom should be made in August. Then should follow an advance to the early days of September; decline to September 25th; then advance into the early part of October, with the low point around the 15th and 16th.

The general trend after the October break should be up until the end of the year, many stocks making highest prices during the month of December. In fact, quite a boom will take place near the end of the year.

DATES TO WATCH FOR CHANGE IN TREND

The following dates will show when there should be important changes in the trend of the market. If low prices are made on the date indicated, you may expect high prices at the next date, but if there is a reversal and prices are high on a low date, then expect them to be low on the next high date. To illustrate: January 9th indicates high—If prices are low instead of high, then expect January 17th to be high, and so on.

However, the dates given will not always mark extreme high and low prices, but some kind of a rally or decline may be expected around these dates.

January 9 high; 17 low; 23-24 high; 29-30 low.

February 7-8 high; 14-16 low; 23 high.

March 2 low; 10 high; 16-17 low; 23-24 high; 30-31 low.

April 8-9 high; 14-15 low; 21-22 high; 29-30 low.

May 6-8 high; 13-14 low; 21-22 high; 30-31 low.

June 5-6 high; 12-13 low; 19-20 high; 27-28 low.

July 4-5 high; 11-12 low; 19-20 high; 27-28 low.

August 3-4 high; 8-10 low; 17-18 high; 25-26 low.

September 2-3 high; 9-10 low; 16-17 high; 25-26 low.

October 1-2 high; 8-9 low; 16-17 high; 23-24 low; 30-31 high.

November 7-8 low; 14-15 high; 21-23 low; 28-29 high.

December 6-7 low; 14-15 high; 21-22 low; 29-30 high.

JANUARY: The general outlook is unfavorable. There will be poor earnings on railroads and strikes are threatened.

The month starts with an advancing market, high prices being made around the 3rd and 4th, where you should sell out and go short. Quite a severe decline around the 9th and 10th; rally around 11th and 12th; decline 19th and 20th; rally 21st and 22nd; decline 24th and 25th; then advance to end of the month.

FEBRUARY: This month indicates a very depressing influence for general business conditions. Reduction in steel prices, cuts in dividends, decline in Steel and Railroad stocks. The low prices for the year on U. S. Steel will be made this month.

February 1st to 3rd a slight advance; 4th to 10th a rapid decline, where bottom should be made, although Steel and Railroad stocks likely to make bottom around 12th or 14th. Rally on 15th and 16th; decline 19th and 20th; advance to end of the month.

Quite a sharp advance will take place in many stocks during the closing days. It will be the starting of the Spring Bull campaign. This is the time to buy stocks to hold for the April boom.

MARCH: Industrial stocks will have slow, steady advances, but in a narrow range. There will be depression in business. Bad weather will delay starting of crops. Unsettled financial conditions in foreign countries will cause depression here.

March 9th to 10th advance; decline 14th to 15th; rapid advance 22nd to 23rd; decline to 26th. Month closes strong with Railroads leading the advance.

APRIL: A much better outlook for both Rails and Industrials. There will be war or war talk, but the markets will advance even on unfavorable news.

Advance to April 4th; decline 8th and 9th; rally 16th to 20th; decline 21st to 23rd; strong advance to the 30th, where many stocks will make tops. Part of the Industrial stocks will reach high on April 16th; decline to the 19th; then advance to the end of the month.

Do not fail to sell out long stocks on this strong market.

MAY: This month falls in a very depressing cycle, threatening strikes, labor troubles, disputes with England, Mexico and Japan, if not actual warfare. The people will become very much dissatisfied and there is danger of revolutionary outbreaks. The markets are likely to become somewhat panicky.

May 1st to 3rd high; severe decline 9th to 10th; rally to the 13th; decline 14th; rally to 18th-19th; severe decline 21st to 25th; followed by a rally to the end of the month.

JUNE: Bad crop news, general unrest and labor troubles will be in evidence. The markets will be slow and dull, moving in a narrow range.

Rails will be more active than Industrials. The high point of Industrials should be reached around June 17th and the low point around the 25th. Rails—advance to the 4th; decline around 9th and 10th; advance 16th-17th; decline 19th-20th; advance 23rd-24th; decline 26th-27th; then advance to the end of the month.

JULY: Railroad earnings will improve, but disturbing financial conditions in New York City will cause some declines.

July 1st to 5th—high; decline, making low for month around 15th-16th; rally to 18th-19th; decline to 23rd; advance to end of the month.

AUGUST: This month falls in a very depressing bearish cycle. There will be danger of strikes and unrest. Reduction in the price of steel and oil. Some rapid declines in Steel and Oil stocks near the end of the month.

Decline August 1st to 8th; advance 12th to 15th; decline 18th and 19th; rally 22nd to 23rd; decline 24th to 26th; followed by an advance to the end of the month.

SEPTEMBER: We will have trouble with Japan. Fires and rioting in New York City will cause a decline in Industrials. Railroad earnings will show improvement, and an advance in Railroad stocks will start.

The month starts in strong—High 5th to 6th; severe decline 7th to 10th; Railroad stocks probably not making low until 13th-14th. Then advance 21st to 22nd; decline 26th-27th. Some unexpected bad news will cause railroads to break 28th to 30th.

OCTOBER: Declines in commodities and cost of living greatly reduced. Somewhat improved financial outlook in the early part of the month will help stocks, but a bad break occurs late in the month.

October 1st to 3rd—a slight advance; decline 5th to 7th; rally 10th to 11th; decline 14th to 15th; advance 19th to 21st, some Rails advancing to the 25th-26th. But many stocks will have a bad break between the 24th and 29th. The 27th or 28th will probably be the low day.

From this low price an advance will start which will continue to the end of the year. Buy stocks at this time to hold for the December boom.

NOVEMBER: This month starts a more hopeful outlook. New and beneficial laws will be passed. Good news of some kind will stimulate the markets and cause great activity. Railroad stocks will lead the advance.

November 1st to 12th—strong advancing market; 14th to 15th sharp decline; rally 16th to 18th; decline 19th to 21st; followed by a strong advance to the end of the month. Some Railroad stocks will probably make high around the 22nd to 23rd. U. S. Steel will be high around 27th-28th for a reaction. Great activity and rapid advances during closing days of the month.

DECEMBER: While there will be trouble with foreign countries and war or war rumors, yet stocks will be very active and show rapid advances. In many ways the influences show the strongest markets of the year. Steel and Oil stocks will have rapid advances. Commodities will also advance.

December 1st to 3rd—slight decline; rally 5th to 6th; decline 7th to 8th; advance 9th to 10th; slight decline 12th to 13th; advance to the 20th-21st; slight reaction 22nd-23rd; rapid advance to the end of the month. You can expect some sensational advances around the 17th to 21st and from the 25th to 31st. The year closes under a very strong bullish wave.

December 14th, 1920.

W. D. GANN.

The above is an exact copy of my forecast sent out December 14, 1920.

Note under "Important points of the Year" the end of the Spring Bull market was forecasted for April 28 to May 3.—The exact high point on the Dow-Jones' Averages was made on May 3, from which followed a severe decline, as predicted.

Also note that bottom was predicted for the month of August, and that a decline in Steels and Oils was foretold for that month.—Mexican Pete sold at 84½ and Crucible at 49, the extreme low prices, on August 25, 1921.

The Forecast called for an advance from August and the highest prices of the year to be made in December, all of which was remarkably fulfilled.

Forecast of the Stock Market for 1922

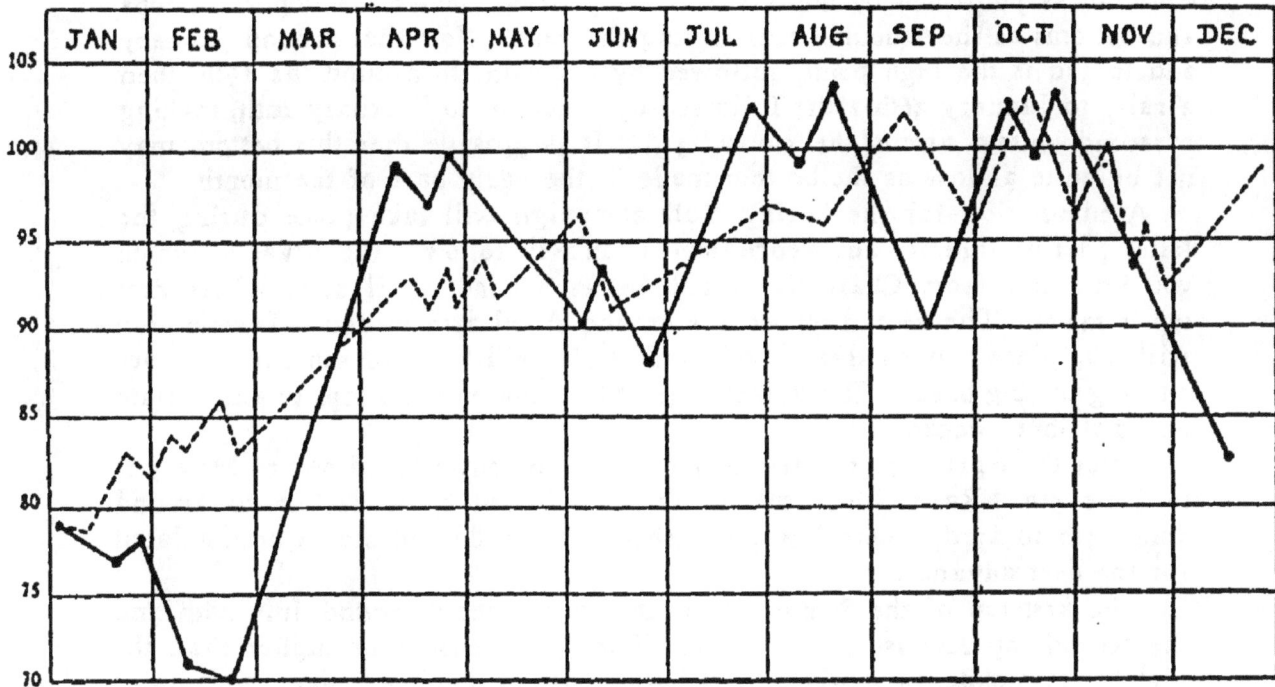

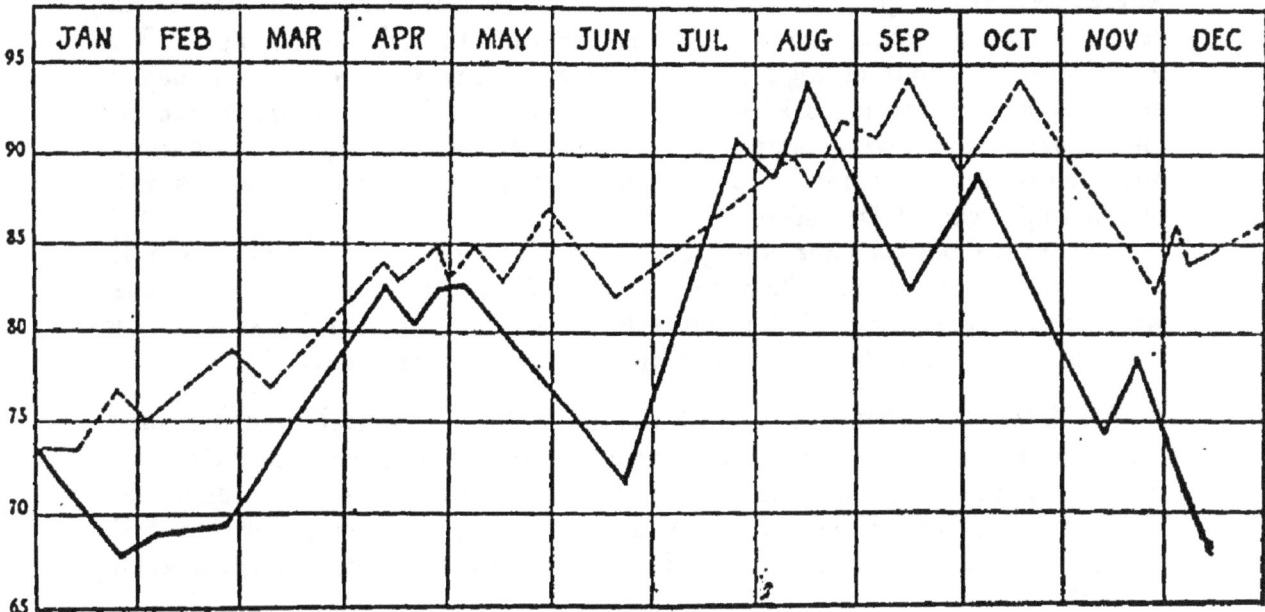

—— W. D. GANN'S FORECAST 1922
------ DOW-JONES AVERAGES

This year indicates a Bull market in stocks, especially the first six to eight months. The latter part of the year is more bearish and some severe declines will take place. The year 1922 promises greater prosperity for this country, improved business conditions, and a much better outlook than was experienced in the latter part of 1920 and in 1921. We will have some unfavorable periods at times and our Government will be confronted with some serious problems. There is danger of war as treachery is shown on the part of some foreign power who is supposed to be our friend. But the major influences favor success and general prosperity.

MAIN TREND AND IMPORTANT SWINGS

INDUSTRIAL STOCKS: Chart No. 1, which is based on the 20 Industrial Stocks published by the Wall Street Journal, shows the important tops and bottoms as they should occur during the year. Note that around January 2nd to 3rd is the high point, followed by a decline to around the 19th, then a rally to January 26th-28th; followed by a decline to February 10th, making a second bottom around February 23rd. It is possible that this bottom may not be quite as low as the bottom made in the early part of the month.

Accumulation for the Spring Bull campaign will take place during the latter part of January and February. Then will follow a big advance, which you will note from Chart No. 1 culminates around April 10th, where first top is made. The second top occurs around April 18th to 26th. Distribution will take place around these levels and stocks will hold for some time before starting the big break. It requires time at both bottoms and tops to accumulate and distribute stocks.

After the April tops the first low point on the down trend occurs May 31st to June 5th. Rally June 10th to 11th; followed by a decline to around June 19th to 23rd, where low point should be made and stocks accumulated for the next advance.

The first top of the Summer Bull campaign occurs around July 26th and the second top August 14th to 19th. These tops should be higher than the high prices made in April. Distribution will again take place and stocks will have a sharp decline, making bottom around September 11th to 15th, where they will again be accumulated for the third and last rise of the year, which culminates around October 8th to 15th and 18th to 24th. This top should be about as high as the July and August tops. Stocks may be held for some time to facilitate distribution, as this should mark the last top before a long Bear campaign. From this time the big trend continues down until December 11th to 15th, where bottom will be made and a rally follow to the end of December.

The range between the low point at the early part of the year and the final highs in August and October should be from 9 to 12 points on averages, which means that some of the active high-priced Industrial Stocks will fluctuate 20 to 30 points between highs and lows during the year.

RAILROAD STOCKS: The Rails have been gradually seeking lower levels every year since the boom in 1909. The lowest prices since 1897 were made in June, 1921. Since that time Rails have shown steady accumulation. They are way behind the Industrials and the curve shows a strong possibility of quite a Bull campaign in 1922 with many of the Rails making considerably higher prices.

Note the main swings of Chart No. 2 indicate high prices around January 2nd to 4th; low prices around January 23rd to 24th; a second bottom around February 5th and a third slightly higher bottom around February 20th to 23rd, from which the Spring Bull campaign starts.

First top April 10th to 12th; second top April 26th to May 2nd, followed by a decline, making bottom June 18th to 24th, from which the second section of the Bull campaign starts, making first top July 26th and second top August 14th.

Then a sharp decline, making bottom around September 15th, followed by a rally, making top October 3rd to 5th. It is possible, if the Rails are leading and are very strong, that the October top may be nearly as high as the August top.

After October the big trend is down. Stocks will be a sale on every rally. The first bottom November 10th to 14th; followed by a quick rally November 21st to 24th; then a severe decline, making bottom around December 10th to 15th, followed by a rally to the end of the year.

The range on the Dow-Jones' averages of 20 Rails, which is shown on Chart No. 2, should be from 10 to 12 points. There is a possibility of them making an even greater range. This would indicate some stocks making a range of 10 to 35 points between the high and low of the year.

JANUARY: The general business outlook is much more hopeful, although there will be some depressing news, which will cause sharp, sudden declines, the Rails probably breaking more than Industrials. Great activity in Steels, Rails, Electric, and Motor stocks indicated.

INDUSTRIAL STOCKS indicate extreme high point of the month around January 2nd-3rd; extreme low point 14th-19th. Minor Swings—4th-5th reaction; 7th-8th rally; 9th-10th decline; 12th-13th rally; 18th-19th first low of reaction; 24th-25th rally; 31st second low of reaction.

RAILROAD STOCKS indicate extreme high January 2nd-5th; extreme low 23rd to 25th. Minor Swings—9th-10th reaction; 12th-13th rally; 13th-14th reaction; 16th-17th top of rally; 18th-19th low; 20th-21st rally to near top made early part of month; 23rd-25th low point; 26th-28th rally.

Dates to Watch for Change in Trend: The swings in the Stock market are based upon a Time factor and my calculations are based upon the commodity curve, money curve and curve of stocks. Sometimes one of these curves will cause a change of trend and the dates given below each month show when there is a possibility of stocks varying from my predicted curve. The dates marked X are the most important points to watch. As a rule the market will have some kind of a rally or a decline around these dates. These changes in time apply to both rails and industrials. January 6th-7th low; 13th-14th high X; 19th-20th low; 26th-27th high X.

FEBRUARY: Slow accumulation will take place in stocks. Foreign affairs will cause some concern. There will be some war talk which will be unsettling for a short period. Railroad earnings will improve. Oils and shipping shares will be active and have quite a strong rally around the 12th-13th.

INDUSTRIAL STOCKS indicate extreme low point around the 5th, 9th and 10th; extreme high of the month 26th-27th. Minor Swings—4th-5th low; 7th-8th high; 9th-10th low; 13th-14th high; 18th-21st last low before Spring rise starts; rally to 26th-27th.

RAILROAD STOCKS indicate extreme high 10th-15th; extreme low 5th and 20th to 23rd. Minor Swings—10th-11th high; 12th-13th low; 15th-16th high; 23rd-26th nearly as low as the 5th; rally to end of month,—Spring rise starts.

Dates to Watch for Change in Trend: February 4th-5th low; 12th-13th high X; 18th-19th low; 26th-27th high X.

MARCH: Some unfavorable weather will delay crops in parts of the country. Foreign affairs will improve and become more peaceful. General business affairs will show steady improvement. Great activity in Rails, Steels, and Motor Stocks; some quick declines followed by quick rallies.

INDUSTRIAL STOCKS indicate extreme low around 1st and 11th-12th; extreme high point 30th-31st. Minor Swings—2nd-4th high; 5th-6th reaction; 26th-27th high; 29th-30th low.

RAILROAD STOCKS indicate extreme low around 1st and 10th-11th; extreme high 27th-28th. Minor Swings—4th-6th high; and if stocks have had a good advance, they may get a sharp reaction; 10th-11th low; 23rd-24th high; 25th-26th low; 27th-28th high; 29th low.

Dates to Watch for Change in Trend—6th-7th low; 12th-13th high X; 19th-21st low,—important change in trend due,—should be up; 27th-28th high X.

APRIL: This month indicates great activity and improved business conditions; plenty of work and the unemployed satisfied. Some war talk and disputes with a foreign country, probably Japan. The stock market will be active and the public will come in and buy stocks. All kinds of good news will be brought out to create a big buying wave. Distribution will start around the 9th to 10th, and if the second top occurs with a strong market around April 18th to 26th, you should sell out all long stocks and put out short lines for the next decline.

INDUSTRIAL STOCKS indicate extreme high around April 10th and 18th to 24th; extreme low 13th-14th. Minor Swings—1st high; 3rd-4th react; 10th, first top of Spring rise; 13th-14th react; 15th-16th rally; 18th-19th low; 25th-26th last top of Spring rise.

RAILROAD STOCKS indicate extreme low April 1st-2nd; extreme high 9th-10th and 26th. Minor Swings—9th-10th high; 11th-12th low; 15th second top; 19th-22nd low; 26th-29th last top of rally.

Dates to Watch for Change in Trend—April 4th-5th low; 11th-12th high X; 18th-19th low; 26th-27th high X.

MAY: General business good. More peaceful state of affairs. Railroads will show increased earnings. Crops will make good progress. Much good news will be brought out, but remember the stock market has discounted it. Expect some sharp declines in stocks around the 7th, 19th and 24th.

INDUSTRIAL STOCKS indicate extreme high May 1st-2nd; extreme low 18th-19th. Minor Swings—5th-6th low; 12th-13th high; 18th-19th low; 20th-21st high; 22nd-23rd low; 26th-27th high.

RAILROAD STOCKS indicate extreme high May 1st-2nd; extreme low 19th-20th. Minor Swings—May 5th-6th low; 14th-15th high; 19th-21st low; 25th-26th high; 31st low.

Dates to Watch for Change in Trend: May 3rd-4th low; 11th-12th high X; 18th-19th low; 26th-27th high X.

JUNE: Some reports of dull business in parts of the country and good business in others. There is danger of a sharp decline in Railroad stocks. Bad crop news will cause an advance in Cotton and Grain. Stocks will become dull and narrow at bottom of declines as accumulation will be taking place. Some great progress on peaceful relations with foreign countries will be made and something will happen to boom copper stocks. Money will be easy and the Summer advance in stocks will start.

INDUSTRIAL STOCKS indicate extreme high June 10th-11th; extreme low 5th-7th and 14th-19th. Minor Swings—June 3rd-4th low; 9th-10th high; 19th-23rd low; 29th high.

RAILROAD STOCKS indicate extreme high June 25th-26th; extreme low 5th-7th and 17th-19th. Minor Swings—June 4th-5th low; 7th-8th high; 14th-19th low; 25th-26th high; 29th-30th low.

Dates to Watch for Change in Trend—June 3rd-4th low; 9th-10th high X; 17th-19th low; 24th-25th high X; 29th low.

JULY: Bad weather in the Eastern states will retard progress of crops and cause an advance in the price of Cotton. Some trouble on account of foreign affairs. Threatened strikes in connection with railroads and shipping. The stock market will be quite active and advance. There is danger of a sharp reaction around the 10th to 14th, but it will be followed by a quick rally. Great activity in oils and shipping stocks. Railroads will show increased earnings and their shares should lead the Summer Bull campaign. Copper stocks will also advance. Something will happen to cause great speculative activity. There will be some war talk.

INDUSTRIAL STOCKS indicate extreme high July 26th-28th; extreme low 10th-12th. Minor Swings—2nd-3rd high; 5th-6th reaction; 9th-10th high; 12th-13th low before big rise starts; 24th-26th high; 29th-31st low.

RAILROAD STOCKS indicate extreme low July 3rd-5th; extreme high 26th. Minor Swings—July 2nd-3rd high; 11th-12th low; 26th top; 30th-31st low.

Dates to Watch for Change in Trend—July 1st-3rd low; 9th-10th high X; 16th-19th low; 24th-26th high X; 30th-31st low.

AUGUST: Business improves; good crop news. Railroad stocks very active and advancing. Steels, Oils, Shipping and Agricultural stocks will also rise. Sugars and late movers will advance, but remember that distribution will take place and that stocks should be sold on rallies and shorts put out for the September break. If the top of the rally comes around the 6th-7th, there may be a sharp reaction around 9th-10th, followed by a quick rally 14th-15th. Stocks may hold and make top around the 19th.

INDUSTRIAL STOCKS indicate extreme high 14th-19th; extreme low 1st-3rd and 23rd-25th. Minor Swings—3rd-4th low; 14th-15th top; 18th-19th low; 21st-22nd high; 24th-25th low; 27th-28th high.

RAILROAD STOCKS indicate extreme high August 14th and 19th; extreme low 29th-30th. Minor Swings—7th high; 9th-10th low; 14th-15th high; 24th-25th low; 27th high.

Dates to Watch for Change in Trend—August 7th high X; 12th-13th low; 21st-22nd high X; 29th-30th low.

SEPTEMBER: Good business, but stocks will have discounted most of it. Coppers, Sugars, and late movers will be brought forward to facilitate distribution in other stocks. War talk, complicated foreign affairs, or danger of strikes connected with railroads or shipping will cause a severe decline in stocks. A bad break occurs between the 10th and 16th. Oils, Rails, and active leaders will decline rapidly.

INDUSTRIAL STOCKS indicate extreme high 6th-9th; extreme low 11th-15th. Minor Swings—1st-3rd low; 5th-6th high; 11th-15th low; 17th-18th rally; 19th-20th react; 21st-22nd high; 24th-25th low; 26th-27th high; 29th-30th low.

RAILROAD STOCKS indicate extreme high 6th-7th; extreme low 13th-15th. Minor Swings—6th-9th high, some stocks holding up and probably making high around the 9th,—be careful about buying as a big break is coming; 11th-13th low; 18th-21st last rally before another big break; 27th-29th low.

Dates to Watch for Change in Trend—5th-6th high X; 13th-14th low; 21st-23rd high X;—from this change in trend stocks will sell very much lower before December; 27th-28 low.

OCTOBER: Good reports of railroad earnings will continue and stocks will be advanced to help distribution. General business quite good. Some complications with foreign countries. Labor will be satisfied and peaceful. Danger of some trouble with Mexico. Watch stocks around the 5th-6th, as this may be the last high before a big decline. October 18th-21st some stocks will make top in a very active market; 23rd-27th sharp decline, with rails breaking badly.

INDUSTRIAL STOCKS indicate extreme high 3rd-5th and 15th-18th; extreme low 25th-27th. Minor Swings—3rd-5th high; 12th-13th low; 18th-20th last rally before big break; 27th-28 sharp decline.

RAILROAD STOCKS indicate extreme high 3rd-5th; extreme low 13th-14th and 26th-27th. Minor Swings—3rd-5th last high before big decline; 13th-14th low; 17th-18th rally; 26th-27th sharp decline.

Dates to Watch for Change in Trend—October 5th-6th high X; 13th-14th low; 20th-21st high X; 26th-27th low.

NOVEMBER: Some very disturbing and depressing conditions; falling off in business; danger of strikes and trouble with foreign countries. Oils and Steels will have some spurts of activity and advances, but they should be sold on every rally. November 4th-5th will be high, from which a big decline will take place; 10th-14th panicky break; 19th-26th another severe decline, with bad breaks in oils and active leaders.

INDUSTRIAL STOCKS indicate extreme high 5th-6th; extreme lows 12th-13th and 25th-26th. Minor Swings—5th-6th high; 12th-13th low; 20th-21st high; 25th-26th low.

RAILROAD STOCKS indicate extreme high 4th-5th; extreme lows 13th-14th and 24th-25th. Minor Swings—5th-6th high; 13th-14th low; 19th-20th rally; 26th-27th low.

Dates to Watch for Change in Trend—November 4th-5th high X; 12th-13th low; 19th-20th high X; 26th-27th low.

DECEMBER: Very unsettled conditions prevail. War talk, if not actual war. Danger of strikes. Bad business conditions will cause panicky declines in stocks. The public who bought stocks at the top of the boom will now be forced to sell regardless of price, causing a big decline and many stocks making lowest prices of the year. Industrial stocks will break before the Rails. The Railroads and some Oils may hold up and rally to around December 10th-11th, but a severe decline takes place around the 10th to 15th, where bottom will be reached; 23rd-26th indicates a sharp decline in Rails, Motors, and Electric stocks, followed by a strong rally to the end of the month.

INDUSTRIAL STOCKS indicate extreme low 10th-15th; extreme high 31st. Minor Swings—1st-3rd high; 10th-13th low; 15th-16th rally; 17th-18th low; rally to December 31st.

RAILROAD STOCKS indicate extreme low 10th-15th; extreme highs 21st and 30th-31st. Minor Swings—1st-3rd high; 10th-14th low; 19th-21st high; 24th-26th low; 31st high of rally.

Dates to Watch for Change in Trend—December 3rd-5th high X; 12th-13th low; 18th-19th high X; 25th-26th low.

November 30th, 1921.

W. D. GANN.

This is an exact copy of my Forecast on Stocks for 1922 as sent out on November 30th, 1921.

A chart or projected curve was sent out with the 1922 Stock Forecast, as reproduced here. The heavy line shows my forecasted trend and the dotted line the Dow-Jones' Averages. You can see how accurately it worked out.

The Forecast called for three tops on Industrial stocks. It indicated a first top for April, a second top for August, a third and final top for the Bull market between October 8 and 15.—The extreme high prices were made on October 14, from which followed a big decline as forecasted.—Under the month of November the Forecast read: "10th-14th panicky break," which was fulfilled with remarkable accuracy.

The Railroad stocks indicated final top for the year on August 14.—The high was made on August 21 and the same level reached on September 11 and October 16, from which a big decline took place, as outlined in the Forecast.

In September, 1922, I issued a supplement telling subscribers that bottom would be made September 30, instead of September 15. Again, the latter part of November, I issued another supplement advising that stocks were bottom and that they would advance in December, and not decline in the early part of the month. With these two corrections, the Forecast was 90 per cent correct. The important and valuable feature about the Forecast was the way it called exact date—October 14—for final high, the Averages reaching the exact point forecasted. No other man that I know of has ever made such accurate long-range forecasts.

Jul 27-
Aug 3

240

220   Nov   Dec
            20-26   23

200

180

160

140

120   Apr 26-
      May 1 May   Nov
100   10-12   5-7   Dec
                            June   5-6
      May   May 18-21   Sep 19-
80   27   31   10-12 21

60   10-12

40   May   23-24   15
      24
                             Aug
20   May   May Jun   16-18
      3-6   30   3-7
                             Aug
0   30-31

20   3-5
      Apr
                                        Oct
40   18-24

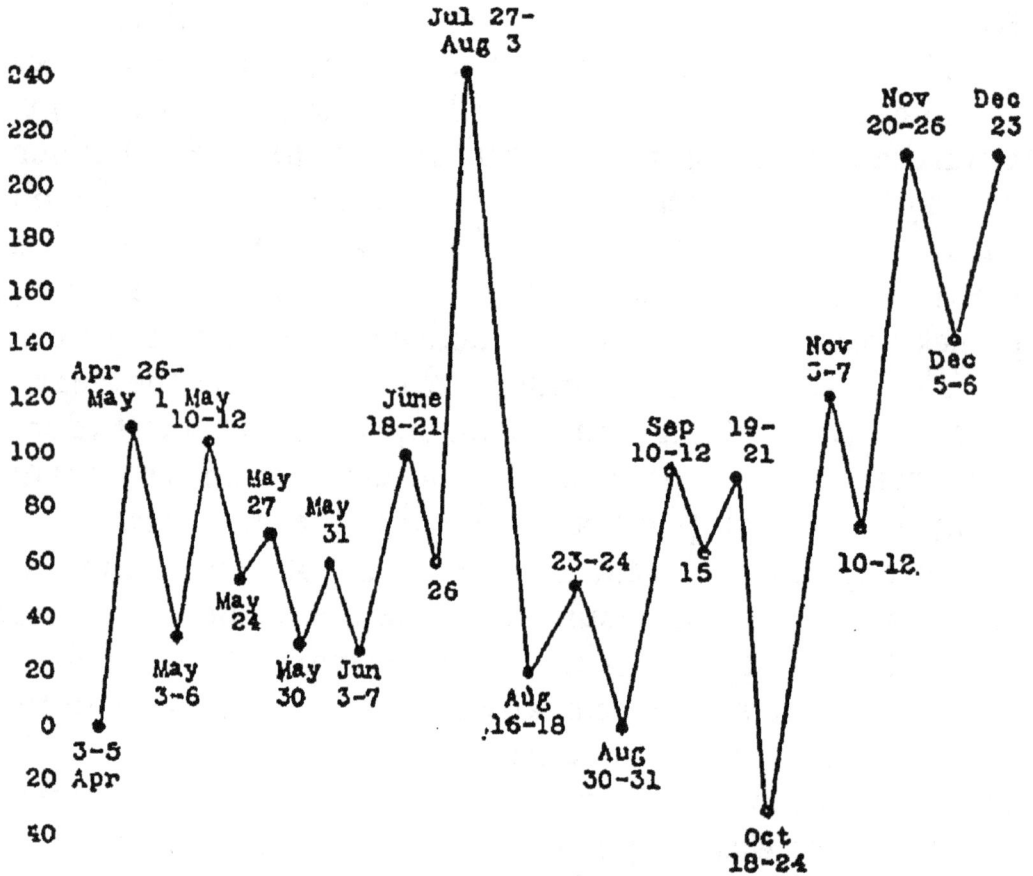

The indications this year are for a range of prices considerably above the average of normal years. An advance takes place in the Spring; then a reaction of about 60 to 100 points until the early part of June, when the market becomes very active and advances, making high of the year on July 28th to August 2nd.

News of crop damage during July will cause a big advance. There is a probability of a drought in Texas and too much rain in the southern and eastern belts. The reports of damage will be very much exaggerated, as usual, and will force prices to a level which can not be maintained.

Better crop news and increased estimates of a larger yield will be in evidence the latter part of August, causing a severe decline. The low of the Fall swing occurs around October 18th to 23th. After this date damage by frost and increased demand for spot cotton will cause another rapid rise which will culminate November 10th to 15th. Then follows a reaction to around December 3rd to 5th; then a rally to December 22nd to 24th.

The enclosed chart shows the major swings of the market. Note from the low of April 5th the advance runs up to April 26th to May 1st; then a reaction to around May 5th to 6th, followed by a rally which will carry prices to the level of May 1st and probably higher by May 10th to 12th.

After this date the fluctuations are narrow until June 3rd to 7th, when the Government crop report will start an advance. The real Bull move will not start until near the end of June, when bad crop news begins to come in. The advance which culminates the latter part of July and early part of August will be very rapid, and the decline which follows will also be very rapid..

After the break starts, rallies of 30 to 40 points are about all that is indicated until the bottom is made around August 30th to 31st. Prices should then be down to the level of the early part of April and possibly lower.

Then follows a sharp rally of about 100 points, making top around September 10th to 13th. After this date the long swing is down to October 18th to 25th, when prices should be 50 to 60 points below the level of the early part of April. The November rally, which culminates around the 10th to 15th, should carry prices to within 50 or 60 points of the high prices made at the top in July and August.

MAY: During this month cold, rainy weather will delay the progress of the growing crop, but the demand for spot cotton will be light and the market will not show great activity until the latter part of the month.

May 26th to 30th—Some bad news should cause increased activity and a quick rally.

JUNE: Reports of dry weather in the western and extreme southern belt, and too much rain in the eastern belt, will start an advance in the October option. June 11th to 15th and 26th to 30th—Around these dates great activity is indicated, and if an advance starts, it will continue for some time.

JULY: Reports of crop damage will be more numerous this month than any other time. A wild buying wave by the public and increased demand for spots will cause wide fluctuations and a big advance. July 26th—Around this date an exciting market and wild fluctuations are indicated. It may mark the first top of the Bull swing.

AUGUST: The early part of the month is bullish, but the big decline will take place in the latter part. August 19th—A very important date to watch for a change in trend. If a rally starts at this time, it may be quite sharp, although it will not hold.

SEPTEMBER: The early part of the month is bullish. There will be bad crop news and a great demand for spots, but if there is a sharp advance around the 10th to 12th, you can expect a decline the balance of the month. September 26th to 30th—A very active market when prices should decline.

OCTOBER: 5th to 6th—Very important; watch for change in trend. There may be some rally at this time, but it is not likely to hold. 16th to 22nd—Indicates a sharp decline, and if the break is quite severe, it is likely to mark last bottom before big advance starts. 27th to 30th—Very active; some important news will come out to affect prices. There is possibility of a sharp decline, but it will not last, and prices will recover rapidly.

NOVEMBER: Reports of a shorter crop than expected will cause an advance. A better foreign demand for spots will also help the rise in prices. November 5th to 6th and 17th to 20th—Are very important dates that will mark changes in trend and indicate great activity.

DECEMBER: A decline takes place in the early part of the month. Bottom should be made on 3rd to 5th, but there is a possibility of a break around the 10th to 13th. The Government estimate on the total crop will be larger than expected, but it probably will have been discounted.. The spot demand will be good, and a sharp advance will take place the latter part of the month.

IMPORTANT DATES TO WATCH FOR CHANGE IN TREND

The following dates are very important and you should watch them for changes in the major or minor trend: April 26th to 27th; May 26th; June

2nd to 4th and 24th to 26th; July 3rd, 9th to 10th, and 24th to 25th; August 22nd to 23rd; September 4th to 7th; 21st and 22nd; October 5th and 6th; 20th to 21st; November 3rd to 4th; 19th to 22nd; December 14th; 18th to 19th.

BEST OPTIONS TO TRADE IN

During the Spring and Summer the October and July options should follow closely the trend outlined on the chart. After September, the December and January options should follow the Forecast the best. During November and December, if the March option is active, it will probably be the best one to trade in.

April 25th, 1922.

W. D. GANN.

This is an exact reproduction of the Cotton Forecast sent out April 25, 1922.

Note that the Forecast called for low prices April 3-5.—The last reaction and low price was made on April 2, after which the trend continued up, subject to reactions, until August 1.

You will see that the top for the summer bull campaign was predicted for July 27 to August 3.—The exact high price was made on August 1, from which a big decline followed, as forecasted.

A correction was made in the October Supplement, which advised that the trend had turned up and that prices would not come down to the level indicated for October 18-24.

The Supplement for November called for the top and change in trend for about November 8.—The exact high price was made on November 9, when the trend turned down.

Cotton made exact low price on December 6 and rallied to December 23, as predicted in the Forecast.

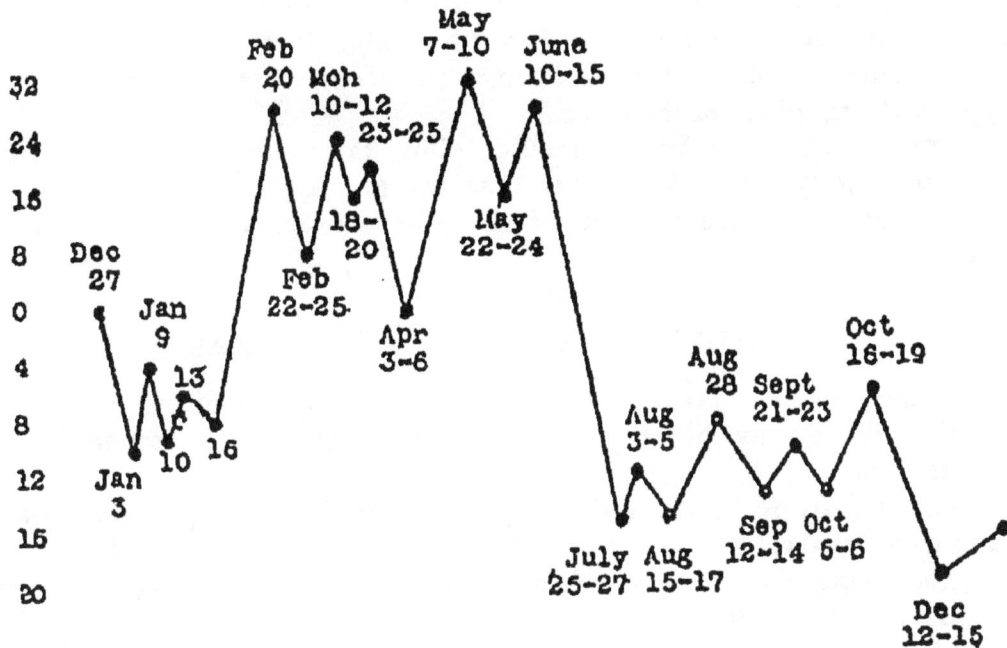

FORECAST ON GRAIN FOR 1922.

Projected Curve and Trend which Wheat should follow:-

This forecast is made up principally for Wheat, although Corn should follow it very closely, making tops and bottoms about the same dates as Wheat does, but, of course, working in a narrower range.

The chart attached gives you the Major and Minor moves as they will occur during the year. The point on the Chart marked "O" is the price at the end of December, or the high price of December 27th. The figures above and below "O" represent cents per bushel, as you will see.

Note that the decline from December 27th high to January 3rd low was about 10 cents per bushel, as indicated on the chart. Note that the low price after February 20th rally occurs on April 3rd to 6th, when prices should be down about 12 cents per bushel from the high price around February 20th.

From the April bottom follows the strongest advance of the year, when prices should run up about 16 cents per bushel, where top should be made around May 7th to 10th.

Highest prices of the year are indicated for the month of May; then the big swing down, making low around July 25th to 27th, which should be about 20 cents per bushel down from the high price reached in May. Notice that a small rally takes place up to around August 3rd to 5th; then follows a decline, making a second bottom about as low as the bottom made on July 25th. Second bottom should be made around August 15th to 17th.

After that time the trend should be up until October 16th to 19th, and the rise from July and August bottoms should be about 8 or 9 cents per bushel on Wheat.

Then follows a long down trend to December 12th to 15th, when prices should reach the lowest of the year. In my judgment they will be below 90 cents per bushel.

The decline from October 16th to December 15th should be about 12 to 13 cents per bushel.

The extreme range on Wheat, between the high of the year and the low of the year, should be between 30 and 35 cents per bushel. However, you must not depend too much on the number of cents per bushel up or down in the major or minor swings. The main thing to watch is the dates for tops or bottoms, and if the market comes out pretty close to these, you should buy or sell regardless of the price.

The May option of Wheat should follow the predicted trend closest up until about May 10th. After that time use the July option until the early part of July. For the balance of the year the September and December options.

IMPORTANT SWINGS OF THE YEAR

January 3rd low; January 16th next low point before big up swing starts.

February 20th top of rally; followed by a reaction to around February 22nd to 25th.

Then a rally to March 10th-12th, which should carry prices to near top made in February.

Long swing down, making low around April 3rd to 6th, when prices should be much lower than in January.

REMEMBER THIS POINT: If May Wheat sells at 1.08 after January 25th, it will indicate much lower prices and probably a decline to around 95 to 92 cents per bushel.

From April 6th a sharp rally up to May 7th to 10th.

Then the long swing down, making bottom July 25th to 27th.

From the July bottom the trend will work up to around October 16th to 19th.

Then follows a long swing down to December 12th to 15th, November being a very bearish month.

DATES TO WATCH FOR CHANGE IN TREND

The most important dates to watch for major changes in trend are: March 20th to 24th; June 21st to 23rd; September 20th to 24th.

The following dates will mark moves of minor importance. You can watch them for reversals. If prices should be low on a date that I have indicated as high, then the next is likely to come out low instead of high. Minor fluctuations and some kind of a small rally or decline will occur around these dates:

January 3rd low; 9th high; 16th low; 28th top of rally for small reaction.

February 5th low of minor reaction; 20th-21st top of major swing; 24th-25th low; 27th top of small rally.

March 7th low of reaction; 12th-13th top of rally; 19th-20th low of reaction; 27th-28th top of rally.

April 4th-5th low of major move; 11th-12th high for reaction; 18th-19th low of reaction; 27th high for small reaction.

May 3rd-4th small reaction; 10th-11th high of major move; 18th-19th low of reaction; 27th high of rally.

June 2nd-3rd reaction; 9th-10th high; 17th low; 24th-25th high.

July 2nd-3rd low; 8th-9th high of rally; 16th-17th low; 20th-21st small rally; 24th-25th low; 27th-28th small rally; 30th-31st low.

August 7th-8th small rally; 15th-16th low; 22nd-23rd high; 28th-29th low for rally.

September 5th-6th high; 13th-14th low; 20th-21st high; 27th-28th low of reaction.

October 5th-6th rally; 13th-14th minor reaction; 18th-19th top of major swing; 26th-27th low for rally.

November 5th-6th top of rally; 11th-12th low; 18th-19th rally; 25th-26th low of reaction.

December 3rd-4th top of rally; 11th-15th low of major swing; 17th-18th rally; 25th-26th low; 30th-31st high of rally.

A supplement will be mailed you each month, giving any changes that are indicated, if the market is not following closely the trend as outlined.

January 31st, 1922.

W. D. GANN.

The above is an exact copy of my Forecast on Grain for 1922 sent out on January 31st, 1922.

The Forecast called for extreme low to be made January 3.—May Wheat made the low—108½—on January 3. Minor reactions occurred on January 10 and 16 as forecasted.

Then followed a big advance, May Wheat reaching 147½ on February 21. The extreme high of the year—149⅞—was made on February 27.—The Forecast was only seven days off from the exact high point.

The Forecast called for 42 points' advance from January 3 to February 20, and the actual advance was 42⅜ points from January 3 to February 27.

The decline occurred during June and July as forecasted, and the low price—104½—was made on September 14.—The Forecast indicated September 12-14 for bottom.

A top was indicated for October 16-19, and the high prices occurred on October 18, from which a 4-cent reaction took place.

A Supplement was issued at the end of October advising that if May Wheat rallied to 116, the trend would reverse and no further big decline could be expected.—The trend did reverse and the market advanced up to the end of December.

These Forecasts are proof conclusive of the great value of long-range predictions, which tell you when extreme high or low prices on stocks, cotton or grain will be reached and enable you to buy or sell before the important moves start.

The big money in the markets is made on the long swings and not by day to day trading. The major moves of the stock and commodity markets recur as regular as the sap rises in the trees in the springtime and the leaves fall in the autumn.

Over twenty years' study and investigation places me in a position to make Forecasts which are dependable and enable you to make profits.

Even Squares for Cotton & Eggs
Time and Price

Master 360° Circle Chart

		1	2	3	4	5

Left vertical axis labels (top to bottom):

12 24/23, 11 22/21, 10 20/19, 9 18/17, 8 16/15, 7 14/13, 6½ 13/12, 6 12/11, 5 10/9, 4½ 9/8, 4 8/7, 3½ 7/6, 3 6/5, 2½ 5/4, 2 4/3, 1½ 3/2, 1 2/1, 1/1

Angle / fraction column (reading down):

Angle	Fraction
30°	1/12
60°	1/6
90°	1/4
120°	1/3
150°	5/12
180°	1/2
210°	7/12
240°	2/3
270°	3/4
300°	5/6
330°	11/12
360°	0
30°	1/12
60°	1/6
90°	1/4
120°	1/3
150°	5/12

O. GANN, President

CABLE Address: GANWAOE, NEW YORK.

SMALL SUPPLY
LARGE DEMAND
RISING PRICES

LARGE SUPPLY
SMALL DEMAND
FALLING PRICES

SCIENTIFIC ADVICE
ON
STOCKS, COTTON, GRAIN.

ANALYTICAL REPORTS
ON
MARKET CONDITIONS

W. D. GANN SCIENTIFIC SERVICE INC.
78 WALL STREET, NEW YORK

1929 ANNUAL STOCK FORECAST

Projected Curve #1 and Main Trend which the 30 Industrial Stocks
should follow:-

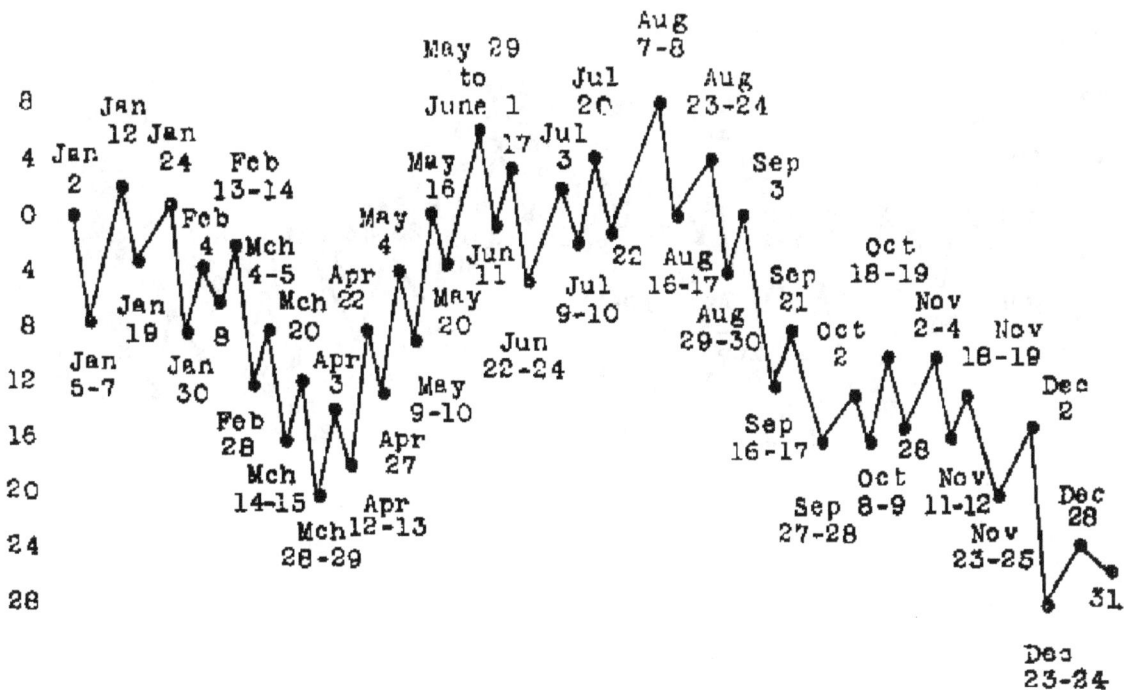

Projected Curve #2 which Industrial Stocks in strong position should
follow:-

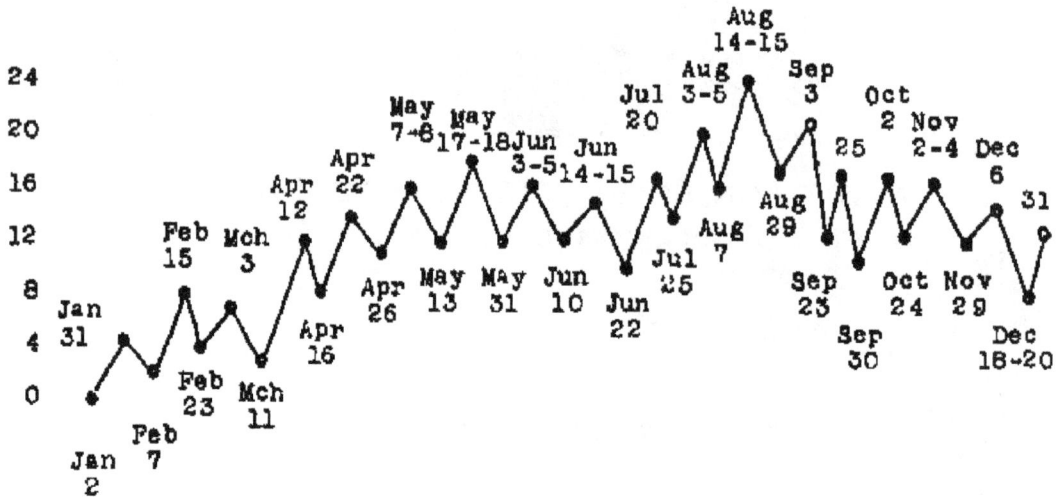

Aug
14-15
24
Jul   Aug   Sep
20   3-5   3
May May   Oct
7-8 17-18 Jun Jun   2   Nov
20   Jun 14-15   25   2-4 Dec
Apr   6
16   Apr 22   31
12
Feb Mch   Aug   Aug
15   3   7   29
Apr   May May Jun   Sep   Oct Nov
12   16   26   13   31   10   Jul   23   24   29
Jan   25
8   Jun
31   22   Sep   Dec
4   30   18-20
0   Feb   Mch
Feb 23   11
7
Jan
2

Projected Curve which Railroad Stocks should follow:-

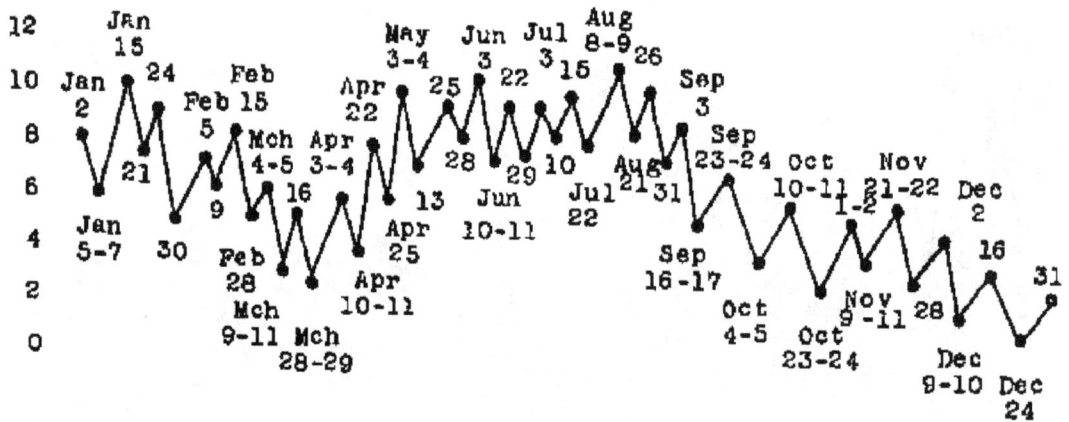

12   Jan
15
Jan   24   May   Jun Jul Aug
10   2   Feb   3-4   15   8-9 26
Feb 15   25   3   22   Sep
8   5   Mch Apr   Apr   3
4-5   3-4   22   Sep
6   9   16   28   29   10   Aug 23-24 Oct   Nov
Jan   13   Jun   Jul   21 31   10-11 21-22 Dec
4   Jan   30   Apr   10-11   22   1-2   2
5-7   Feb   25   Sep   16
2   28   16-17   Oct   Nov   31
Mch   Apr   4-5   Oct   9-11   28
0   9-11 Mch   10-11   23-24   Dec
28-29   9-10 Dec
24

Industrial Curve No. 1, shown below, is an exact copy of my Forecast, sent out on November 3, 1928, for the year 1929. Curve No. 2 is an exact copy of the projected trend for stocks in strong position which led the advance. The charts of 30 Industrials and 20 Rails will show you how closely the Dow-Jones Averages followed my Forecast. Note how the Forecast called for the big decline which culminated in March and indicated bottom; how it advised buying for a big advance to last until August. Most stocks made top within a few days of the date forecast. You will see that the Forecast indicated September 3 as last day that stocks should be top and a big decline follow. On September 3, the Dow-Jones 30 Industrial stock averages reached the highest of the year and the highest in history, from which a big decline followed, as indicated in the Forecast.

Do you know of any other economic, investment or advisory service that was able to predict the 1929 stock panic one year in advance? My Forecast was based on my Master Time Factor and mathematical interpretation of the return of cycles. It was not based on guesswork or human judgment. If it had been, I would have been just as wrong as other people who guessed. You cannot afford to depend on guesswork when you are risking your money in the market. What others think makes no difference. You want to follow someone who knows. When you know the future, you have no fear and can trade with confidence.

My Annual Stock Forecast will help you to know when to buy and sell at the right time and will prove of great value to you. We have a chart reproducing my Annual Forecasts from 1919 to date and a comparison with the Dow-Jones averages, which we will be glad to send to anyone interested, also literature, testimonials and newspaper comments on the service. My Annual Forecasts on Grain, Cotton, Coffee, Sugar, Cocoa and Rubber have proven very accurate for many years.

1929 ANNUAL STOCK FORECAST

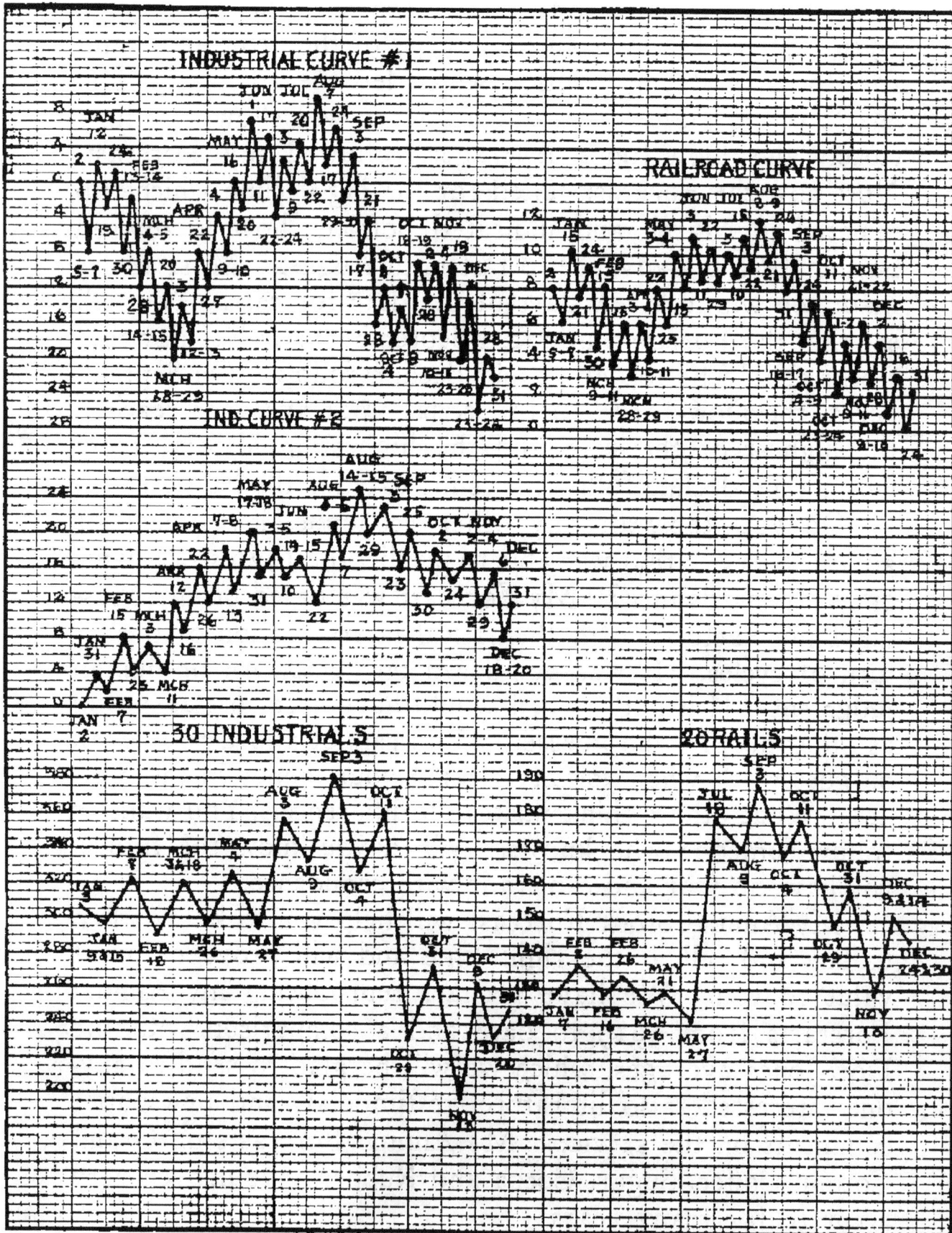

This year occurs in a cycle which shows the ending of the bull market and the beginning of a prolonged bear campaign. The present bull campaign has lasted longer than any other previous campaign in the history of this country. The fact that it has run longer and prices have advanced to such abnormal heights means that when the decline sets in, it must be in proportion to the advance. The year 1929 will witness some sharp, severe panicky declines in many high-priced stocks.

The history of the stock market has always been that it discounts prosperity and that in doing so prices always advance too far. In other words, the stock market runs too far ahead of prosperity and the first decline is only a readjustment back to what stocks should sell according to their merit and investment return. Then, when business depression sets in and earnings start to show a falling off, stock prices continue to go lower, discounting unfavorable business conditions.

But such groups of stocks as the oils, sugars, rubbers and some of the agricultural stocks, which have been depressed and declined while other stocks advanced, will record much higher prices in 1929. New and popular industries will continue to prosper, such as, radio, airplane, chemical and electrical concerns. This is the electrical age. People take quickly to new inventions, especially those which provide for the convenience and comfort of living. This will increase the earnings of concerns manufacturing new electrical appliances.

Many stocks will be distributed and will work lower while the stocks in strong position work higher. With such a varied list of stocks representing so many industries in different parts of the country, it is not reasonable to suppose that they would follow the same trend by any means.

More and more business is getting into the lines of mass production, mergers and consolidation. The big companies are getting the business while the smaller companies find it harder to get business enough to return a fair amount on their capital stock.

During the early part of the year, business conditions will not be up to general hopes and expectations. In the Spring and Summer business will improve and the outlook generally will be cheerful. But again in the Fall of the year depression will set in and unfavorable business conditions will cause big declines in stocks. Money rates will be high the greater part of the year.

During the year 1928 the public have entered the stock market on the largest sale ever known in history. Foreigners have bought our stocks more than at any time since or prior to the outbreak of the World War. The American public is no longer making safe investments in stocks. They have the gambling fever and are buying everything regardless of price, simply buying on hope that stocks will continue to go up. This is a dangerous situation and has always resulted in a big decline. There will be no exception in this case.

The man who makes money buying stocks in 1929 will have to use greater discrimination than ever before in selecting the right stocks to buy. When once stocks have reached final top and start on the way down, they will continue to work lower and rallies will get smaller. Those who hold on and hope will have big losses. The markets will move over a very wide range and sharp, severe declines will be followed by quick rallies. It will be necessary most of the time for a trader to be very nimble and change position quickly in order to take advantage of the opportunities as they develop in an active market.

WHAT WILL CAUSE THE NEXT DEPRESSION IN BUSINESS AND DECLINE IN STOCKS?

Prosperity!—The great wave of prosperity which this country has experienced during the past few years has been in many ways responsible to the stock market. The great increase in the value of stocks has increased the borrowing power of various companies and has permitted expansion and even inflation. The pendulum has swung so far in one direction that many people have forgotten that it can ever swing back in the other direction, but one extreme always follows another and it will not fail at this time. Stocks, like water, always seek their level.

The great earnings of many large corporations during the past year can not be expected to continue. Over-confidence is just as bad as extreme pessimism. It is just as easy for a big man to make a mistake as it is a little man. In my judgment many of the wisest speculators who have made large fortunes out of this bull campaign will overstay their market and be caught just the same as they have in the past. Then when the decline gets under way and they try to liquidate in a bear market, they will bring about a real smash in prices. It is one thing to mark stocks up to dizzy heights and quite another thing to be able to sell all of them near top prices. As stocks decline, forced selling both by pools and the public always comes into the market and causes prices to go lower than they naturally would if there had not been over-speculation. The public never has been considered good leaders in a bull market. The fact that they are now in the market in greater numbers than ever before makes the technical position of the market more dangerous.

Inflation.—The volume of trading on the New York Stock Exchange during 1928 was the largest in history and at this writing the total sales for the year have exceeded 750,000,000 shares and will approach 900,000,000 by the end of the year. Stock Exchange seats have had the greatest advance in history. Brokers' loans doubled in 1927 and 1928. Such enormous volume of trading at extreme high levels with feverish markets and wide fluctuations can mean only one thing,—that the pools and insiders have taken advantage of public buying to liquidate stocks and when once they have sold all they have to sell, they will not support the market. With the public so heavily involved in such large numbers and being unable to support the market, when once the decline gets under way, it will be more sharp and severe than ever before. Loans will be called and bankers will make new loans only on the very best security. We will hear of many stocks being thrown out of loans.

Another contributing factor to inflation was our large holding of gold but this has changed materially during 1927 and 1928 when more than half a billion of gold has flowed out to foreign countries and there are no prospects that it will not continue during the next few years.

Instalment Buying.—People are still living beyond their means and instalment buying continues on a large scale. We believe it will yet prove to be the greatest menace to business and to the prosperity of the country. When depression sets in and unemployment increases and people are unable to pay for goods which they have bought on a credit, buying power will be reduced and many companies will not only lose business but will lose money on goods sold on a credit.

Agricultural Situation.—Has been so unfavorable during the past few years that the Government has had to devise means to help the farmer and no doubt President Hoover will see that some law is passed to remedy this condition. However, we are in a cycle which is likely to produce crop failures or a series of small crops for some years to come. This will reduce the purchasing power of the farmer and help to bring about deflation in stocks.

Prosperity Complex.—The recent wave of seeming prosperity has been due to the psychological effect on people. They have watched stocks go wild in the past three years until they are hypnotized into believing that every concern and everybody is prosperous, but facts do not confirm it. During 1927 about 45 per cent of all concerns making income tax returns showed a loss in business and 1928 will not be much better. It is now a survival of the fittest. The small businesses are failing more every year. Conditions are changing so fast that many old firms are being forced out of business. Electricity and oil are taking the place of coal and wood. Automobiles supplanted the horse, and the railroads, despite the large increase in population and business, have not shown as great earnings as they did 20 years ago. Many industries have not been prosperous for some time. The textile, coal and agricultural industries have suffered. The oil situation has been bad until recently. The rubber industry has been demoralized by low prices. Sugar has been at low levels for the past two years. When people realize that prosperity is not general and confined to only a few lines, then they will have the "panic complex."

Public Confidence.—As long as the public believes that everything is all right, they will hold on and hope, but when public buying power has exhausted itself and the largest number of stock gamblers in history lose confidence and all start to sell, it requires no stretch of imagination to picture what will happen. When the time cycle is up, neither Republican, Democrat, nor our good President Hoover can stem the tide. It is a natural law. Action equals reaction in the opposite direction. We see it in the ebb and flow of the tide and we know that from the full bloom of summer follows the dead leaves of winter. Gamblers do not think; they always gamble on hope and that is why they lose. Investors and traders must pause and think, look and listen, and get out of stocks before the great deluge comes.

War.—Our great prosperity has caused jealousy throughout the world, and as conditions get worse in foreign countries, greed and jealousy will lead to war. It is the hungry dog that starts the fight. A study of the rise and fall of nations shows that when any country enjoys unusual prosperity for a long period of time, war is one of the main causes of the start of depression. While we hear a lot of talk about peace, the facts show that many of the leading foreign countries as well as our own country, are spending more money preparing for war than ever before in their history. When a man or a country is armed and gets ready to fight, he usually gets what he is ready for.

Foreign Competition.—Germany is rapidly coming back and competition for trade will be keener in the coming year. Many of the other foreign countries are making desperate efforts to regain their pre-war trade and will make progress along these lines, which will hurt our business.

INDUSTRIAL STOCKS

Main Trend or Major Swings

The Industrial Curve this year is based on the Dow-Jones' 30 Industrial Stock Averages. Previously the Dow-Jones' Averages, which are published by the *Wall Street Journal*, were based on 20 industrial stocks, but in the latter part of 1928, they changed from 20 to 30 and our Curve is based on the 30 Industrial Stocks. The stocks now used in these Averages are: Allied Chemical, Am. Can, Am. Smelting, Am. Sugar, Am. Tobacco B, Atlantic Refining, Bethlehem Steel, Chrysler, Gen. Electric, Gen. Motors, Gen. Ry. Signal, Goodrich, Int. Harvester, Int. Nickel, Nash Motors, Mack Trucks, North American, Paramount, Postum, Radio, Sears Roebuck, Stand. Oil of N. J., Texas Corp., Texas Gulf, Union Carbide, U. S. Steel, Victor Tk., Westinghouse, Woolworth, Wright Aero.

From the low level in August, 1921, to the high level in November, 1928, the 20 Industrial Stocks recorded an advance of about 230 points, the greatest advance in history. The fact that these Averages advanced nearly 100 points during 1928 is unparalleled in history. This year is like 1906, 1916, and 1919, when such violent fluctuations were witnessed and large volume of trading took place, only to be followed the year after by a panicky decline.

The minimum between extreme high and extreme low during 1929 for the 30 Industrial stocks will not be less than 50 points and the maximum fluctuation may be as much as 90 to 100 points. This means that many of the high-priced stocks will fluctuate 150 to 200 points between extreme high and extreme low prices. The lower-priced stocks will move in a narrower range and will not make as much as the minimum between extreme high and low.

Most of the Dow-Jones' 30 Industrial Stocks will follow Curve No. 1 very closely. The high point for most of these stocks will be reached around January 12th. After that time prices should gradually work lower and the trend should be down until around March 28th to 29th, when bottom will be reached for another bull campaign. Many stocks will reach bottom around March 14th to 15th and remain in a narrow trading range until the bull campaign starts in April. When the advance gets under way, some stocks will reach top for the year in May, others in June and some of the others which are behind the market will reach final high in August as shown by Curve No. 1 and Curve No. 2. A large majority of stocks will not go any higher than the highs reached in the month of July. After July and early August, the main trend will be down and some sharp declines will take place, prices working lower and reaching first bottom around September 27th to 28th. From this level follows a fair-sized rally and a trading market running into the early part of November. After that, the big bear campaign will get under way and stocks continue to work lower, reaching extreme low level for the year around December 23rd to 24th.

There are now over 1500 stocks listed on the New York Stock Exchange and often in one day over 800 different issues are traded in. Therefore, the 30 Industrials and 20 Rails do not always represent the main trend or curve of the market and many stocks will run in opposition to this trend. That is why I am giving you Curve No. 1 and Curve No. 2 on Industrial stocks.

Industrial Curve No. 2 represents the stocks which are in strong position and many of which are not included in the Dow-Jones' 30 Industrials. Many of these stocks have declined during 1928 and have been accumulating. They will advance while other stocks decline. Curve No. 2 indicates low around January 2nd followed by an advance up to January 31st; a decline to February 7th and high of next rally around February 15th. Then prices will work lower, making bottom around March 11th. Watch the stocks that make bottom at this time as they will be the ones to lead the advance. After the low in March, this Curve continues to work higher with only moderate reactions until high is reached around May 17th to 18th. From this top a bigger decline will take place. The last low is indicated around June 22nd. From this level the stocks which are in strong position and behind the market will gradually work higher, some of them reaching top during July while others will not reach final top until August 14th to 15th. After this top is reached heavy liquidation will start and prices will work lower from every rally. First decline culminates around September 30th; then a rally making top on October 2nd, followed by a decline to October 24th; then a final top around November 2nd to 4th, followed by a big decline, reaching bottom around December 18th to 20th; then a rally to the end of the year.

Below is a list of stocks in strong position which should follow closely Industrial Curve No. 2. They will be the best stocks to buy on reactions:

Ajax Rubber	Cont. Baking A	Loft	Sinclair Oil
Amerada	Cont. Motors	Lee Rubber	So. Porto Rico Sug.
Am. Agri. Ch.	Cuban Am. Sug.	Lehn & Fink	Spicer Mfg.
Am. Beet Sug.	Curtiss Aero.	Louisiana Oil	S. O. of Calif.
Am. Bosch Mag.	Davison Chem.	Mack Trucks	S. O. of N. J.
Am. Brake Sh.	Dome Mines	Magma	S. O. of N. Y.
Am. Drug	Elec. Pr. & Lt.	Mallinson	Sun Oil
Am. & For. Pr.	Elec. Storage	Maracaibo	Superior Oil
Am. Ship & Com.	Fisk Rubber	Marland	Tennessee Cop.
Am. Steel Fdy.	Foundation	Mex. Seab.	Texas Corp.
Am. Sugar	Glidden	Mid-Cont. P.	Texas Pac. C. & O.
Am. Woolen	Goodrich	Nat. Pr. & Lt.	Texas Gulf Sul.
Anaconda	Goodyear	Nevada Cons.	Transcont. Oil
Armour A	Granby	N. Y. Airbrake	U. S. Rubber
Assd. Dry Gds.	Gt. Nor. Ore	Otis Steel	U. S. Smelt.
Austin Nichols	Gt. West. Sug.	Packard	Va. Car. Chem.
Barnsdall A	Hupp	Panhandle	Ward Baking B
Beechnut	Indian Ref.	Pan Pete B	Warner Pictures
Bethlehem St.	Inspiration	Park Utah	Westinghouse Elec.
Booth F.	Int. Comb. Eng.	Pathe Ex. A	White Eagle
Briggs	Int. Mar. Pfd.	Phillips P.	White Motors
Cal. & Hecla	Jones Tea	Pillsbury Fl.	Willys Overland
Central Alloy	Kelsey Hayes	Reo Motors	Wilson & Co.
Cerro de Pasco	Kelvinator	Republic Iron	Worth Pump
Chandler Clev.	Kennecott	Reynolds Spg.	Wright Aero
Chile Copper	Kresge, S. S.	Royal Dutch	Yellow Truck
Congoleum	Lago Oil	Shell Union	Producers & Ref.
Cons. Textile	Loews	Simms Pete	

The stocks given in the list below are the ones which have been distributed and are the best to sell short around the dates indicated for top on Curve No. 1. These stocks will have the greatest declines, especially in the early part of the year and again from August to December when a big bear campaign is indicated.

Allis Chalmers	Chrysler	Int. Harvester	Timken
Allied Chemical	Coca Cola	Kroger	Tobacco Products
American Can	Cont. Can	Mathieson Al.	Union Carbide
Am. Intern'l	Corn Products	Mont. Ward	U. S. Ind. Alcohol
Am. Linseed	Dupont	Reynolds "B"	U. S. Steel
Am. Locomotive	Gen. Electric	Sears Roebuck	Vanadium
Am. Radiator	Gen. Motors	Shattuck F. G.	Victor Talking
Am. Smelting	Hudson Motors	Stewart Warner	Woolworth
A. M. Byers	Houston Oil	Studebaker	

RAILROAD STOCKS

Main Trend or Major Swings

The Railroad Curve is based on the Dow-Jones' 20 Railroad Stock Averages published by the *Wall Street Journal*. The issues used in these Averages are as follows: Atchison, Atlantic Coast, B. & O., Canadian Pacific, Ches. & Ohio, Rock Island, Del. Lackawanna & Western, Erie, Illinois Central, Louisville & Nashville, N. Y. Central, New Haven, Norfolk & Western, Northern Pacific, Pennsylvania, Pere Marquette, Southern Pacific, Southern Railway, Texas & Pacific, and Union Pacific.

From the low in June, 1921, to the high in November, 1928, these Railroad Averages advanced nearly 80 points. They have made the highest price in history, getting above the extreme high level recorded in 1906. The fact that they advanced into new territory in the latter part of 1928 shows the possibility of many rails which are in strong position going higher during 1929. But the fact that during prosperous times the railroads have been unable to earn an average of 6 per cent on their capitalization does not make them very attractive from a speculative standpoint. Only those which have merit and show large earnings will have very big advances during 1929.

The fluctuations between extreme high and extreme low during 1929 are not likely to be less than 20 points and the average may be as high as 30 to 35 points, which means that many high-priced stocks will fluctuate 50 to 75 points between extreme high and low.

The Rails as a rule follow the forecast trend better than the Industrials because they represent only one group of stocks while the Industrials represent fifteen or twenty different groups. The Dow-Jones' 20 Railroad Stock Averages are representative of the railroad group and most of the railroads will follow Curve No. 1 very closely, therefore it is not necessary to give Curve No. 2 this year.

Railroad Curve No. 1, you will notice on page 12, runs down from January 2nd and bottom is indicated around the 5th to 7th. Top for the month of January is indicated around the 15th and after this date the main trend is down, prices working lower and reaching first bottom around March 9th to 11th and second bottom around March 28th to 29th. Accumulation should take place around this time and a bull campaign should start. First top is indicated around May 3rd to 4th; then a decline, followed by an advance with second top, possibly a little higher, around June 3rd. Then another decline and irregular market, reaching low level around June 28th and 29th. After that prices will work higher until around July 15th; then decline to the 22nd, followed by an advance to around August 8th to 9th, when final top on rails should be made for another big decline. After this top, prices will work lower from every rally. A big decline is indicated for September; another sharp decline in October, reaching bottom around the 23rd to 24th; then a rally running to around November 21st to 22nd followed by a decline to December 24th, when the 20 Rails will reach the lowest price of the year.

The following Rails are in the strongest position and should have the greatest advances at the times when the bull campaigns are indicated:

Atlantic Coast Line	Del. Lackawanna & W.	Missouri Pacific
Bangor & Aroostook	Erie	New Haven
Brooklyn Man. Transit	Gt. Northern Pfd.	Northern Pacific
Chicago Gt. Western	Hudson & Manhattan	Seaboard Air Line
C. M. & St. Paul Com.	Kansas City Southern	Wabash Common
C. M. & St. Paul Pfd.	Mo. Kansas & Texas	Western Maryland

The Railroad stocks given below are those which are in the weakest technical position; have had advances and show distribution. They will be the best short sales on rallies during the times that the Forecast indicates declines.

Atchison	Lehigh Valley	Pittsburgh & W. Va.
Baltimore & Ohio	Louisville & Nash.	Reading
Canadian Pacific	N. Y. Central	St. Louis & San Fran.
Chesapeake & Ohio	Norfolk & Western	St. Louis & S. W.
Rock Island	Pere Marquette	Southern Pacific
Delaware & Hudson	Texas & Pacific	Southern Railway
	Union Pacific	

POSITION OF THE VARIOUS GROUPS

With the large number of stocks now listed on the New York Stock Exchange representing the various industries throughout this country and foreign countries, and as these different groups of stocks are affected by supply and demand and the varying conditions in the different parts of the United States and by events which transpire in foreign countries, it is impossible for them to all reach extreme high or extreme low on the same date or even in the same year or the same month. The different time element of the various stocks and groups of stocks will cause some to advance while others decline. Therefore it is well to watch the individual stocks. Watch those that make top in May, those that make top in June and those that make top in August. The ones that make top in the early part of the year and fail to reach higher levels in July or August, will be the ones to lead the decline, because they will have had longer time for distribution. Guard against selling short the late movers until they have had time to complete distribution. You will receive a list of stocks in strongest position and those in weakest position with the Supplement on the first of each month.

The Dow-Jones' 30 Industrial stocks are representative of the active industrials and most of them will follow the Industrial Curve very closely, but some of the individual stocks which are in strong or weak position will vary from this Curve and make tops and bottoms at different times. These special stocks and their position will be covered in the Supplements each month.

The New York *Herald Tribune* Averages on 70 stocks are a more active and reliable trend guide now than the Dow-Jones' 30 Industrials. I am giving the stocks used in these Averages because I will often refer to them in the Supplements issued on the first of each month during the year. The range of these 70 stocks between extreme high and low should not be less than 40 points and will probably reach as high as 70 to 80 points. They take in the representative stocks from the following groups:

COPPERS.—Am. Smelting, Anaconda, Cerro de Pasco, Calumet & Ariz., Greene Cananea, Kennecott and Tennessee Copper & Chemical.

EQUIPMENTS.—Am. Car & Fdy., Baldwin Loco., Gen. Ry. Signal, Pullman.

FOODS.—Am. Sugar Pfd., Armour & Co. of Del. Pfd., California Packing, Corn Products, Nat. Biscuit.

MANUFACTURING.—Allied Chemical, Allis Chalmers, Am. Can, Am. Radiator, Am. Tobacco, Burroughs Add. Machine, Chicago Pneumatic Tool, Coca Cola, Columbian Carbon, Eastman Kodak, Endicott Johnson, General Electric, Int. Bus. Machine, Int. Harvester and U. S. Rubber.

MOTORS.—General Motors, Chrysler Motors, Chrysler Motors Pfd., Jordan, Hudson, Mack Truck, Stewart Warner, Stromberg, Studebaker, White.

OILS.—Atlantic Refining, California Petroleum, Houston, Maryland Oil, Pan-American Pete "A", Pure Oil Pfd., Standard Oil of Calif., Standard Oil of N. J., Texas Company and Union Oil of Calif.

STEELS.—Bethlehem, Crucible, Gulf States, Sloss Sheffield, U. S. Steel, Vanadium.

STORES.—Gimbel Bros., Macy, Montgomery Ward, Sears Roebuck and Woolworth.

UTILITIES.—American Express, Am. Tel. & Tel., B'klyn Edison, Columbia Gas, Cons. Gas, Detroit Edison, Peoples Gas, Western Union.

A review of the above groups showing those in the strongest and weakest position will be sent with the Forecast or given in the Supplements each month.

IMPORTANT DATES FOR CHANGE IN THE MAJOR TREND

The following dates should be watched for important changes in the major trend of both Industrial and Railroad stocks. If any stock makes top or bottom around any of these dates, you can expect a reversal in trend, especially if there is a sharp decline or a sharp advance around these dates: Feb. 8th to 10th, March 21st to 23rd, May 3rd to 7th, June 20th to 24th, August 3rd to 8th, Sept. 21st to 24th, Nov. 8th to 11th, Dec. 20th to 24th. These dates are based upon a permanent cycle which does not change. Important tops and bottoms are made in many stocks every year around these times. Watch the stocks that reach extreme high or low levels around these dates.

DATES FOR ACTIVITY AND WIDE FLUCTUATIONS

The following dates indicate times when stocks will be very active and have wide fluctuations, making tops and bottoms. While all stocks will not make tops and bottoms around these dates, some of the most active ones will and if you watch the ones that turn around these dates, it will prove helpful in your trading:

January 5th to 7th, 12th to 15th, 18th to 24th.
February 9th to 12th, 20th to 22nd, and 27th to 28th.

March 10th to 11th, very important for change in trend; 21st to 22nd important; 28th to 29th another very important date for change.

April 3rd, 9th to 10th, 13th to 15th, 21st to 23rd.

May 3rd to 4th—watch stocks that make top around this date; 9th to 11th another important date when some stocks will make bottom and other stocks will make top. 22nd to 23rd and 29th to 31st—very important dates for change in trend; watch for stocks that will make top around this date.

June 1st to 2nd—quite important; 7th to 10th another important change; 21st to 23rd a more important change.

July 3rd to 5th—very important for change in trend; 9th to 10th also quite important; 21st to 24th more important.

August—One of the most important months for change in trend. Many stocks will start on their long down trend. 7th to 8th—quite important; 16th to 17th important; 23rd to 24th important; 29th to 30th of minor importance.

September 2nd to 3rd important; 16th to 17th important, should be bottom of a panicky decline. 21st to 24th important for top; 27th and 28th important for bottom of a big break.

October 2nd; 8th to 9th; 18th to 20th very important—watch stocks which start to decline and go with them; 26th to 28th minor importance.

November 10th to 22nd—a very important period for wide fluctuations. Airplanes, radio and some electrical stocks may have sharp advances. Other important dates for changes are 1st to 2nd, 17th to 19th, and 24th to 25th.

December 1st to 2nd important; 16th to 17th of minor importance; 23rd to 24th greater activity and of major importance.

The above dates are not only important for changes in trend and times when bottoms and tops should be reached, but on these dates important news is indicated and some will be of a sudden, unexpected nature, at times favorable and at other times unfavorable, but causing stocks to be active and fluctuate, making tops and bottoms and changing trend.

HOW TO TRADE WITH THE FORECAST

The time given for tops and bottoms is the most important factor for you to know and watch. It makes no difference about the price a stock is selling at. So long as you KNOW WHEN it will reach low or high levels you can buy or sell and make money. When the Forecast indicates bottom at a certain date and stocks decline, you should buy the ones given as in strong position or the ones we recommend buying and place a stop loss order 3 to 5 points away according to the price the stock is selling at. With stocks that sell at $200 to $300 per share, it is often necessary to use a stop loss order 10 points away because you have an opportunity to make large profits and can afford to take a greater risk.

Watch the action of stocks around the dates when the Forecast shows that tops or bottoms are indicated and when they hesitate for a few days and fail to make new high or low levels, you should get out and reverse position. Keep up charts and follow the rules in my book, TRUTH OF THE STOCK TAPE, and you will be able to follow the Forecast to better advantage and make more profit.

Do not expect the Averages or individual stocks to advance or decline as many points as shown on the graph or Projected Trend. This is only a guide to show you when big swings and activity are indicated. For example: Industrial Curve No. 1 begins at "O" on January 2nd and runs down to "7" on January 5th to 7th, a decline of 7 points on Averages. Some high-priced stocks may decline 10 to 20 points at this time while other low and medium-priced stocks will decline only 2 to 5 points. While some stocks which are late movers and in very strong position will follow Curve No. 2 and move up during January at the same time that high-priced leaders decline, the main thing is that Curve No. 1 shows a sharp advance from January 5th to 7th up to January 12th and Curve No. 2 shows up trend all the month of January. Therefore you should watch for a decline and buy the strong stocks around January 5th to 7th; then watch for top January 12th to 15th, sell out and go short of the stocks which are in our short sale list. Then on January 30th, if there has been a big decline as shown by Curve No. 2, you should cover shorts and buy for a rally and if stocks advance to February 13th to 15th, watch for top, sell out longs and go short because Curve No. 1 indicates a big decline the last half of February and during March.

The big buying opportunity will come in March. Around March 10th to 11th and 28th to 29th, you should buy the best stocks to hold for the Spring bull campaign into late May. Both Curve No. 1 and No. 2 indicate a big decline from July and August to December, therefore from July and August you should play the short side and wait for rallies to sell short rather than buy on breaks because the main trend will be down and you should never buck the trend but go with it.

Remember you must buy and sell at the right time regardless of prices. No matter how high stocks are, if they are going higher, you should buy. It makes no difference how low they are; if the trend is down and they are going lower, you must sell short and go with the trend. Take a loss quickly if you see that the Forecast is off or you have picked the wrong stock. Do not hold on and hope. Delays are dangerous. It is easy to make back small losses, but hard to regain big ones. Follow the rule—cut short your losses and let your profits run. Learn to act quickly. How much better to take action now than to trust to uncertain time. You can always get in the market again so long as you have money. New opportunities always come if you have patience and cash to take advantage of them.

1929 PREVIEW

JANUARY, FEBRUARY AND MARCH

While the new year opens under favorable conditions and you will hear much about great prosperity and the newspapers will be optimistic for the future, the bright outlook is likely to be clouded with war or complications in foreign countries. Trouble is threatened to the United States through Mexico or Japan. Peace pacts are likely to be broken. Spain and France will arouse opposition. Agitation over religion in some of the foreign countries will disturb peaceful conditions.

Great storms are indicated in the south and southwestern parts of the United States during the early Spring. Much loss and damage by fire. In March when President Hoover takes office, if some law has not already been passed, he will advocate having one passed to help the farmers. This will cause an advance in commodities and in turn help agricultural stocks. Airplane concerns will make rapid progress in the Spring and from a panicky depressed stock market in February and March, a Spring bull campaign will take place.

Steel business will be quite active. Electrical concerns will do a large business and there will be a boom in oil stocks.

APRIL, MAY AND JUNE

The Spring Quarter indicates unfavorable weather for starting crops. Storms and rains and danger of a tidal wave along the Gulf of Mexico. Commodity prices will advance and business in general will improve. A wild wave of speculation in oils, coppers, rubbers, sugars and airplane stocks will make this a very active period. Along in May or June foreign competition will begin to hurt business in some lines in this country. This will cause a depressing effect on stocks and they will decline.

JULY, AUGUST AND SEPTEMBER

During this period some of the foreign countries will prosper and we will have great competition to face. War or trouble with foreign countries is threatened. A very mixed market during this period with some stocks advancing while others decline. Speculation will shift from stocks to commodities on account of short crops. Foreign crops will be short in some of the countries. Storms and unseasonable weather will cause damage.

August will be marked by many electric storms and damage by fire. Some new discoveries will help chemical stocks around this time. Germany and France will make great strides in aviation.

September.—A great change in business conditions will set in around this time which will cause a severe decline in the stock market. Textile and woolen stocks will prosper and these will be among the last stocks to advance. During the months of April, August, September, and October, there is danger of war and trouble through foreign countries.

OCTOBER, NOVEMBER AND DECEMBER

Settlement of the debt question with France will again come to the front. Other countries will arrange some favorable agreement in regard to trade which will cause business depression here. A great change in the business outlook will set in as we near the end of the year. Corporation earnings will show depreciation and be disappointing.

The month of October indicates some advance in mining stocks. The oil and sugar stocks will be among the last to advance around this time. During November the chemicals and oils will have a boom for a short time and make final top. In December foreign business with South American countries will be good, but we will have competition from some of the European countries.

MONTHLY INDICATIONS

JANUARY

The new year starts off under favorable conditions, but profit-taking will start and stocks will sell off sharply the first few days. Then good buying will appear and an advance will start. The oils, rubbers, chemicals, and airplanes will lead the advance, reaching top around the 12th to 15th. Around the 18th to 24th some rails, electrics and steels will advance. Some trouble in foreign countries, probably Germany or France, will have an unfavorable effect and will help to start the decline here. Watch for top; sell out long stocks and go short. Quite a decline will take place to the end of the month.

Industrial Stocks indicate extreme high for the month around the 12th to 15th; extreme lows around the 5th to 7th and 30th. Minor moves: January 2nd decline should start; 5th to 7th bottom of decline. Heavy buying should start around this time and a sharp advance should take place, making top around the 12th. 19th bottom of decline; 24th top of rally; then follows heavy selling and a sharp decline, reaching bottom around the 30th.

Railroad Stocks indicate extreme high for the month around the 15th; extreme low around the 5th to 7th and 30th. Minor moves: January 2nd top, when decline should start; 5th to 7th bottom for quite a rally; 15th top of strong rally, when another decline should start; 21st bottom of decline; 24th top of rally. From this top a big decline should take place reaching low for the month around the 30th.

Dates to watch for change in trend: The dates marked "XX" are the most important and indicate a major change in trend. You should watch for important changes around these dates. The dates marked "X" only indicate minor changes in trend which will only last for a few days. January 5th–7th XX, 11th–12th X, 25th–26th XX, 31st X.

FEBRUARY

Business will fall off and we will hear some discouraging reports. The Federal Reserve Bank will make some change or threaten to curb speculation. There will be talk of new banking laws, which may be adverse to speculation. The general list of high-priced stocks will decline this month, although the market will be mixed. Sugars, rubbers and late movers will have some advances. The railroad, airplane, radio, and electric stocks will rally from every decline. Around the 12th to 13th of the month some of the oils, rubbers and sugars will be quite strong. The general list of old time leaders, however, will work lower from every little rally.

Industrial Stocks indicate extreme high for the month around the 13th to 14th and extreme low around the 28th. Minor moves: 1st to 4th advance; then follows a decline to the 8th, when bottom should be reached for another quick rally; 13th to 14th top, sell out and go short. Expect heavy liquidation and a sharp, severe decline reaching bottom around the 28th for a moderate rally.

Railroad Stocks indicate extreme high for the month around the 15th and extreme low around the 28th. Minor moves: 1st to 5th advance and make top for a moderate decline; 9th bottom of decline; expect quick rally in some rails, reaching high around the 15th, followed by a sharp decline making bottom around the 28th.

Dates to watch for change in trend: 9th to 12th XX; 19th to 20th XX; 23rd to 24th X, 28th X.

Mr. Hoover will take the office of President of the United States this month and in the early part of the month there will be a demonstration in stocks and quite an advance, but it will not hold and a sharp, severe decline will take place in many stocks before the end of the month. Some trouble is likely to come up in connection with Spain or Mexico which will upset the market. Airplane stocks will be quite strong during the dates indicated for advances to take place. The oils, sugars and chemicals will hold up better than other stocks. Traction stocks will be strong and there is likely to be some development in connection with the subway fare which will cause an advance in New York traction stocks. The steels, motors, rails, and electrical issues will break during the early and latter part of the month.

Industrial Stocks indicate extreme high for the month around the 4th to 5th; extreme low around the 28th to 29th, although some stocks will reach low for the month around the 14th to 15th. Minor moves: 1st to 5th strong advance. The market will be discounting President Hoover's inauguration. A sharp decline follows, making first bottom around the 14th to 15th; then a quick rally in many stocks reaching top around the 20th, followed by heavy liquidation and a sharp decline to around the 28th or 29th when final bottom will be reached for another bull campaign. This is the time to buy the stocks in strong position as they will have sharp advances and work higher into the summer.

Railroad Stocks indicate extreme high for the month around the 4th to 5th; extreme low around the 9th to 11th and 28th to 29th. Minor moves: 1st to 5th strong market. Stocks behind the market will lead the advance. From the top around the 4th to 5th quite a sharp decline will take place, culminating around the 9th to 11th; then follows a moderate rally reaching top around the 16th; then another decline, making final bottom around the 28th to 29th when you should buy the stocks in strong position for an advance which will last into the early days of May.

Dates to watch for change in trend: 4th to 5th X; 10th to 11th XX; 16th X; 21st to 23rd X; 28th to 29th XX.

The public will again come into the market on a large scale and there will be a wild wave of speculation, especially in the oils, coppers, rubbers, sugars and airplane stocks. The chemicals, airplanes and radio stocks will have rapid advances. Some action by the Government or law passed will cause a break which will run down to around the 15th. Money rates will be quite high. 16th to 30th, General news will be more favorable and stocks will have better advances. Foreign trade will increase, especially with the South American countries.

Industrial Stocks indicate extreme low for the month around the 12th to 13th and extreme high around the 20th to 22nd. Minor moves: 1st to 3rd top of quick advance; 12th to 13th bottom for another big advance; 20th to 22nd top of sharp rally; then follows a decline making bottom around the 26th to 27th when steels should be bought for another advance, running to the end of the month and continuing into May.

Railroad Stocks indicate extreme low for the month around the 10th to 11th and extreme high around the 20th to 22nd, although they will be quite strong and some will make higher just at the end of the month. Minor moves: 1st to 3rd–4th quick advance; then follows a moderate decline, reaching bottom around the 10th to 11th, when a sharp advance will take place, stocks running up fast and making top around the 20th to 22nd, followed by a reaction to the 25th; then a strong advance to the end of the month.

Dates to watch for change in trend: 2nd to 3rd X; 9th to 10th X; 13th to 15th XX; 21st to 23rd XX; 26th to 27th X.

MAY

This is a month for great activity in the stock market. We will hear some very bullish news about general business conditions. There will be some large combines, consummation of mergers; large financial deals will take place and there will be much talk of continued prosperity, all of which will cause the public to buy stocks at the top. General news will be very bullish and stocks will fluctuate over wide ranges. Some stocks will reach high around the early part of the month and have a break around the middle of the month. There will be a boom in rubbers, sugars, oils, airplanes, radio and electrical stocks. These will be the leaders. Watch for top and sell out. Do not overstay your market as a big break will take place in June.

Industrial Stocks indicate extreme high for the month around the 29th to 31st and extreme low around the 9th to 10th. Minor moves: 1st to 4th quick rally, making top for a sharp reaction; 9th to 10th bottom of decline; buy for another sharp advance; 16th top of rally, but only for a minor reaction; 20th bottom of reaction. Stocks in strong position will have a rapid advance between the 10th and 29th. Watch for top around this time.

Railroad Stocks indicate extreme high for the month around the 3rd to 4th; extreme low around the 11th to 13th, although some issues will go to extreme high around the end of the month. Minor moves: 1st to 3rd strong market, making top around 3rd to 4th. Then follows a decline, making bottom around the 11th to 13th, followed by an advance making first top around the 25th for a moderate reaction to the 28th; then rally to the end of month.

Dates to watch for change in trend: 3rd to 4th X; 9th to 10th XX; 22nd to 23rd X; 29th to 31st XX.

JUNE

A sharp decline and heavy liquidation in many stocks is indicated for this month. There will be war in foreign countries or war rumors. Strikes at home as well as abroad. Crop news will be unfavorable. Storms or earthquakes on the southern border and in Mexico will do damage and help to unsettle the market. The outlook for the summer business will be very much mixed. One of the major cycles and time factors runs out this month and a very important change in trend is indicated. High-priced stocks will have rapid declines and many stocks will make extreme high for the year.

The tin, oils and agricultural stocks and also the chemicals will break badly after reaching top in the early part of the month. Motors will also decline sharply.

Industrial Stocks indicate extreme high for the month around June 1st; extreme low around the 22nd to 24th. Minor moves: 1st to 2nd advance and make top for a big decline; 10th to 11th bottom of sharp decline; then follows a moderate rally reaching top around the 17th, followed by heavy liquidation and sharp decline making bottom 22nd to 24th. From the 24th to the end of the month many stocks will have quite a rally.

Railroad Stocks indicate extreme high for the month around the 3rd; extreme low around the 10th to 11th and 28th to 29th. The rails will not move in a very wide range this month, except a few of the very high-priced issues. Minor moves: 1st to 3rd advance; 4th to 10th–11th sharp decline; then follows a moderate rally, reaching top around the 21st to 22nd followed by liquidation and lower prices, making bottom for the month 28th to 29th.

Dates to watch for change in trend: June 1st to 2nd XX; 7th to 10th X; 21st to 23rd XX; 28th X.

JULY

Another advance will take place this month and many stocks will have sharp rallies and reach the final high for the year. The airplane companies will prosper and their stocks will advance. Electrical and chemical stocks will also record sharp advances. Pools will rush up stocks as fast as they can to unload. The late movers will be brought into line while distribution is taking place in the old time leaders. Sugars and rubbers should have some sharp advances. A very important major time factor ends at this time and indicates the starting of a big prolonged bear campaign. Remember that the last high for the year will occur in many stocks. A great deluge and panicky decline will follow the top at this time, resulting in a "Black Friday" in September. There are likely to be some labor troubles and strikes in the west and south which will interfere with the business outlook.

Industrial Stocks indicate extreme high for the month around the 20th; extreme low around the 9th to 10th. Minor moves: 1st to 3rd strong market, making top for a quick decline; 9th to 10th bottom of sharp decline; then follows a rapid advance, making top on the 20th; decline, reaching bottom on the 22nd; followed by a strong market to the end of the month.

Railroad Stocks.—The rails will move in a comparatively narrow range this month. Extreme low is indicated around the 9th to 10th and 22nd; extreme high around the 15th. Minor moves: 1st to 3rd advance; then follows a decline making bottom around the 9th to 10th; a quick rally to the 15th; then follows a sharp decline reaching bottom on the 22nd, followed by an advance to the end of July.

Dates to watch for change in trend: 3rd to 5th XX; 10th X; 21st to 24th XX; 30th to 31st X.

AUGUST

A few of the late movers will advance this month and reach final high. Chemical stocks will be among the last to advance. The steels and oils will be strong for awhile and the sugars and rubbers will make final top. Unfavorable news will develop which will start sharp declines and the long bull campaign will come to a sudden end. Money rates will be high and final top will be reached for a big bear campaign. Stand from under! Don't get caught in the great deluge! Remember it is too late to sell when everyone is trying to sell. There will be electric storms which will cause damage to crops and heavy losses are indicated through fires.

Industrial Stocks indicate extreme high for the month around the 7th to 8th; extreme low 29th to 30. Minor moves: The first of the month starts in strong and prices run up fast reaching top around the 7th to 8th; then heavy selling will take place and a sharp decline will follow, bottom being reached around the 16th to 17th, but only for a small rally; 23rd to 24th top of rally, followed by heavy liquidation and lower prices, making bottom for the month around the 29th to 30th.

Railroad Stocks indicate extreme high for the month around the 8th to 9th, although some industrial stocks and rails among the late movers will hold up and not make top until the 14th to 15th as indicated on Curve No. 2. Extreme low for the month for rails indicated around the 30th to 31st. Minor moves: 1st, advance will start and prices will run up fast, making top around the 8th to 9th; then follows a fast decline, reaching bottom around the 20th to 21st followed by moderate rally to around the 25th; then a sharp decline making low for the month on the 30th to 31st.

Dates to watch for change in trend: 7th to 8th XX; 16th to 17th X; 23rd to 24th XX; 29th to 30th XX.

SEPTEMBER

One of the sharpest declines of the year is indicated. There will be loss of confidence by investors and the public will try to get out after it is too late. Storms will damage crops and the general business outlook will become cloudy. War news will upset the market and unfavorable developments in foreign countries. A "Black Friday" is indicated and a panicky decline in stocks with only small rallies. The short side will prove the most profitable. You should sell short and pyramid on the way down.

Industrial Stocks indicate extreme high for the month around the 2nd to 3rd; extreme low 27th to 28th. Minor moves: 2nd to 3rd top of moderate rally. Heavy liquidation will break out around this time. Unfavorable news will develop and a sharp, severe decline will take place, reaching first bottom around the 16th to 17th, but only for a small rally. 20th to 21st top of moderate rally followed by another heavy wave of liquidation, carrying prices down to extreme low levels around the 27th to 28th, from which level a moderate rally will follow.

Railroad Stocks indicate extreme high for the month around the 3rd; extreme low at the end of the month. Minor moves: 1st to 3rd advance. Liquidation will start around this time and a sharp decline will follow, carrying prices down to around the 16th–17th; then a moderate rally on short covering with top around the 23rd—24th, followed by a sharp decline running down to the end of the month.

Dates to watch for change in trend: September 2nd to 3rd XX; 16th to 17th XX; 21st to 24th X; 27th to 28th XX.

OCTOBER

General business conditions will be getting worse and the country will suffer from the over-speculation. Money rates will be high and bankers will call loans, causing some sharp declines in stocks after rallies. The chemical, electrical and airplane stocks will hold up and have some quick rallies around the dates indicated for advances.

Industrial Stocks indicate extreme high around the 18th to 19th; extreme low around the 8th to 9th and 26th to 28th. Minor moves: October 2nd top of small rally from which a sharp decline will take place; 8th to 9th bottom of decline, when a better advance will take place, especially in the stocks in strong position; 18th to 19th top of rally. Stocks in weak position will have a sharp decline, running down to the 26th to 28th; then follows a moderate rally to the end of the month.

Railroad Stocks indicate extreme high for the month around the 10th to 11th; extreme low 23rd—24th. Minor moves: 1st to 4th decline and make bottom for a moderate rally; 10th to 11th top of rally; then follows a heavy wave of liquidation and lower prices making bottom around the 23rd to 24th, followed by a moderate advance to the end of the month.

Dates to watch for change in trend: 2nd to 4th XX; 8th to 9th X; 18th to 20th XX; 26th to 28th X.

NOVEMBER

The oils, chemicals and rubbers will have a final advance this month and make top for another decline. Business conditions will be growing more unfavorable. There are likely to be earthquakes in Mexico or California. This will disturb the stock market and depress business. This is the month for war news from foreign countries and some great leader abroad will show his power. The latter part of the month is very unfavorable and some sharp declines will take place. But the airplane, radio and electrical companies and some of the rails will have an advance around the 10th to 22nd.

Industrial Stocks indicate extreme high for the month around the 2nd to 4th; extreme low around the 23rd to 25th. Minor moves: 1st to 4th advance and make top for a sharp, severe decline; then follows heavy selling and a sharp decline, reaching bottom around the 11th to 12th, but only for a moderate rally; 18th to 19th top of advance. From this level there will be another sharp, severe decline carrying prices down to low levels around the 23rd to 25th. Then follows a moderate rally to the end of the month.

Railroad Stocks indicate extreme high for the month around the 21st to 22nd; extreme low around the 27th to 28th. Minor moves: 1st to 2nd top of moderate rally; then follows a decline, reaching bottom around the 9th to 11th; then a quick rally, making top around the 21st to 22nd followed by heavy liquidation and a sharp decline, making bottom around the 27th to 28th.

Dates to watch for change in trend: 1st to 2nd XX; 11th to 13th X; 17th to 19th XX; 24th to 26th X.

DECEMBER

Our business in some of the foreign countries will increase. Speculation will shift from stocks to commodities. The U. S. Government is threatened with great opposition, if not danger of war. General business outlook will grow very much more unfavorable. Panicky declines in stocks will take place.

Industrial Stocks indicate extreme high for the month around the 2nd; extreme low around the 23rd to 24th. Minor moves: 1st to 2nd advance; then follows a sharp, severe decline and heavy liquidation with only small rallies indicated lasting one to two days, reaching extreme low around the 23rd to 24th; then follows a quick rally reaching top on the 28th followed by decline to the 31st.

Railroad Stocks indicate extreme high for the month around the 2nd; extreme low around the 24th. Minor moves: 1st to 2nd advance; 3rd to 10th sharp decline, making bottom for only a moderate rally; 15th top of rally; then heavy liquidation and a decline running to the 24th; then follows a rally to the end of the month.

Dates to watch for change in trend: 1st to 2nd XX; 16th to 17th X; 23rd to 24th XX; 28th X.

This Forecast is PRIVATE AND CONFIDENTIAL and for your personal use only. For your own protection do not permit others to copy or use it.

W. D. GANN.

November 23rd, 1928.

TIME FACTOR AND FORECASTING METHOD

After you have learned all of the rules laid down in TRUTH OF THE STOCK TAPE and WALL STREET STOCK SELECTOR and have learned how to apply them, I am sure you will agree that I have given you more than your money's worth in these books. You will then be ready for a post-graduate course and will probably want to know how to forecast according to my Master Time Factor, and determine the years when stocks will have big advances and reach final tops and also the years and the cycles when panicky declines are indicated.

I teach all of these rules with my complete Forecasting Methods, showing how to determine the major and minor swings according to the time element. I can teach you how to determine the wave lengths of different stocks so you will know about how many points they are going to advance when they go into new territory and about how many points they are going to decline when they break out of the zone of distribution. With my Forecasting Methods, you can make up a forecast for the average market one or more years in advance and also make up a yearly forecast on individual stocks. Each stock moves according to its individual time limit and makes top and bottom at different times, because the vibration and wave length varies on the different stocks.

I teach Courses of Instruction on Cotton, Wheat, Corn, Oats, Rye, Lard, Coffee, Sugar, Cocoa, Rubber, Silk and other commodities, but I only impart these Methods to people who are willing to comply with my requirements. They are too valuable to be broadcast or put in the hands of people who cannot use them to advantage. Therefore, I only teach them to people who want them for their own use and do not intend to publish them or sell them to others. I will not teach my Forecasting Method to anyone unless I feel sure that they can make a success with it after they learn it. Some men cannot make a success with any kind of a method or rule. I would not take a man's money and teach him something that I did not think would benefit him.

The man who expects to succeed in speculation or investments must study and learn all that he can about the market. It has been well said, "Where knowledge begins, speculation ceases." Therefore, the aim and object of every man who wants to make success in speculation or investing should get as much scientific knowledge as possible and then he will be able to make profits.

W. D. GANN SCIENTIFIC SERVICE

My method of determining the trend of the stocks and commodity markets has stood the test of time. I have been in New York City for 22 years and have always done business under my own name. This Service possesses many superior advantages over other classes of service, because it has the one thing lacking in all other services—the *time element*. My discoveries of a Master Time Factor and the Great Cycle enable me to forecast markets years in advance. I do not depend on space charts based on space movements alone, because these would make errors and cause losses. I use volume combined with the proper time charts, which help me to determine the technical position of the stocks much better and a long time before the statistical position is shown. Time tells on all things. The fact that I have been selling my Forecasts all over the United States and in many of the foreign countries for the past 15 years, proves that they are valuable, because people continue to subscribe to them year after year. Investors and traders are always willing to pay for what will help them to make a greater success. It pays to get the best scientific knowledge, because the best is always the cheapest in the long run and you cannot expect to get something good for nothing. Experience has taught me that the best way to help others is to show them how to help themselves, and if I can get subscribers to read my books and learn my Methods, they make a greater success following my Service.

Supply & Demand Letter.—The object of this Service is to give you valuable advice based on scientific methods and to show you how to help yourself. Only a fool makes mistakes without learning something. I have benefited because I have made mistakes in the past and made losses. I can show you how to avoid the mistakes that most of the traders make in Wall Street.

The Busy-Man's Service.—Many bankers, merchants, manufacturers, lawyers, doctors and business men in all walks of life have no time to study the market and do their own forecasting. Therefore, our Service provides expert analysis for the man who cannot find time to do it himself. The busy-man's service which we furnish is really a personal service. We supervise accounts, constantly watching your stocks, advise when to buy or sell specific stocks; write personal letters, and send telegrams when necessary, but you do your own trading. We do not buy or sell for anyone and will not handle discretionary accounts under any conditions. We have nothing to sell but Service.

Being out of the market and not buying or selling anything or handling any promotions, I can give you better expert opinion, based on mathematical science and my time factors, than any banker, broker or other service. To succeed we must keep subscribers making money. There can be no loss in good service; it is all pure gain. The more we help others, the greater we are benefited.

CHARTS ON STOCKS AND COMMODITIES

We keep up charts on hundreds of different stocks and are prepared to make up daily, weekly and monthly high and low charts on almost any stock with or without the volume of sales. These charts are very valuable for traders to study. Every trader and investor should have a chart on the stocks that he trades in. The charts that we make up are not blueprints, but are made by hand on cross-section ruled paper and can be continued. With these charts and the rules and methods given in TRUTH OF THE STOCK TAPE and WALL STREET STOCK SELECTOR, you will make a greater success.

Prices for making up charts:

Monthly high and low chart for three years................ $1.00
     or ten years back for.................................... 3.00
Weekly high and low chart for one year................... 2.00
     or with volume.. 3.00
Daily high and low chart for one month................... 2.00
     six months or more at $1.00 per month or one year for.... 9.00

We also make up charts on cotton and grain options and other commodities at the same prices.

PERMANENT CHART

1	2	3	4	5	6	7	8	9	10	11	12	13	14	15	16	17	18	19	20
20	40	60	80	100	120	140	160	180	200	220	240	260	280	300	320	340	360	380	400
19	39	59	79	99	119	139	159	179	199	219	239	259	279	299	319	339	359	379	399
18	38	58	78	98	118	138	158	178	198	218	238	258	278	298	318	338	358	378	398
17	37	57	77	97	117	137	157	177	197	217	237	257	277	297	317	337	357	377	397
16	36	56	76	96	116	136	156	176	196	216	236	256	276	296	316	336	356	376	396
15	35	55	75	95	115	135	155	175	195	215	235	255	275	295	315	335	355	375	395
14	34	54	74	94	114	134	154	174	194	214	234	254	274	294	314	334	354	374	394
13	33	53	73	93	113	133	153	173	193	213	233	253	273	293	313	333	353	373	393
12	32	52	72	92	112	132	152	172	192	212	232	252	272	292	312	332	352	372	392
11	31	51	71	91	111	131	151	171	191	211	231	251	271	291	311	331	351	371	391
10	30	50	70	90	110	130	150	170	190	210	230	250	270	290	310	330	350	370	390
9	29	49	69	89	109	129	149	169	189	209	229	249	269	289	309	329	349	369	389
8	28	48	68	88	108	128	148	168	188	208	228	248	268	288	308	328	348	368	388
7	27	47	67	87	107	127	147	167	187	207	227	247	267	287	307	327	347	367	387
6	26	46	66	86	106	126	146	166	186	206	226	246	266	286	306	326	346	366	386
5	25	45	65	85	105	125	145	165	185	205	225	245	265	285	305	325	345	365	385
4	24	44	64	84	104	124	144	164	184	204	224	244	264	284	304	324	344	364	384
3	23	43	63	83	103	123	143	163	183	203	223	243	263	283	303	323	343	363	383
2	22	42	62	82	102	122	142	162	182	202	222	242	262	282	302	322	342	362	382
1	21	41	61	81	101	121	141	161	181	201	221	241	261	281	301	321	341	361	381

SUPPLY AND DEMAND LETTER

I issue the SUPPLY AND DEMAND LETTER tri-weekly covering advice on Stocks. This letter advises you the best and most active stocks to trade in; tells when to buy and sell and about what prices. I also advise where to place stop loss orders.

There is only one way to determine price movements, and that is the way I do it,—by the study of SUPPLY and DEMAND and a TIME FACTOR. SUPPLY and DEMAND tell what everybody is doing; not one set of men or the public. SUPPLY and DEMAND show where the balance of power rests, and if the DEMAND from the public is greater than the SUPPLY from the so-called insiders, stocks advance, and *vice-versa*. But remember the public never run a market for very long, because they are not organized; have no leader and the final result is a collapse and loss. I study the market daily to determine a change in SUPPLY and DEMAND and to locate the balance of power, in order that my subscribers may get the benefit of big moves.

The average man who guesses what the market will do or follows inside tips, or so-called "real" inside information, loses all in the end. I tell you it is impossible to get inside information; only "fools and suckers" expect it. Do you suppose men who make markets are going to tell you when they buy and sell? They would be fools if they did. They have to buy from some one and when they want to sell they must find a buyer. Do not delude yourself; the insiders use every means possible to keep secret their operations.

A frequent mistake made by many people is to subscribe to my Market Letter for one month. The market may be in an accumulation or distribution stage and no big moves take place for the month; then they quit and criticize my letter. Remember I do not make the market; I only follow manipulation and when big moves are ready I get you in. If you follow my service long enough to get acquainted with my methods, you will appreciate its value and become a permanent subscriber.

Another mistake people make is to subscribe for the letter, get a line on the future of the market, then discontinue their subscription, saying, "Oh, well, I know what the trend of the market is now, I don't need a letter." Then, suddenly I see a change in the market and advise my subscribers to sell out, and those who did not get my letter still hold and do not know the trend has changed; therefore, lose money and blame me.

People often write for my opinion on Baldwin, U. S. Steel, General Asphalt or some special stock. I judge the stock by the position of Time and Volume as it is today. If in a few days I see a large amount of Volume up or down, I change my position, so *it is not always what I think of a stock today, but what I am going to think of it later that counts.* That is why I issue a tri-weekly letter because the market changes and I can advise my subscribers to change their position and protect themselves against losses. If the market never reversed its trend, there would be no need of a tri-weekly letter.

People often write me and say "You were bearish on a certain stock at such and such a date; now in your tri-weekly letter you are bullish on it." My answer is "A wise man changes his mind, a fool never." The man who can change quickly when he sees a reason to do so is the man you want to follow, for he will protect you against losses. A bull-headed, stubborn man who holds on, hopes and ignores facts, will end in ruin. Go into the market to make money and be ready to change sides when the occasion demands it.

The subscription price of the SUPPLY AND DEMAND LETTER is $15 per month; three months $40; six months $75; or $150 per year—payable in advance.

In Friday's issue each week I give an outline of the market for the following week. This feature is invaluable to traders at distant points. The SUPPLY AND DEMAND LETTER is the only one that publishes such accurate advance information.

Price of the Weekly Letter alone $6.00 per month; $60.00 per year.

The Tri-weekly Commodity Letter is separate from the Stock Letter. It is issued every Monday, Wednesday and Friday, covering cotton, cottonseed oil, wheat, corn, oats, rye, lard, coffee and sugar. Weekly letter issued every Friday, covers the same commodities. Subscription rates same as Stock Letter.

TELEGRAPH SERVICE

For subscribers living at distant points who can not be reached by letter in time for the market next day, I have a special telegraph service. A code is furnished and telegrams sent collect, either by night message or fast day message. A telegram of 10 to 15 words gives all the advice necessary on stocks, cotton and grain.

Price of this wire service is $30.00 per month.

ANNUAL FORECAST ON STOCKS

My Annual Forecast on Stocks is issued in the month of December each year. This forecast gives the trend of stocks for the following year; gives dates each month when high and low prices will be made; tells when extreme highs or lows of the year can be expected; and also informs whether stocks are in a Bull or Bear cycle. This forecast is based on a "time" factor which I discovered. I have been able to forecast every important campaign for the past twenty years. Copies of Forecasts of recent years mailed free.

The price of the Annual Forecast is $100.00 per year. A Supplement is mailed to subscribers the first of each month.

ANNUAL FORECASTS ON COTTON AND GRAIN

In the month of December each year, I issue an annual Forecast covering Cotton for the following year. It contains a chart or projected curve which the Future Options should follow, and gives dates when high or low prices should be made. Price of the Forecast $100.00, including supplements issued once a month, or more often if necessary.

The Grain Forecast covers wheat, corn, oats, rye and lard.
Coffee, sugar and cocoa are combined in one Forecast.
The Rubber Forecast covers rubber futures.
The above Forecasts are $100.00 each.

We make up on request forecasts on silk, hides, burlap, jute and bags, and other commodities. Also make up Annual Forecasts on individual stocks on request.

SUBSCRIPTION RATES

Annual Stock Forecast $100.00 per year.

Annual Grain Forecast $100.00 per year.

Annual Cotton Forecast $100.00 per year.

Annual Coffee, Sugar & Cocoa Forecast $100.00 per year.
Supplements to all Forecasts are issued on the first of each month.

Tri-weekly Stock Letter $150.00 per year;
6 months $75.00; 3 months $40.00; one month $15.00.

Tri-weekly Commodity Letter $150.00 per year;
6 months $75.00; 3 months $40.00; one month $15.00.

Tri-weekly Stock and Commodity Letters combined $25.00 per month.

Weekly Stock Letter $60.00 per year; 6 months $33.00; one month $6.00.

~~Tri-weekly Stock Letter $60.00 per year; 6 months $33.00; one month $6.00.~~

Weekly Commodity Letter $60.00 per year;
6 months $33.00; one month $6.00.

Weekly Stock and Commodity Letters combined $10.00 per month.

Daily Telegraph Service, including Tri-weekly Letter $30.00 per month.
All messages sent collect in Private Code which is furnished free.

Telegrams on important changes sent collect to subscribers to the Annual Forecasts or market letters at the rate of $7.50 per month extra.

Personal Service $60.00 per month or $500.00 per year.

All subscriptions payable in advance.
The above subscription rates are subject to advance without notice.

"Wall Street Stock Selector," $6.00 per copy.

"Helpful Hints for Stock Traders," free to subscribers.

W. D. GANN SCIENTIFIC SERVICE INC.
99 [99] WALL STREET   NEW YORK, N. Y.

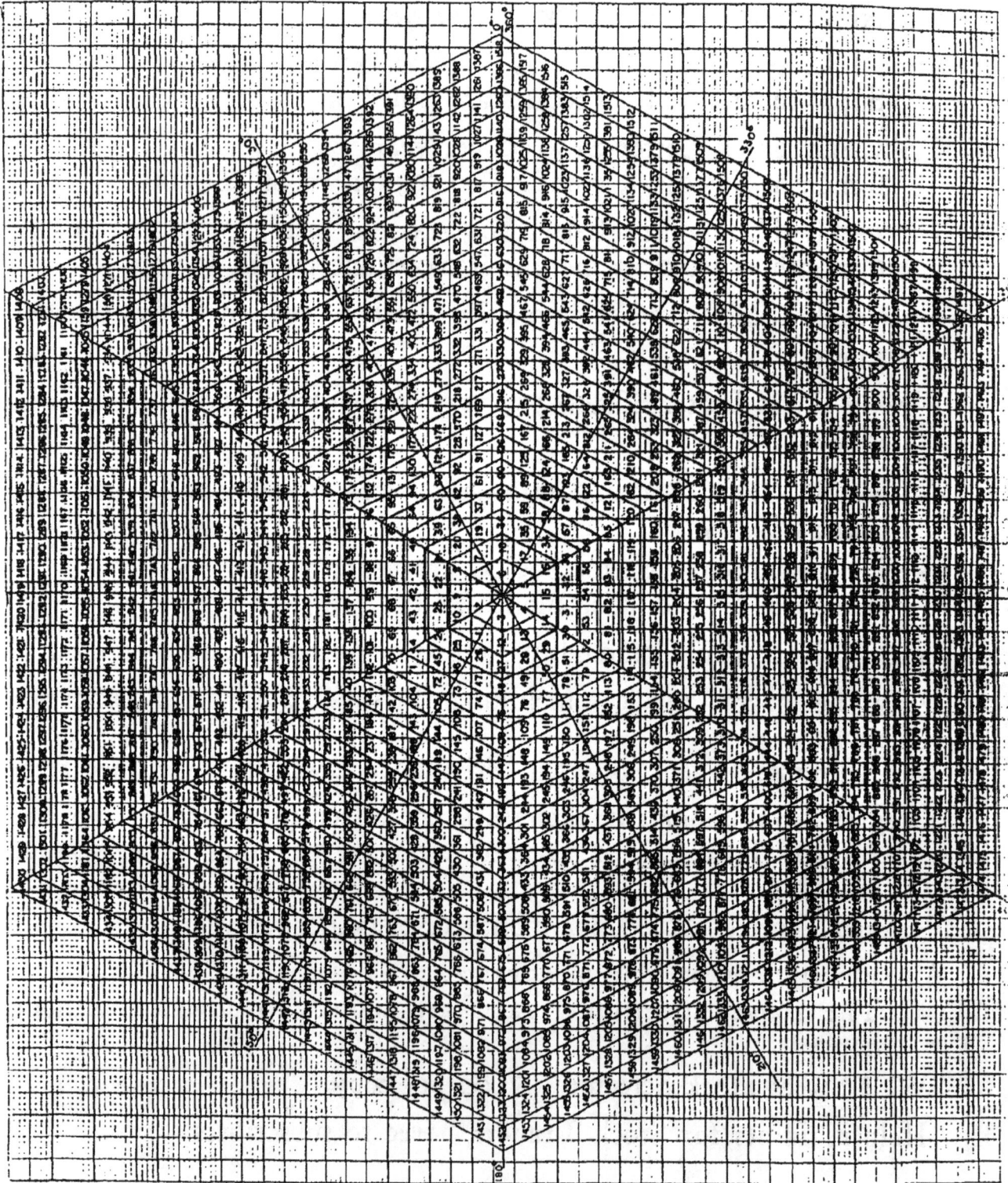

Eggs October Low May 28 1932

Oct 15 /33

	5560 164	5575 163	5550 162	5525 161	5500 160	5475 159	5475 158	5425 157	5425 156	5375 155	5350 154	5375 153	5300 152	5275 151	
	5725 165		4400 116	4375	4350 114	4325 113	4300	4475	4450 110		4200	4475	4500 166	5250 150	
Nov 157½ /9½	5750 166	4450 118	3450 78	3425 77	3400 76	3375 75	3350 74	3325 73	3300	3275	3250 70	3225 69	4175 165	5775 149	27½ June ½
	5675 167	4475 79	3475 47	3675 46	3650 45	3625 44	3600 43	3575	3525	3500 40	3200 68	4100 162	5700 148	200
	5700 168	4600	3500 82	2700 48	2700	2650	2625	2600	1975 19	2400 39	3175 67	4075 103	5775 147	6575 199
	5725 169	4575 81	3525	2750 45	2700	1700 8	1675 7	1650	1425 18	2475 38	3150 66	4050 107	5750 146	6550 198
160	5750 170	4550 82	3550 50	2750 26	1750 10	1750	1625	1625 6	1725 17	2475 37	3175 65	4025 101	5175 145	6575 197 ½ 2
Nov 29	5775 171	4575 83	3575 5	2775	2775	1775	1575	3000	1900 16	3100 36	4000 100	5100 144	6500 196	3600 /18
	5600 172	4600 12	3600 84	2700 52	1600	1600	1605 13	1850 14	1875	1775 35	3075 63	3475 99	5075 143	6475 195
	5675 173	4625	3625 65	1700 53	2600	2425 30	2775 31	2300 32	2575 33	3250 34	3050 62	3950 98	5050 142	6450 194
202½ Dec 31	5650 174	4650 156	3650 86	2650 54	2675 55	2700 56	1475 57	4750 58	1475 59	3000 60	3625 61	3925 97	5075 141	6475 193	337½ May 9
	5875 175	4675	3675 87	3700 88	3725 89	3750 90	3775 91	3800 92	3825 93	3850 94	3875 95	3900 96	5000 140	6400 192	
	5900 176	4700	4725 129	4750 130	4775 131	4800 132	4825 133	4850 134	4875 135	4900 136	4925 137	4950 138	4975 139	6375 191	
	5925 177	5950 178	5975 179	6000 180	6125 181	6150 182	6175 183	6700 184	6225 185	6750 186	6475 187	6300 188	6325 189	6350 190	

570

465 July 14

160

202½ Dec 31

337½ May 9

Jan

July 4

570

March

815

INVESTORS!

UP-TO-DATE

PRACTICAL

COMPLETE

WALL STREET

EDUCATION

FROM

TRUTH OF THE STOCK TAPE

WALL STREET STOCK SELECTOR

NEW STOCK TREND DETECTOR and

HOW TO MAKE PROFITS TRADING IN
PUTS AND CALLS

BY W. D. GANN

HAVE YOU LOST MONEY IN STOCKS?

These books will show you why . . . and how to make profits!

Anyone who knows the right stocks to buy and sell will make a success in Wall Street. If you have lost money in stocks, it is because of ignorance of when to buy and sell and what stocks to buy and sell. The only way to overcome this ignorance is with knowledge.

These practical books by W. D. Gann . . . written in plain, direct language . . . will give you a complete Wall Street education. They will teach you the things you need to know—the relation of price, time, volume and velocity—how to detect minor and major trends—when to place stop loss orders—how to divide your capital—how to pick leaders—and give you a practical demonstration of their success.

You have probably spent years of study and training to achieve success in your profession or business. You could not succeed otherwise. You must do the same thing for success in Wall Street. Luck is a poor substitute for knowledge.

"Truth of the Stock Tape and Wall Street Stock Selector" and "New Stock Trend Detector" are written by a man who has developed these rules and knows that they work because he has made a practical success in Wall Street using them. These books will help you to help yourself in practical every day Wall Street.

The price of the complete set is $8.00 and they have proven worth a hundred and a thousands times the price. Read what they contain. Read what others say. Then read these books and be on your way to success.

TRUTH OF THE STOCK TAPE	WALL STREET STOCK SELECTOR
This book was published in 1923 and is bound together with	which was published in 1930. Price of combined books, $5.00

These two books contain 41 charts proving the rules and also high and low prices by months from 1914 to 1929. Many of the rules were previously sold by the author in courses for $1,000.

TRUTH OF THE STOCK TAPE

Part I—Preparation for Trading

What is tape reading? How to read the stock tape. How the tape fools you. How stocks are sold. Essential qualifications for successful trading.

Part II—How to Trade

Rules for successful trading. Methods of operating. Charts and their use. Habits of stocks. Different classes of stocks.

Part III—How to Determine the Position of Stocks:

Position of stocks. General trend of the market. How to tell the stocks in strongest position. How to tell when stocks are in weak position. Judging final tops and bottoms.

Part IV—Commodities:

How to trade in cotton. Proper way to read the cotton tape. How to determine a change in trend. Wheat and Corn trading. Judging accumulation and distribution zones.

WALL STREET STOCK SELECTOR

1. **New Era in Stocks or Changed Cycles.**
   How traders were fooled on cycles. How cycles repeat. Panics from 1814 to 1929.

2. **Twenty-Four Never-Failing Rules.**

3. **Time Charts and Trend Changes.**
   Time records prove cause and effect. Trend according to Time charts. Monthly dates for change in trend. Months to watch for change in trend.

4. **Successful Stock Selecting Methods.**
   How to balance a stock. The Rule of Three. Volume of Sales. Determining right time to sell.

5. **How Investors Should Trade.**
   When investors should take profits. What investors should watch. Buying old or seasoned stocks. What to do with old stocks that work opposite the trend.

6. **How to Select the Early and Late Leaders.**
   The various groups of stocks are analyzed, with weak and strong stocks shown, as chemicals, coppers, foods, motors, oils, public utilities, steels, etc.

7. **Stocks of the Future.**
   Airplane stocks. Stocks to watch for future opportunities.

NEW STOCK TREND DETECTOR
Published in January, 1936
Price $3.00

Some of the subjects considered are:
A New Deal in Wall Street
Foundation of Successful Trading
History Repeats
Individual Stocks vs. Averages
New Rules to Detect Trend of Stocks
Volume of Sales
A Practical Trading Method
And 14 Charts proving the rules
Also monthly high and low prices on a list of active stocks; bringing stocks in the first two books up to date.

HOW TO MAKE PROFITS TRADING
IN PUTS AND CALLS

This booklet was published in July, 1937. . Price $1.00

It tells clearly what Puts and Calls are:

How and when to buy them.

Definite rules for successful trading in both high and low priced stocks with Puts and Calls.

It adapts Put and Call trading to the fundamental rules laid down in the other books.

WHAT OTHERS SAY

Bombay, India, Oct. 23, 1937:—"I do not know how I should adequately express my feeling of entire satisfaction I had when I finished the studies of all your four books. I am confident anyone who masters the definite yet simple principles laid down therein and follows them to the last letter will come out a very successful speculator."
B. G. S.

Norfolk, Va., Aug. 10, 1937:—"Your $6.00 book caused me to sell completely on Friday preceding the bad break on Tuesday in July, 1933. It was worth $2,000 to me."
P. H. O'H.

Grand Rapids, Mich., June 14, 1937:—"Have read your book NEW STOCK TREND DETECTOR and find it better than any book I have ever studied."
M. H.

South Bend, Ind., April 24, 1937:—"I wish to mention that I am the proud possessor of Mr. Gann's books TRUTH OF THE STOCK TAPE, WALL STREET STOCK SELECTOR, and NEW STOCK TREND DETECTOR. I have learned very much from them and continue to read them from time to time."
T. J. H.

Philadelphia, Pa., March 5, 1937:—"Have read practically everything written on the Stock Market and must say that your books are the most comprehensive and thorough of all."
G. R.

Greensburg, Pa., January 30, 1937:—"Be advised that I have read your last three books from cover to cover and found them wonderful. I must say that every word and every page answered questions that have arisen in my mind at one time or another in my six years of experience in the stock market. They not only answered my questions, but enlightened me on many other things I knew nothing about. I have read many books on finance, and looked for information but yours I found to be the key to all of them. I could go on and write a letter, page for page, praising your wonderful knowledge of the Stock Market but this would take up your precious time to read, so I will stop and ask fr your latest literature on books by you, and your services and their price."
J. A. B.

Charlotte, N. C., October 5, 1936:—"Have received a great deal of valuable information through the study of this book. I would like to personally thank you for giving me the benefit, in book form, of your extensive experience in stock trading. It is difficult to estimate just what some of the information contained in your book might be worth. For instance, your rule with reference to previous support points is, in my estimation, most valuable."
I. R. B.

St. Louis, Mo., May 9, 1936:—"This new book is another great accomplishment added to your fine work. . . . I wonder how many people will appreciate the hours that it required to gather so much information and for so little as $3. Not many will be able to see and understand and I will go so far as to say that most readers will be too lazy to investigate and prove your theory."
J. A. J.

New York, N. Y., April 25, 1936:—"Your new book is the best you have written so far, full of vigor and straight from the shoulder. I wonder how many people realize that the advice contained in those pages is the result of a tremendous amount of hard work, and also represents the crystalized wisdom gained through actual operations during your 35 years in Wall Street."
M. D.

Roslindale, Mass., February 10, 1936:—"I am still a very small trader but I have increased my capital 500% since I finished your book two years ago."
W. A. F.

Plainfield, N. J., September 7, 1935:—"It certainly is a wonderful book, and should be used by business men all over the country as a text book. I am carefully reading it through and studying it for the third time, and every time I go through it I seem to find something new."
J. H. P.

Salisbury, N. C., January 2, 1935:—"For the past year and a half I have been studying your excellent book, WALL STREET STOCK SELECTOR. I have derived a great deal from it, and consider it the finest of all texts on securities."
A. R.

Los Angeles, Calif., October 27, 1933:—"I really am unable to express myself in writing as to what I feel in regard to such a remarkable volume, of what I consider the greatest truth ever presented by any one man at any time in the history of Wall Street."
M. A. M.

St. Louis, Mo., November 12, 1930:—"Mr. Gann in these works has disclosed a factor that is unknown to and unsuspected by the majority of traders, ignorance of which is responsible for swift and sudden losses. He has formulated a number of principles and rules to safeguard first the investor's capital. He shows by example how to recognize opportunity and to safeguard profits. Mr. Gann's works, I have just heard, are being used as a supplementary text-book by Washington University here in the School of Commerce and Finance. I have examined the statements and opinions of Mr. Gann since 1921 and the subsequent history of the market proves that he is entitled to great respect."
A. K.

TESTIMONIALS

COMPLETE SET ------------------------------$8.00

TRUTH OF THE STOCK TAPE ----------------$3.00

TRUTH OF THE STOCK TAPE AND
WALL STREET STOCK SELECTOR-----------$5.00

NEW STOCK TREND DETECTOR-------------$3.00

HOW TO MAKE PROFITS TRADING IN
PUTS AND CALLS----------------------------$1.00

FINANCIAL GUARDIAN PUBLISHING CO.
82 Wall Street
New York, N. Y.

Even Squares for Cotton & Eggs
Time and Price

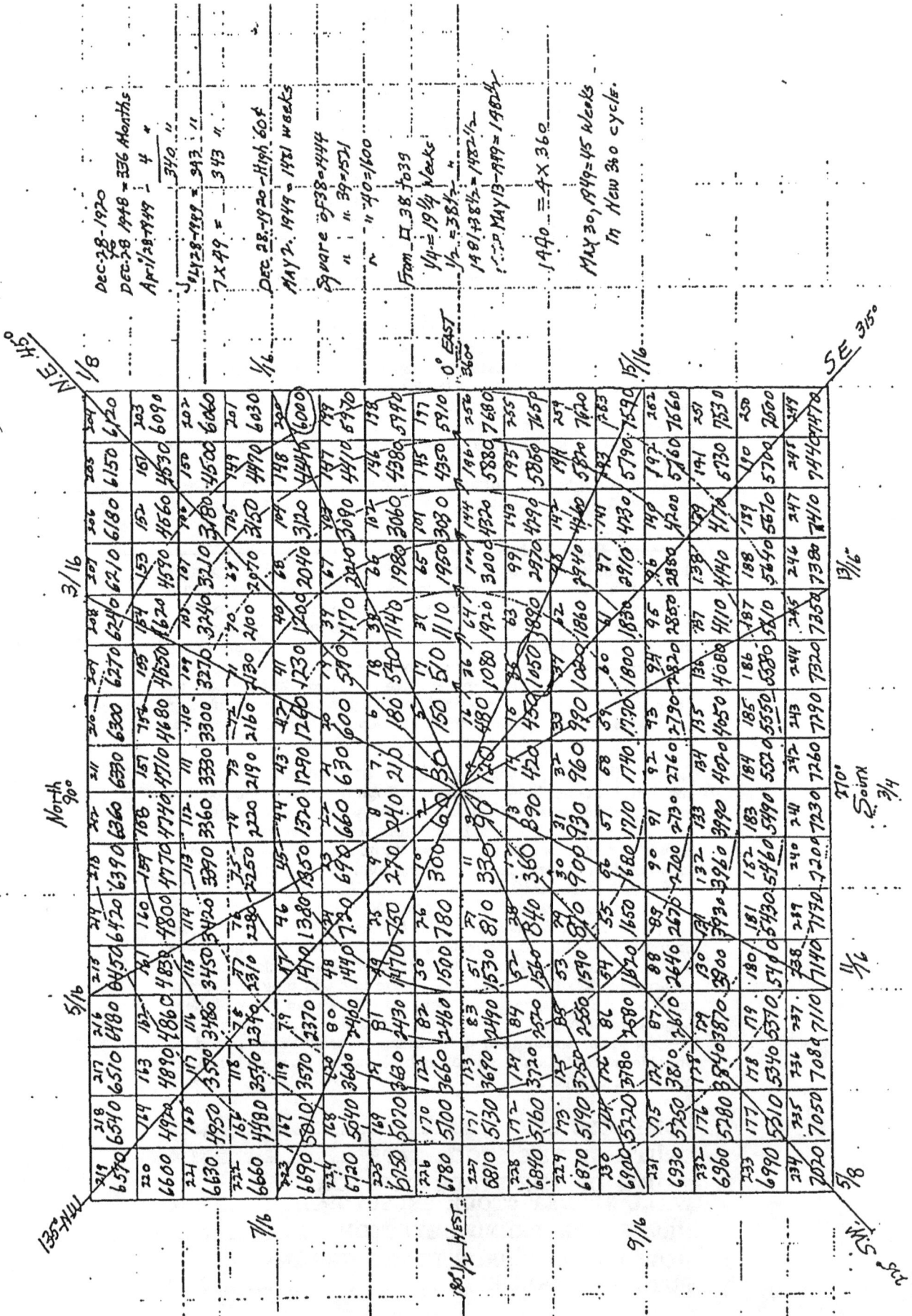

Directional labels around the square: N.E. 45°, North 90°, NW 135°, 0° EAST, 360°, South 270°, SW 225°, SE 315°

Fractional divisions: 1/8, 3/16, 1/4, 5/16, 3/8, 9/16, 5/8, 11/16, 3/4, 13/16, 7/8, 15/16

Annotations (right margin):

DEC-28-1920
DEC-28 1948 = 336 Months
Apr/28-1949 4 "
              4
              340

JULY28-1989 = 943 "
7×49 = 343 "

DEC 28-1920 — High '04
MAY2-1944 — 181 weeks

From II 38.639
1/4 = 19 1/4 weeks
1/2 = 384 —
MAY2-1944=481-1841=1989
7×49=343+1841=

4×49=

4×49 = 360
1841+4=1845

MAY30-1845 weeks
in New 360 cycle.

LEARN BEFORE YOU LOSE

OR

WHY YOU LOSE MONEY ON STOCKS

AND

HOW TO MAKE PROFITS

LEARN BEFORE YOU LOSE

OR

WHY YOU HAVE LOST MONEY IN STOCKS

AND HOW TO MAKE IT BACK

Why do the great majority of people who buy and sell stocks lose?

There are three main reasons:

1. They over-trade or buy and sell too much for their capital.

2. They do not place stop loss orders or limit their losses.

3. Lack of Knowledge. This is the most important reason of all.

Most people buy a stock because they hope it will go up and they will make profits. They buy on tips, or what someone else thinks, without any concrete knowledge of their own that the stock will advance. Thus they entered the market wrong and did not recognize this mistake or attempt to correct it until too late. Finally they sell because they fear the stock will go lower and often they sell out near low levels, getting out at the wrong time, making two mistakes, getting in the market at the wrong time and getting out at the wrong time. One mistake could have been prevented, they could have gotten out right after getting in wrong. They do not realize that operating in Stocks and Commodities is a business or a profession, the same as engineering or the medical profession.

Why You Should Learn to Determine the Trend of the Market

You may have tried to follow market letters and like many others either lost money or failed to make profits, because the market letters gave a list of too many stocks to buy or sell and you picked the wrong one and lost. A smart man cannot follow another man blindly even though the other man is right, because you cannot have confidence and act on advice when you do not know what it is based on. You will be able to act with confidence and make profits when you can SEE and KNOW for YOURSELF why STOCKS should go UP or DOWN. That is why you should take a Course of Instructions and prepare yourself to act independent of the advice of others.

Why I Teach My Methods

Long years in practical market trading and experience in teaching others has taught me what others need for success in speculation. They must learn a rule and how to apply it before they take up the second lesson or set of Rules. When you first went to school you had to learn your A, B, Cs before you could read and when you started to study arithmetic you had to learn the four fundamental rules, addition, multiplication, division and subtraction.

Then you were prepared to take up higher mathematics, algebra and geometry.

My Course or Lessons starts you in the same way, leading you step by step and adding more rules when you are ready and can understand them.

I have made a success in Wall Street and have all the income that I need, this fact can be proven by the records. I find real pleasure in helping others who are trying to help themselves. Money it not everything in life, when I teach a young man or woman how to protect and preserve their capital I am giving them valuable knowledge that they cannot lose, and no one can steal it or take it from them.

You should never buy a method from a man who has not made money with it.

W. D. GANN

THIRTY-ONE YEARS IN WALL STREET

The Founder and president of W. D. Gann & Son, Inc. has devoted 35 years exclusively to the study of stock and commodity markets and has spent over $300,000.00 developing a worthwhile, practical method of Stock Forecasting.

During the past 31 years W. D. Gann has been in business for himself and under his own name in New York City. He is a member of the Commodity Exchange, Inc. of New York, New Orleans Cotton Exchange and is a Christian and a member of the Masonic fraternity.

The Record of Forecasts—
Highlights through the years

1909—W. D. Gann's record as a forecaster dates back 30 years. We reprint part of an article written by the late Richard D. Wyckoff and published in the Ticker Magazine. This article is dated December 1909 and attests to Mr. Gann's remarkable ability as a forecaster over 30 years ago.

WILLIAM D. GANN
An Operator Whose Science and Ability Place Him in the Front Rank—
His Remarkable Predictions and Trading Record.

Sometime ago the attention of this magazine was attracted by certain long pull stock market predictions which were being made by William D. Gann. In a large number of cases Mr. Gann gave us in advance the exact points at which certain stocks and commodities would sell, together with prices close to the then prevailing figures which would not be touched.

For instance, when New York Central was 131 he predicted that it would sell at 145 before 129.

So repeatedly did his figures prove to be accurate, and so different did his work appear from that of any expert whose methods we had examined, that we set about to investigate Mr. Gann and his way of figuring out these predictions, as well as the particular use which he was making of them in the market.

The results of this investigation are remarkable in many ways.

It appears to be a fact that Mr. Gann

7

has developed an entirely new idea as to the principles governing stock market movements. He bases his operations upon certain natural laws, which, though existing since the world began, have only in recent years been subjected to the will of man, and added to the list of so-called modern discoveries.

We have asked Mr. Gann for an outline of his work and have secured some remarkable evidence as to the results obtained therefrom. We submit this in full recognition of the fact that in Wall Street a man with a new idea—an idea which violates the traditions and encourages a scientific view of the proposition—is not usually welcomed by the majority, for the reason that he stimulates thought and research. These activities said majority abhors.

Mr Gann's description of his experience and methods is given herewith. It should be read with a recognition of the established fact that Mr. Gann's predictions have proved correct in a large majority of instances.

"After years of patient study I have proven to my entire satisfaction as well as demonstrated to others that vibration explains every possible phase and condition of the market."

In order to substantiate Mr. Gann's claims as to what he has been able to do under this method, we called upon Mr. William E. Gilley, an Inspector of Imports, 16 Beaver Street, New York. Mr. Gilley is well-known in the down-town district. He himself has studied stock market movements for twenty-five years, during which time he has examined every piece of market literature that has been issued and procurable in Wall Street. It was he who encouraged Mr. Gann to study out the scientific and mathematical possibilities of the subject. When asked what had been the most impressive of Mr. Gann's work and predictions, he replied as follows:

"It is very difficult for me to remember all the predictions and operations of Mr. Gann which may be classed as phenomenal, but the following are a few: In 1908 when Union Pacific was 168⅛ he told me that it would not touch 169 before it had a good break. We sold it short all the way down to 152⅝, covering on the weak spots and putting it out again on the rallies, securing twenty-three points profit out of an eighteen-point move.

"He came to me when United States Steel was selling around 50 and said 'This Steel will run up to 58 but it will not sell at 59. From there it should break 16¾

points. We sold it short around 58⅜ with a stop at 59. The highest it went was 58¾. From there it declined to 41¼ —17½ points.

"At another time wheat was selling at about 89c. He predicted that the May option would sell at $1.35. We bought it and made large profits on the way up. It actually touched $1.35½.

"When Union Pacific was 172, he said it would go to 184⅞ but not an eighth higher until it had had a good break. It went to 184⅞ and came back from there eight or nine times. We sold it short repeatedly with a stop at 185 and were never caught. It eventually came back to 172½.

"Mr. Gann's calculations are based on natural law. I have followed his work closely for years. I know that he has a firm grasp of the basic principles which govern stock market movements, and I do not believe any other man on earth can duplicate the idea or his method at the present time.

"Early this year he figured that the top of the advance would fall on a certain day in August and calculated the prices at which the Dow-Jones averages would then stand. The market culminated on the exact day and within four-tenths of one per cent. of the figures predicted."

"You and Mr. Gann must have cleaned up considerable money on all these operations," was suggested.

"Yes, we have made a great deal of money. He has taken half a million dollars out of the market in the past few years. I once saw him take $130, and in less than one month run it up to cover $12,000. He can compound money faster than any man I ever met."

"One of the most astonishing calculations made by Mr. Gann was during last summer (1909) when he predicted that September wheat would sell at $1.20. This meant that it must touch that figure before the end of the month of September. At twelve o'clock, Chicago time, on September 30th (the last day) the option was selling below $1.08, and it looked as though his prediction would not be fulfilled. Mr. Gann said 'If it does not touch $1.20 by the close of the market it will prove that there is something wrong with my whole method of calculation. I do not care what the price is now, it must go there.' It is common history that September wheat surprised the whole country by selling at $1.20 and no higher in the very last hour of the trading, closing at that figure.

So much for what Mr. Gann has said and done as evidenced by himself and others. Now as to what demonstrations have taken place before our representative:

During the month of October, 1909, in twenty-five market days, Mr. Gann made, in the presence of our representative, two hundred and eighty-six transactions in various stocks, on both the long and short side of the market. Two hundred and sixty-four of these transactions resulted in profits; twenty-two in losses.

The capital with which he operated was doubled ten times, so that at the end of the month he had one thousand per cent. of his original margin.

In our presence Mr. Gann sold Steel common short at 94⅞, saying that it would not go to 95. It did not.

On a drive which occurred during the week ending October 29th, Mr. Gann bought Steel common at 86¼, saying that it would not go to 86. The lowest it sold was 86⅛.

We have seen him give in one day sixteen successive orders in the same stock, eight of which turned out to be either the top or the bottom eighth of that particular swing. The above we can positively verify.

Such performances as these, coupled with the foregoing, are probably unparalleled in the history of the Street.

James R. Keene has said, "The man who is right six times out of ten will make his fortune." Here is a trader, who, without any attempt to make a showing (for he did not know the results were to be published), establishes a record of over ninety-two per cent profitable trades.

Mr. Gann has refused to disclose his method at any price, but to those scientifically inclined he has unquestionably added to the stock of Wall Street knowledge and pointed out infinite possibilities.

We have requested Mr. Gann to figure out for the readers of The Ticker a few of the most striking indications which appear in his calculations. In presenting these we wish it understood that no man, in or out of Wall Street, is infallible.

Mr. Gann's figures at present indicate that the trend of the stock market should, barring the usual rallies, be toward lower prices until March or April, 1910.

He calculates that May wheat, which is now selling at $1.02, should not sell below 99c. and should sell at $1.45 next spring.

On cotton, which is now at about the 15c. level, he estimates that, after a good reaction from these prices, the commodity should reach 18c. in the spring of 1910. He looks for a corner in the March or May option.

Whether these figures prove correct or not, will in no sense detract from the record which Mr. Gann has already established.

Mr. Gann was born in Lufkin, Texas, and is thirty-one years of age. He is a gifted mathematician, has an extraordinary memory for figures, and is an expert Tape Reader. Take away his science and he would beat the market on his intuitive tape reading alone.

Endowed as he is with such qualities, we have no hesitation in predicting that within a comparatively few years Wm. D. Gann will receive full recognition as one of Wall Street's leading operators.

R. D. W.

Note—Since the above forecast was made, Cotton has suffered the expected decline, the extreme break having been 120 points. The lowest on May wheat thus far has been $1.01⅝. It is now selling at 1.06¼.

•

In 1912 Mr. Gann forecast the election of Woodrow Wilson and has been correct in forecasting the election of every President since that time. Many of these forecasts have been published in newspapers throughout the country.

In the spring of 1918 Mr. Gann forecast the end of the World War. This forecast was sent out to newspapers throughout the country, and in January, 1919, the New York Herald and other papers gave Mr. Gann credit for forecasting the end of the war and the Kaiser's abdication.

In his 1919 Annual Stock Forecast, issued late in 1918, he forecast a big bull market for 1919 and especially referred to a boom in oil stocks.

His Stock Forecasts for 1920 and 1921 indicated a bear market with sharp declines. The 1921 Forecast called the exact date for bottom on stocks in August, 1921.

In 1923 Mr. Gann wrote "Truth of the Stock Tape" and forecast a big advance in chemical and airplane stocks, which followed during the Coolidge bull campaign. This book has been reviewed by newspapers and magazines throughout the country and favorably commented on by college professors, business men, investors and traders, all of whom agree that it is the best book ever written on the subject.

His Stock Forecasts for 1924 and 1925 outlined the bull market which followed.

In the spring of 1927, Mr. Gann wrote "The Tunnel Thru the Air, or Looking back From 1940," which contained many remarkable forecasts in regard to stocks and commodities and world events which have been fulfilled. In this book Mr. Gann said that from 1929 to 1932 there would be the worst panic in the world's history. Writing under date of "October 3, 1931" on page 323, he said, "The New York Stock Exchange closed to prevent complete panic because the people were panic-stricken and selling stocks regardless of price." It is a matter of history that the New York Stock Exchange did consider closing on October 3 to 5, but decided to stop short selling. The low of that panicky decline was reached on October 5 and a rally of 33 points in industrial stock averages followed to November 9, 1931.

His 1929 Stock Forecast, issued on November 23, 1928, and based on his Master Time Factor, indicated the end of the bull market in August and early September, 1929. He stated in no uncertain terms that the panic would start in September, 1929, and that it would be a great deluge with a Black Friday. We quote from the Forecast:

"AUGUST—A few of the late movers will advance this month and reach final high. * * * Unfavorable news will develop which will start declines and the long bull campaign will come to a sudden end. Money rates will be high and final top will be reached for a big bear campaign. Stand from under! Don't get caught in the great deluge! Remember it is too late to sell when everyone is trying to sell. * * *

"SEPTEMBER—One of the sharpest declines of the year is indicated. There will be loss of confidence by investors, and the public will try to get out after it is too late. Storms will damage crops and the general business outlook will become cloudy. War news will upset the market and unfavorable developments in foreign countries. A 'Black Friday' is indicated and a panicky decline in stocks with only small rallies. The short side will prove the most profitable. You should sell short and pyramid on the way down."

In the spring of 1930, Mr. Gann wrote "Wall Street Stock Selector," which was published in June, 1930. In this book he had a chapter headed, "Investors' Panic," which described conditions just as they occurred during 1931, 1932 and 1933. We quote from the book, pages 203-04:

"The coming investors' panic will be the greatest in history, because there are at least 15 to 25 million investors in the United States who hold stocks in the leading corporations, and when once they get scared, which they will after years of decline, then the selling will be so terrific that no buying power can withstand it. Stocks are so well distributed in the hands of the public that since the 1929 panic many people think that the market is panic-proof, but this seeming strength is really the weakest feature of the market. * * *

"Love of money has been the cause of all financial troubles and depressions in the past, and the coming panic will be the greatest the world has ever known, because there is more money in the United States than ever before, therefore more to fight for."

Thousands of people have bought this book and profited by reading and studying it. The book has been favorably commented on by such papers as The Financial Times of London, England, Wall Street Journal, New York Daily Investment News, Coast Investor, and many other newspapers and magazines throughout the world.

On February 10, 1932, Mr. Gann said that stocks were bottom for a big rally. His 1932 Stock Forecast, issued October 21, 1931, called March 8 for last top for another big decline. During the latter part of June, 1932, and early July he strongly advised buying stocks, stating that final bottom had been reached, as shown by his market letter issued July 8, the day that most stocks reached final bottom. We quote from page 6 of the 1932 Forecast:

5

"The latter part of June, July, August and September are the most active and bullish months of the year, when sharp advances will be recorded. First extreme high is indicated around September 20 to 21, when stocks should make extreme high for the year. Then follows a decline, reaching bottom around October 4 to 5."

Between July 8 and September 8 many stocks advanced 20 to 60 points. The market reached high of a secondary rally on September 23, from which a big decline followed, making low in the latter part of November and early December, as indicated in the Forecast.

On March 1, 1933, by the use of his Master Time Factor Mr. Gann forecast bottom for stocks and commodities and advised buying for a big advance, as shown by the market letters issued March 1 and 3 given below. This is another proof of the great value of Mr. Gann's discovery of a Master Time Factor.

KEEPING UP TO DATE

Mr. Gann has always been progressive and believes in keeping up to date. In April, 1933, he bought a specially equipped airplane for making crop surveys. Many of the newspapers throughout the country commented on this progressive step. The following article appeared in the New York Daily Investment News, May 26, 1933:

NEW YORK DAILY INVESTMENT NEWS

GANN TO TOUR COUNTRY BY PLANE
FOR BROAD BUSINESS SURVEY

Wayne, Mich., May 25.—W. D. Gann, stock market analyst, of 99 Wall St., today left here for New York with the first 1933 model Stinson Reliant plane, piloted by Elinor Smith, woman aviator.

Mr. Gann will use the plane for an extensive tour of the country during which he will study cotton, wheat and tobacco crop and business conditions. He will leave on this tour early in June.

The forecaster expects to make speed in the gathering of first hand information on business conditions by use of the airplane.

The plane is equipped with blind-flying apparatus, extra-large fuel tanks to afford a flying range of 750 miles and with radio receiving equipment. The plane is powered with a Lycoming engine and is capable of 135 miles per hour.

By receiving radio advices on market conditions, Mr. Gann calculates that he will be able at all times to gauge his operations in the markets and send up-to-the-minute advise to his clients, even though he is many miles away from his Wall Street office.

As far as is known, Mr. Gann will be the first Wall Street adviser to use a plane as part of his equipment in studying market conditions.

The recent burst of activity in the markets, following the closing of the banks and leading stock and commodity exchanges, prompted the analyst to buy the plane.

He decided that rapid-changing conditions made it necessary for him to gather his data on crops and business at first hand.

Mr. Gann is a member of the Commodity Exchange, Inc., and also of the New Orleans Cotton Exchange. During his tour of the country he will visit the cotton belt in the south and southwest, the tobacco fields in the south, and the wheat stand in the middle west.

At all times during the trip he will communicate regularly with his office by wire and by radio. He expects to make talks in various cities to Kiwanis and Rotary Clubs, chambers of commerce and other business organizations.

His itinerary will include the following cities:

Washington, D. C.; Richmond, Va; Raleigh, N. C.; Atlanta, Ga; Birmingham, Ala; Memphis, Tenn.; New Orleans, La.; Little Rock, Ark.; Houston and Dallas, Texas; St. Louis, Detroit and Chicago.

1933 STOCK FORECAST:

Mr. Gann's 1933 Stock Forecast called for top July 17 and a sharp decline to July 21. Stocks reached high on July 17 and a wide-open break followed, with the average down 25 points in 4 days.

1934 STOCK FORECAST:

His 1934 Forecast indicated top for February 13th and the high was reached on averages February 5th and 15th. The next low was indicated for May 11th to 12th, and the market made low on May 14th. The next top was indicated for June 22nd; stocks reached high on June 19th. The last low for 1934 was forecast for July 21st to 23rd and the extreme low of the year was reached on July 26th. The Forecast called for the last top for September 8th to 10th, and stocks reached top of the rally on September 6th. A reaction followed to September 17th, the exact date indicated in the Forecast for low. The next top was forecast for October 5th and 6th and the industrial averages reached top October 11th. The next bottom was called for October 23rd to 24th and the lows were reached October 26th. The next top was indicated, according to the Forecast, for December 4th to 5th. The averages reached top on December 6th and a reaction followed. The Forecast indicated high for the end of December and the averages reached high for the month on December 31st.

•

A CROP SURVEY IN SOUTH AMERICA

In the early part of March, 1935, Mr. Gann made a trip to South America to study crop conditions and get first hand information on the increase in production of cotton in Peru, Chile, Argentine, and Brazil. On this trip he covered about 18,000 miles by airplane and more than 1,000 miles by automobile, driving into the country to see the conditions of soil and the possibilities for increased production of Wheat, Corn and Cotton, which will influence prices in the United States market by underselling, due to lower cost of labor in Argentine and Brazil. While in South America, Mr. Gann was interviewed by many newspapers.

We reproduce part of an article which appeared in the Beunos Aires Herald, March 21, 1935.

BEUNOS AIRES HERALD

Thursday, March 21, 1935

SCIENCE AND STOCK

—

An Astonishing Claims

—

Records of 1,000 Years

The man who guesses and gambles on hope is sure to lose while the man who follows science makes profits. There is cause and effect for everything and by time element and the cycle theory everything can be mathematically determined.

Mr. W. D. Gann, member of the New Orleans Cotton Exchange and the Rubber Exchange of New York, who stated that he has devoted over 30 years to study of time cycles and spent $300,000 (U.S.) to develop a dependable method based on mathematical science that will determine the trend of stocks and commodities. The success attending his methods he asserts, are borne out by his own good fortune on the American markets, and his accuracy in forecasting the futures markets for the past twenty years has been very widely commented upon in the Press in all parts of the United States.

Mr. Gann told a HERALD reporter yesterday that he has carried his records of grain back over 1,000 years and cotton records nearly 400 years. The former he was able to gather the most accurate information about from old British records, while in his search for cotton cycles he visited Egypt and India. More recently he has used his own aeroplane extensively in America for getting round the country quickly to make forecasts on the cotton crops.

•

1935 Stock Forecast:

His 1935 Forecast indicated first top for January 9th to 10th and the high was reached on January 7th. The next top was forecast for February 13th. The actual highs were reached February 18th, from which a sharp decline followed, making low for the year on March 18th. The Forecast called for the last low on March 28th, and the averages made a second low on March 25th. From the low in March, the Forecast indicated a big advance of at least 32 points in the Dow-Jones Industrial averages.

August 28th and 29th indicated top for a reaction. The averages reached top on August 27th and then reacted. The Forecast called for the next top September 12th to 15th. High on the averages was reached September 11th. The Forecast indicated the next bottom for September 24th to 25th; the last low was made September 20th and 26th.

The Forecast called for top October 26th to 28th, and the averages reached high on October 28th, which was the high of the year up to that time. The Forecast indicated November 15th to 16th as the last high of the year. The actual high of the Dow-Jones 30 Industrial averages was reached on November 20th, from which a reaction of 10 points on averages followed. The Forecast called for low December 9-10th and 23rd. The low of the reaction was made on December 16th and 19th. The Forecast called for a rally to December 31st, and this rally took place.

Mr. Gann has also been issuing Annual Forecast on Cotton, Wheat and other commodities for many years. These Forecasts have shown the same percentage of accuracy that the Stock Forecasts have.

These Annual, Forecasts on Stocks, Cotton, and Grain are issued in October and November each year for the following year.

NEW STOCK TREND DETECTOR

In December 1935, Mr. Gann wrote a new book, NEW STOCK TREND DETECTOR, bringing "Wall Street Stock Selector" up-to-date, with new rules never before published and a method of trading that formerly sold for $1000.00. This book covers changed conditions caused by the new Securities Exchange laws. It gives an example of trading in Chrysler Motors from 1925 to the end of 1935 and new rules on Volume of Sales. This book with the two former books will give you a valuable stock market education.

W. D. GANN MAKES PROFITS TRADING ACCORDING
TO HIS OWN METHODS

Many ask the question, "If Mr. Gann can forecast the market accurately, why does he sell service or write market letters?" He has answered that question before, that he finds pleasure in giving his knowledge to help others who need help; money is not everything in life.

Below we publish a record taken from brokers' statements, showing the trades made by Mr. Gann for 3 years. This is proof that he can and does make money by following his own rules and methods. Before you buy a course of instructions, get the record of actual trading by the man who is behind it, if he has not made money following his own advice, why should you pay money for it and follow it and risk your money?

W. D. GANN'S TRADING RECORD FOR 1933

From August 1 to December 31:

Total number of trades—135—of which 112 showed profits and 23 losses.

Percentage of accuracy on the total number of trades.. 83%

Percentage of profits to losses.. 89.9%

Total number of trades for the entire year of 1933: 479 trades, of which 422 were profits and 57 showed losses.

Percentage of accuracy 88.1%

Percentage of profits on capital used.. 4000% or 40 for 1

TRADING RECORD FOR 1934

From January 1 to December 31: Total number of trades—362.

Cotton	— 147 trades, of which 135 showed profits and 12 losses
Grain	— 170 " " " 161 " " " 9 "
Rubber	— 23 " " " 21 " " " 2 "
Silver	— 7 " " " 7 " " " 0 "
Silk	— 4 " " " 3 " " " 1 "
Stocks	— 11 " " " 10 " " " 1 "

Total for yr. 362 trades, of which 337 showed profits and 25 losses.

Percentage of accuracy on the total number of trades.......................... 93.09%

Percentage of profits to losses... 93.10%

Percentage of profits on capital used.. 800% or 8 for 1

TRADING RECORD FOR 1935

Commodities:

Total trades in Cotton, Grain and Rubber—98—of which 83 showed profits and 15 showed losses.

Percentage of accuracy on total number of trades....................................... 85%

Percentage of profits to losses.. 82%

Percentage of profits on capital used... 336%

Stocks:

Total number of trades—34—of which 29 showed profits and 5 losses.

Percentage of accuracy on total number of trades.. 85.5%
Percentage of profits to losses.. 83%
Percentage of profits on capital used.. 100%

Such a record of accuracy proves that W. D. Gann has discovered a Master Time Factor and Cycle Theory that works and can be depended upon in future.

1936—"New Stock Trend Detector" was written by W. D. Gann. This book was a further advance over "Truth of the Stock Tape" and "Wall Street Stock Selector" and contained an actual trading record for 10 years in Chrysler Motors according to the rules set down in these books.
Bought Special built all-metal Airplane, "The Silver Star" for making crop surveys.

1937—Wrote and published a book, "How to Make Profits Trading in Puts and Calls" Scientific Stock Forecasting again proved equal to the test of predicting a bear year, sharp declines coming in March and September. A maximum decline of 80 points was called for and the actual decline from the March high to the November low was 82 and a fraction points. We reprint an article from the Milwaukee Journal giving further details.

PREDICTED STOCK MARKET CRASHES OF 1929, 1937

Gann Says There'll Be Another Decline in November and an Upturn in December of This Year

NEW YORK, N. Y.—W. D. Gann, who forecast the 1929 stock market crash one year in advance and predicted the exact date, September 3, 1929, when the panic would start, has made another hit.

His 1937 Stock Forecast, issued November 18, 1936, is just as accurate. On page 2 he said—General Outlook for 1937":

This year comes under a time cycle which definitely indicates a bear year in most stocks and a panicky decline in the first half of the year and another panicky decline in the last half of the year. Fluctuations will be wide. Sudden, unexpected events of an unfavorable nature will occur from time to time which will upset the market and rallies will fail to hold. Action by the government and laws changed or passed by congress will have a great influence on business conditions and stock prices.

*   *   *

"Many people are still buying stocks or holding stocks and hoping for the day when inflation will come and they will be able to sell at high prices. Inflation has been going on ever since 1933 and one of these days people will wake up and find that deflation has set in and then they will realize that inflation had already existed.

*   *   *

The securities and exchange commission is getting more drastic in its regulations of operations on the exchange and there is likely to be more legislation in 1937. This will cause less support to the market in the future because there will be less buying by floor traders and specialists, and probably less short selling, therefore less support from short sellers when a panic takes place. The final result of all this regulation is likely to do more harm than good as far as the public is concerned."

A Matter of Record

It is a matter of record that the Dow-Jones 30 industrial stock averages reached extreme high on March 8, 1937, and Mr. Gann's forecast called March 6-8 as last high of the year. The decline lasted until June 18, when the Dow-Jones averages were down 32 points. His forecast called for a decline of 32 points and indicated June 23-25 as last low before a rally into August. The forecast said last high would be reached August 25-27 before a panicky decline would start. The Dow-Jones averages reached high August 14, up 27 points from June lows, and on August 25 the market had the last rally and the decline started.

Long Bear Wave

In his forecast for August on page 15 he said: "This should be one of the active months for the stock market. Sudden, unexpected events of an unfavorable nature will cause some sharp breaks and, in fact, this is the month when the market should start on its long bear wave again. The newspapers will try to make it appear that business is improving but it will be far from good. There will be disturbing conditions at Washington and some trouble over crop control or shortage of crops due to government action. Stocks will rally from time to time but the short side is where the big money will be made."

The bear market started in August as predicted. Mr. Gann's forecast called for low October 14-15 and the extreme lows were reached on October 19, just four days later, when there was a panicky decline, culminating in one of the worst declines in the history of the stock exchange, with the Dow-Jones averages down 79.65 points. The most uncanny prediction by Mr. Gann was that the averages could decline a maximum of 80 points.

In his 1937 forecast, page 7, he said: "The range in these industrial averages during 1937 is not likely to be less than 50 to 60 points and may reach a maximum of 80 points."

His forecast called for a sharp advance from October 15 to 30 and the Dow-Jones averages advanced 25 points from October 19 to 30.

Advance in December

Mr. Gann was asked how it was possible to make such an accurate forecast one year in advance. He stated that it was his own discovery of a mathematical master time factor and cycle theory which enables him to tell when certain cycles recur and great panics and booms take place. He said that the extent of an advance was determined by a theory based on the law of averages and that under certain circumstances stocks decline or advance about the same number of points.

* * *

"What about the near future of the stock market?" Gann replied: "My forecast indicates that stocks will back and fill until around November 15, when congress meets. Then they will have another decline and reach low of the reaction about November 26-27, followed by an advance in December."

1938—Predicted bull market to start in the spring or early summer, and called for low of the year for the early part of April. Actual low occurred on March 31st. This Forecast strongly advised buying airplane stocks and said they would lead the market upward. It is now market history that the airplane stocks as a group were the strongest on the New York Stock Exchange, and many of these stocks doubled and tripled in value during 1938.

Again We Repeat:

"Prove all things and hold fast to that which is good."

1939—The Stock Forecast called for high January 3rd, the Dow-Jones Industrial Averages made high January 4th and started to decline.

The Forecast indicated low for January 21st to 23rd, the averages reached low January 26th.

February 4th to 6th indicated high, averages made high February 6th.

February 21st to 23rd indicated low, averages made low February 21st.

March 4th to 6th indicated high, averages made high March 10th.

March 8th to 9th and 24th to 25th indicated low, averages made low March 22nd and 28th.

April 19th to 20th called for last low, averages made low April 11th.

May 16th - 17th indicated high, averages made high May 10th to 15th.

June 7th to 9th indicated high, averages made high June 9th, and a sharp decline followed.

June 23rd to 24th indicated low, averages made low June 29th to 30th.

July 28th to 29th indicated high, averages made high July 25th to 28th.

August 4th to 5th indicated low, averages made low August 5th and 7th.

The 1939 Forecast was issued and mailed to subscribers on November 14th, 1938.

We are sure that anyone will agree that such accurate, long-range forecasting cannot be done by guess-work. You can learn to make forecasts one year or more in advance when you learn how to apply the rules taught with the Master Forecasting Method.

What Others Say of W. D. Gann's Methods:

Below we print copies of letters received from two prominent business men, many other letters on file in our office from people who have used Mr. Gann's Courses of Instruction and followed his advice.

New York, N. Y.
March 16, 1933.

My Dear Mr. Gann:

I am very glad to write you a letter stating my personal observation of the application of your system to trading in Cotton.

On November 30, 1923, starting with a capital of $973.00 you showed a clear profit of over $30,000. at the close of business on January 28, 1924. This profit was made through the purchase and sale of contracts for the delivery and sale of cotton on the New York Cotton Exchange through one of the leading New York brokerage offices. I personally know of all the trades made in this commodity for the account, having received advices of your operations, from the broker on the day following the day each trade was made.

On January 29, 1924, a check for $24,764.04 was drawn against the account and delivered to a person with whom I am personally acquainted.

C. M.

———

New Bern, N. C.
August 23rd, 1937

I have known Mr. W. D. Gann for many years. I have been in his office on Wall Street, have seen him trade with his method and take the money out of the market. With it he has made a fortune in speculation. And he does not need the money he gets for his method or market service any more than Mr. Ford does for sale of cars.

His method has been used by me since 1927, successfully. In my opinion, it is the only one with which one can make money in the market and keep it. If you will follow his method and the rules he lays down, you will also make a success and I can assure you without it you will make a failure.

This statement is made after having read every book I could find on the subject, including the lives of all the big operators of the past and subscribed to every financial paper published and most of the market services.

C. K.

Results of Trading According To Rules

One of the rules is for trading in fast moves after the market gives a definite signal for a big move up or down. This rule gets you in the market when activity starts and keeps you in until the move has run its course, enabling you to make large profits in a comparatively short period of time.

Trading in the Dow-Jones 30 Industrial Averages beginning June 5th, 1897 to July 25th, 1939 you would have been in the market 1283 weeks or 24⅓ years out of a total of 42 years.

Total number of points profit would have been.	2,367.
Average points profit per month	1.84
Profits on 100 shares of stock would have been	$236,700.00

(without pyramiding or ever trading in more than 100 sh.)

Figures do not allow for errors in judgment, commission or interest, making a liberal deduction of 25% to cover same	59,175.00
Net profit on 100 shares, or a capital of $3,000	$177,525.00

You could have started trading in 1897 in 100 shares on a capital of $1,000.00 but according to the methods and rules you should have started with a capital of $3,000.00 for trading in 100 shares.

Should you have traded in the active leading stocks at all times, instead of the averages, the profits would have been much greater because the active leaders moved from one to three times as many points as the average.

Dow Jones 20 Railroad Averages May 1897 to March 1914 and Dow Jones 30 Industrial Averages February 1913 to June 1939, trading according to the rules during the above periods, show possible points:

Advances	2,085.52
Possible decline	2,012.42
Total points	4,097.94
Points made on Advance	1,336.78
Points made on Decline	1,236.13
Total	2,572.91
Percentage of total points made to possible points,	63%
Percentage of all points made on the up-side or Bull Market	64%
Percentage of points made on the down-side or Bear Market	61.4%

Total number of trades made...177

Total number of years...42

Average number of trades per year...4.2
    (Slightly above 4 per year)

Net profit per year on 100 shares..$6,125.74

Net profit on 100 shares from 1897 to 1939..$257,291.00

Figuring an original investment of..$5,000.00

Equity as of June 30th, 1939 would be..$262,291.00

Value of $100. invested in 1897 as of June 1939....................................$5,145.82

COMPARISON OF DOW THEORY AND
W. D. GANN'S METHOD
BASED ON DOW JONES 30 INDUSTRIAL AVERAGES

1897 to September 1937

	Dow's Theory:	Mr. Gann's Method:	Advantage of Mr. Gann's Method:
Total points made	718.54	2,118.03	1,399.49
Points made long side	416.37	1,127.40	711.03
Points made short side	302.17	990.63	688.46
Average number of points per year	17.5	51.66	34.16
Total profit made on 100 shares	$71,854.00	$211,803.00	$139,949.00
Profit per year on 100 shares	1,752.54	5,165.92	3,413.38
$100. invested in 1897 equals	3,602.88	5,177.37	1,574.49
Trades per year average	½ trade of 1 every 2 yrs.	3.4	

The Dow Theory as well as Mr. Gann's Method are subject to the human element and errors in determining when the combination occurs naturally will arise. No deduction from the above figures is made for errors or for commission and expenses. The computation and the results of the Dow Theory is based upon what we believe to be the best opinion. Mr. Gann's Method is based upon his own interpretation of his rules.

How You Can Make Profits

You can become a successful trader or investor if you acquire knowledge and learn the mathematical rules which determine the trend of Stocks and Commodity market movements.

The Bible says "Ye shall know the truth and the truth shall make you free". When you have learned the truth about stocks you will no longer buy on hope or sell on fear, you will face facts and be free to act on judgment based on rules that you know always have worked and always will.

Why I Can Teach You To Succeed

I have paid the price in time and money to discover, test and prove, rules that are, practical and get results. You will agree that 36 years experience is valuable in any line of business and that after I have spent that much time in study and research I can teach you the rules that will take the gamble out of Stock Market trading and make it a safe and profitable business. The man who devotes all the time to any business will learn more about it than the man who only studies it a short time.

If the average man or woman would only spend the first few hundred dollars they lose in the market in acquiring knowledge and learning the rules for buying and selling at the right time, they would then make profits—not losses.

Your Son's or Daughter's Future

A man can leave his son or daughter a million dollars or more and they can lose it quickly if they have not learned the rules how to invest it safely. My Course of Instructions will teach any one how to preserve his capital and make profits. They must be willing to study and work hard.

Forecasting Business
Good Positions For Students

Changed conditions due to Government interference, regulations and changes in Europe, make it necessary for every business man to forecast his own business in order to meet competition. It makes no difference whether a manufacturer of raw material or a seller of the finished product, he must be able to forecast future business conditions and guage future demand as closely as possible in order to make a profit in business. This creates a good position for a man who can accurately forecast business conditions and changes. The young man who prepares himself and becomes an expert in forecasting business, Commodities, Stocks and Bonds, will find a demand for his services. Estates must have an expert to handle their investments and once a man has proven his ability to increase the profits of a large estate he will find he can name his own terms as to salary. Money must have brains and experts to increase its earning power. Large estates can and will pay a man who can keep capital intact and prevent losses. The Investment Counsellor will find the future holds a bright outlook for him if he knows his business and has fully prepared himself.

What the Course Consists of

The Complete Course is in Four Lessons:

LESSON I. Form Reading or Picture Method. A great improvement on the Dow Theory. Formations or how to forecast the trend by certain formations by fixed rules which help to make your judgment accurate. Examples are given to prove the rules. With this lesson you learn from the picture or formation and after experience your eyes will recognize a formation and know what it means.

LESSON II. Resistance Levels. Where stocks meet buying or selling and make bottom and top. Definite mathematical rules, practical and proven that make profits. They are easy to learn and apply. All buying and selling points marked plainly on the charts and rules given why to buy or sell at certain points. Anyone should be able to learn this lesson in three days' time and make substantial profits with this Lesson alone. This method keeps you with the trend and enables you to buy near low levels and sell near top.

LESSON III. Time Elements and Time Rules. There is a definite relation between price and time. When time is up stocks make top and start down. When time is up and the time cycle runs out stocks make bottom and start up. It makes no difference how high stocks are selling, they can go higher until time runs out and no matter how low they are they can go lower until time is up.

Time is the most important factor in determining and forecasting market movements. Very few people understand the time element and its value. With this lesson you learn when the right time comes to buy and you know according to time three important buying points:

1. When near extreme low levels. With limited risk.

2. A safer buying point at a certain time period.

3. The safest buying point after the market gives the third time signal.

These rules give the three selling levels according to time. With this method you will be able to make up a forecast one year or more in advance on the average or individual stock.

LESSON IV. Volume of Sales. New, up-to-date, since the Security Exchange regulation and higher margin requirements have changed volume of sales. The Volume of Sales is the driving power that moves the market but time determines when volume will change at top or bottom. The volume rules are proven by charts, rules and forms on volume never published or used by anyone else.

Results from the Methods

1896 to 1939—43 years with Dow Jones Averages.

No. 1 Course of Instructions

CONSISTING OF TWO LESSONS:

1. Form Reading or picture method. Some Time Rules and Formations. B. W. points.

2. Resistance levels make it easier to operate with first lesson. Gives more mathematical confirmations of why to buy and sell at certain points.

In order to help those who are worthy and trying to help themselves, I am making a very reasonable price on these courses so that young students and people of small means can get started on their Investment Education. At a small cost and with a small capital students may start trading after they have gained knowledge and make profits.

The price is $500.00; payable $300.00 cash in advance. Easy terms on the balance, or can be paid after you make profits.

No. 2 Complete Course of Instructions

CONSISTING OF FOUR LESSONS:

This is a more complete course than I have sold for $5,000.00 in former years and it is worth $5,000.00 or more to anyone who will study it and use it. To help others who need help and are trying to make a success, I am making a low price of $1,000.00 for the Complete Course which includes a Weekly High and Low Chart on Dow-Jones 20 Railroad Averages 1896 to 1914, a Weekly High and Low Chart on Dow-Jones 30 Industrial Averages 1914 to date. A swing Chart on 30 Industrials 1896 to date. Weekly High and Low Charts on five active stocks that you select or we select, these Charts will be for two or three years back, according to the stock and market positions at the time.

Terms arranged if you are not in position to pay all cash in advance.

No. 3 Master Forecasting Method

This Method contains all of the Form Rules, Resistance Level and Volume of Sales and my secret discovery of the Master Time Factor and a new way of Forecasting by Mathematical Rules that are simple and practical.

MATHEMATICAL RULES OR REASONS: It is possible to get as many as nine confirmations or reasons why a stock should be bottom or top at a certain time and the greater number of confirmations the surer the chances of making profits. That is why each of my Lessons and Courses teach you more rules to confirm what you learned in the first Course or previous Lessons.

Master Charts that save time and work go with this Course, Master High and Low Charts ten to forty-five years back. This Course gives mathematical proof of how I forecast the 1929 Bull Market and the Panic which followed to 1932.

Price of complete Master Forecasting Course $2500.00 cash in advance. Terms can be arranged with part cash and balance on monthly payments.

Correspondence Course

Anyone can learn a Course by correspondence because everything is made plain. The buying and selling points are marked on the Charts and Rules why we buy or sell at a certain point. However, you can make greater progress if you can arrange for a few days personal instruction.

WHY YOU CAN MAKE MORE PROFITS TRADING
IN COMMODITIES THAN STOCKS

In trading according to my Mechanical Method & Trend Indicator or according to my 1936 New Master Forecasting Methods on Cotton, Grain, Rubber and other commodities, there are many advantages over trading in stocks:

1. Commodities follow a seasonal trend and are much easier to forecast. They move with supply and demand.

2. It requires much less work to keep up charts and calculations on Commodities. There are 1200 stocks listed on the New York Stock Exchange and you must keep a separate chart on as many of them as you wish to forecast the trend of. With Cotton, you need one to three charts, and the same with Grain.

3. When you have a forecast made up for Cotton or Grain, if you are right, you are sure to make money because all options follow the same trend. There are no cross-currents as in stocks, with some stocks declining to new low levels and other making new highs.

4. In dealing in Futures, there are no heavy interest charges as there are when long of stocks and no dividends to pay as when short of stocks.

5. Dividends can be suddenly passed or declared which will affect stock prices. This cannot happen to commodities.

6. Pools cannot manipulate a commodity as they can a stock.

7. Facts about commodities are general known while many stocks are mystery stocks all the time and some stocks are subject to false rumors.

8. The stages of the business cycle tell more about the prices of commodities than they do about stocks.

9. Commodities are governed only by demand and supply. This is not always true of stocks.

10. Speculation in commodities is more legitimate than speculation in stocks because you are dealing in a necessity.

11. Commodities are consumed. Stocks are not. This has a bearing upon the ease in forecasting commodity prices.

13. Stock prices tend to move by groups of stocks, while commodities move independently.

14. Notable speculators, like Livermore and Dr. E. H. Crawford, have discovered after long experience that they make money with greater certainty in commodities.

15. Stocks go into receivers' hands and go out of business. Commodities go on forever. Crops are planted and harvested each year.

16. There is always a demand by consumers for commodities, which is not the case with stocks.

17. Since the Securities Exchange Law was passed, marginal requirements are much higher on stocks than on Commodities. Therefore, you can make more money on the same capital trading in Cotton, Wheat, Corn, Rubber or other markets.

18. When you learn the rules for forecasting and trading in Commodities, they never change because we will always have wheat, corn, and cotton crops every year, and these crops will be consumed, while stocks change and you have to study new stocks to keep up with changed conditions.

COMMODITY METHODS

The prices of my Commodity Methods are less than Stock Methods because it requires less time to teach them and a small number of charts are needed:

MECHANICAL METHOD AND TREND INDICATION COVERING COTTON OR GRAIN

Price $600.00 Terms: $300.00 cash in advance; balance in monthly payments. Any man can learn this Method easily thru correspondence in a few days. With this Method we furnish weekly charts running back 2 to 3 years, daily charts and a trend chart; instructions how to work the Method; rules for telling where to buy and sell, where to place stop loss orders and when to pyramid. Cotton and Grain Methods combined, price $1,200.00 Terms: $500.00 cash in advance, balance in monthly payments.

FORECASTING METHOD ON COTTON OR GRAIN

Contains Master Time Factor:

Price $1,500.00 Terms: $750.00 cash; balance in monthly payments. With this Method you get charts on cotton back to 1869 (monthly) and with the Grain Method chart running back to 1842 (monthly), also weekly and daily charts, Master tables, Resistance Levels and Resistance Cards. You are taught the Master Time Factor and how to make up a forecast one or more years in advance.

Cotton and Grain Methods combined, price $2,500.00 Terms: $1,500.00 cash in advance, balance in monthly payments.

KNOWLEDGE IS POWER

Webster said: "The man who can teach me something is the man I want to know." You may think my prices are high, but stop to consider that you have the use of these Methods during your entire lifetime and that the knowledge I teach will be worth the money for one week's trading at critical times. You can easily lose in the market the price you would pay for my Course and the market leaves you with no valuable knowledge after your losses. Learn to see and know for yourself what Commodities will do; then you will make a success.

Special Rates in Classes
For College Students

I will make a special rate to students where classes of five or more take the course at the same time.

Time Required to Learn the Course

Time required depends on the student. His education, experience and practical knowledge of stocks and commodities. If you have read my books or kept up charts you will learn in a much shorter time than one who has had no experience or special training. However, anyone who can add, subtract, multiply and divide can learn how to apply my rules. School teachers learn easy. The amount of time you put in studying each day or week will determine how soon you can learn the rules and start trading.

Some learn in one week, some in three weeks and others in three months, but one thing is sure, the longer you study the more you learn. Each year you will know more and practice will make you perfect.

Trade on Paper

I recommend that all students start trading on paper until they are sure how to apply the rules. You learn by doing and mistakes made on paper will prevent actual losses later. Never be in a hurry. Be sure you are right, then act and success is sure.

Health Is Wealth

Good health is essential for success in any business and for active trading in Stocks and Commodities. Keeping your health perfect is just as important as protecting your capital.

Why I Live in Miami

I have learned the value of good health and that is why I have a winter home in Miami, Florida. I give personal instruction to individuals or classes in Miami from October 1st to May 1st every year.

W. D. GANN
820 S.W. 26 Road
Miami, Florida

W. D. GANN

P. O. BOX 223
WALL STREET STATION
NEW YORK 5, N. Y.

New York, N. Y.

Master 360° Circle Chart

		1	2	3	4	5	6	7	8	9	10	11	12	1	2	3	4	5
12	24	360	720	1080	1440	1800	2160	2520	2880	3240	3600	3960	4320	4680	5040	5400	5760	6120
	23	345	705	1065	1425	1785	2145	2505	2865	3225	3585	3945	4305	4665	5025	5385	5745	6105
11	22	330	690	1050	1410	1770	2130	2490	2850	3210	3570	3930	4290	4650	5010	(5370)	5730	6090
7/8	21	315	675	(1035)	1395	1755	2115	2475	2835	3195	3555	3915	4275	4635	4995	5365	5715	6075
10	20	300	660	1020	1380	1740	2100	2460	2820	3180	3540	3900	4260	4620	4980	5340	5700	6060
3/4	19	285	645	1005	1365	1725	2085	2445	2805	3165	3525	3885	4245	4605	4965	5325	5685	6045
9	18	270	630	990	1350	1710	2070	2430	2790	3150	3510	3870	4230	4590	4950	5310	5670	6030
	17	255	615	975	1335	1695	2055	2415	2775	3135	3495	3855	4215	4575	4935	5295	5655	6015
8	2/3 16	240	600	960	1320	1680	2040	2400	2760	3120	3480	3840	4200	4560	4920	5280	5640	(6000)
5/8	15	225	585	945	1305	1665	2025	2385	2745	3105	3465	3825	4185	4545	4905	5265	5625	5985
7	14	210	570	930	1290	1650	2010	2370	2730	3090	3450	3810	4170	4530	4890	5250	5610	5970
1/2	13	195	555	915	1275	1635	1995	2355	2715	3075	3435	3795	4155	4515	4875	5235	5595	5955
6	12	180	540	900	1260	1620	1980	2340	2700	3060	3420	3780	4140	4500	4860	5220	5580	5940
	11	165	525	885	1245	1605	1965	2325	2685	3045	3405	3765	4125	4485	4845	5205	5565	5925
5	10	150	510	870	1230	1590	1950	2310	2670	3030	3390	3750	4110	4470	4830	5190	5550	5910
	9	135	495	855	1215	1575	1935	2295	2655	3015	3375	3735	4095	4455	4815	5175	5535	5895
4	1/3 8	120	480	840	1200	1560	1920	2280	2640	3000	3360	3720	4080	4440	4800	5160	5520	5880
	7	105	465	825	1185	1545	1905	2265	2625	2985	3345	3705	4065	4425	4785	5145	5505	5865
3	1/4 6	90	450	810	1170	1530	1890	2250	2610	2970	3330	3690	4050	4410	4770	5130	5490	(5850)
	5	75	435	795	1155	1515	1875	2235	2595	2955	3315	3675	4035	4395	4755	5115	5475	5835
2	1/6 4	60	420	780	1140	1500	1860	2220	2580	2940	3300	3660	4020	4380	4740	5100	5460	5820
	1/8 3	45	405	765	1125	1485	1845	2205	2565	2925	3285	3645	4005	4365	4725	5085	5445	5805
1	2	30	390	(750)	1110	1470	1830	2190	2550	2910	3270	3630	3990	4350	4710	5070	5430	5790
	1	15	375	735	1095	1455	1815	2175	2535	2895	3255	3615	3975	4335	4695	5055	5415	5775

| | 30° 1/12 | 60° 1/6 | 90° 1/4 | 120° 1/3 | 180° 5/12 | 180° 1/2 | 210° 7/12 | 240° 2/3 | 270° 3/4 | 300° 5/6 | 330° 11/12 | 360° 1/1 | 30° 1/12 | 60° 1/6 | 90° 1/4 | 120° 1/3 | 150° 5/12 |

MATHEMATICAL FORMULA FOR MARKET PREDICTIONS

Time Cycles Tell the Trend of Commodities, Stocks and Business

To make success investing in stocks or speculating in commodities you must have a well defined plan and must know the rules that have stood the test of time for 50 years or more. After you learn the rules you must eliminate guess work, hope and fear and follow rules and you will make profits.

When you buy a course of instructions look up the record of the man who has discovered and developed it and if he has made a success with it and made money you can afford to buy the course and follow the rules.

W. D. GANN'S RECORD FOR 52 YEARS

1902 August 15th made first trade in commodities and started studying mathematical principles to determine the future trend.

1905 September 12th the daily Texarkanian of Texarkana, Texas, printed an article giving Mr. Gann's view on Cotton prices.

1907 he predicted the panic in stocks and the decline in commodities and made large profits.

1908 May 12th left Oklahoma City for New York City. August 8th made one of his greatest mathematical discoveries for predicting the trend of stocks and commodities. Started trading with a capital of $300 and made $25,000. Started another account with $130 and made $12,000 in thirty days time.

1909 December the Ticker magazine (now the magazine of Wall Street) printed an article "remarkable predictions and trading record". The article was written by the late R. D. Wyckoff, owner and editor of the Ticker Magazine at that time.

The following is a copy of part of the article:

"In order to substantiate Mr. Gann's claims as to what he has been able to do under this method, we called upon Mr. William E. Gilley, an Inspector of Imports, 16 Beaver Street, New York. Mr. Gilley is well known in the downtown district. He himself has studied stock market movements for twenty-five years, during which time he has examined every piece of market literature that has been issued and procurable in Wall Street. It was he who encouraged Mr. Gann to study out the scientific and mathematical possibilities of the subject. When asked what had been the most impressive of Mr. Gann's work and predictions, he replied as follows:

" 'It is very difficult for me to remember all the predictions and operations of Mr. Gann which may be classed as phenomenal, but the following are a few: In 1908 when Union Pacific was 168⅛, he told me that it would not touch 169 before it had a good break. We sold it short all the way down to 152⅝, covering on the weak spots and putting it out again on the rallies, securing twenty-three points profit out of an eighteen-point move.

" 'Mr. Gann's calculations are based on natural law. I have followed his work closely for years. I know that he has a firm grasp of the basic principles which govern stock market movements, and I do not believe any other man on earth can duplicate the idea or his method at the present time.

" 'Early this year he figured that the top of the advance would fall on a certain day in August and calculated the prices at which the Dow-Jones averages would then stand. The market culminated on the exact day and within four-tenths of one per cent of the figures predicted.'

" 'You and Mr. Gann must have cleaned up considerable money on all these operations,' was suggested.

" 'Yes, we have made a great deal of money. He has taken half a million dollars out of the market in the past few years. I once saw him take $130, and in less than one month ran it up to over $12,000. He can compound money faster than any man I ever met.

" 'One of the most astonishing calculations made by Mr. Gann was during last summer (1909) when he predicted that September wheat would sell at $1.20. This meant that it must touch that figure before the end of the month of September. At twelve o'clock, Chicago time, on September 30th (the last day) the option was selling below $1.08, and it looked as though his prediction would not be fulfilled. Mr. Gann said, 'If it does not touch $1.20 by the close of the market it will prove that there is something wrong with my whole method of calculation. I do not care what the price is now, it must go there.' It is common history that September wheat surprised the whole country by selling at $1.20 and no higher in the very last hour of the trading, closing at that figure.'

"So much for what Mr. Gann has said and done as evidenced by himself and others. Now as to what demonstrations have taken place before our representative:

"During the month of October, 1909, in twenty-five market days, Mr. Gann made, in the presence of our representative, two hundred and eighty-six transactions in various stocks, on both the long and short side of the market. Two hundred and sixty-four of these transactions resulted in profits; twenty-two in losses.

"The capital with which he operated was doubled ten times, so that at the end of the month he had one thousand per cent on his original margin.

"In our presence Mr. Gann sold Steel common short at 94⅞, saying that it would not go to 95. It did not.

"On a drive which occurred during the week ending October 29th, Mr. Gann bought Steel common at 86¼, saying that it would not go to 86. The lowest it sold was 86⅛.

"We have seen him give in one day sixteen successive orders in the same stock, eight of which turned out to be at either the top or the bottom eighth of that particular swing. The above we can positively verify.

"Such performances as these, coupled with the foregoing, are probably unparalleled in the history of the Street.

"James R. Keene has said, 'The man who is right six times out of ten will make his fortune.' Here is a trader, who, without any attempt to make a showing (for he did not know the results were to be published), establishes a record of over ninety-two per cent profitable trades.

"Mr. Gann has refused to disclose his method at any price, but to those scientifically inclined he has unquestionably added to the stock of Wall Street knowledge and pointed out infinite possibilities.

"We have requested Mr. Gann to figure out for the readers of The Ticker a few of the most striking indications which appear in his calculations. In presenting those we wish it understood that no man, in or out of Wall Street, is infallible.

"Mr. Gann's figures at present indicate that the trend of the stock market should, barring the usual rallies, be toward lower prices until March or April, 1910.

"He calculates that May wheat, which is now selling at $1.02, should not sell below 99c and should sell at $1.45 next spring.

"On cotton, which is now at about the 15c level, he estimates that, after a good reaction from these prices, the commodity should reach 18c in the spring of 1910. He looks for a corner in the March or May option.

"Whether these figures prove correct or not will in no sense detract from the record which Mr. Gann has already established.

"Mr. Gann was born in Lufkin, Texas, and is thirty-one years of age. He is a gifted mathematician, has an extraordinary memory for figures, and is an expert Tape Reader. Take away his science and he would beat the market on his intuitive tape reading alone.

"Endowed as he is with such qualities, we have no hesitation in predicting that within a comparatively few years Wm. D. Gann will receive full recognition as one of Wall Street's leading operators.   R. D. W."

December, 1909—The Commercial West Magazine and other newspapers carried articles about W. D. Gann's successful speculation.

1914—Predicted the World War and the panic in Stocks.

1918, March—Issued a prediction indicating the end of the war and the Kaiser's abdication, 1918. This prediction was accurately fulfilled. The Beaumont Journal, Houston Post, New York Herald and many other leading newspapers commented on this prediction.

1919—The Annual Forecast issued in the fall of 1918 indicated a big boom in oil stocks as well as a general bull market in stocks which was accurately fulfilled.

1920, November—Issued an Annual Forecast on Stocks for 1921 predicting a panic and extreme low for stocks for August. Also predicted improvement in business starting in the summer of 1921. Many newspapers commented on these forecasts.

1922—Predicted better business conditions. The Los Angeles Sunday Times and many other newspapers carried his article.

1922, December 6—The Daily Northside News of New York carried an article headed "Gann Foretold Course of Stocks." The Morning Telegraph also gave W. D. Gann credit for forecasting bull market in stocks for 1922.

The Angelina County News of Lufkin, Texas, Mr. Gann's home town, gave wide publicity to his accurate predictions.

The Boston American, Evening Telegram of New York in March, 1923, commented on W. D. Gann's mathematical ability.

1923—Wrote "Truth of the Stock Tape." This book pronounced by experts as the best book ever written on the Stock Market. It was favorably reviewed by the Wall Street Journal, Financial Times of London and other newspapers in Canada and the United States.

Predicted a crop failure and a big advance in Cotton for 1923. Cotton prices advanced 17c per pound between August and November 30, 1923. Mr. Gann made enormous profits trading in Cotton during this period. Below we quote from a letter:

W. D. GANN STARTED AN ACCOUNT WITH $973.00 AND MADE OVER $30,000.00 IN SIXTY DAYS' TIME
(Read the Letter Below Confirming This)

New York, N. Y., March, 1933

Dear Mr. Gann:

I am very glad to write you a letter stating my personal observation of the application of your system to trading in Cotton.

On November 30, 1923, starting with a capital of $973.00, you showed a clear profit of over $30,000 at the close of business on January 28, 1924. This profit was made through the purchase and sale of contracts for the delivery and sale of cotton on the New York Cotton Exchange through one of the leading New York brokerage offices. I personally know of all the trades made in this commodity for the account, having received advises of your operations, from the broker on the day following the day each trade was made.

On January 29, 1924, a check for $24,764.04 was drawn against the account and delivered to a person with whom I am personally acquainted.

I am glad to add that I had one of your cotton forecasts for the year 1923, and the diagram prepared by you foretold, without exception, the days on which all the major and minor moves of the market would start and finish.

With best wishes, I remain

Very truly yours,

C. M.

1924—Forecast big advance in Wheat.

In the fall of 1925 issued an Annual Forecast predicting a big decline in Cotton for 1926.

December, 1926—Cotton was selling for 12½c per pound. He wrote an article entitled "King Cotton to Regain His Throne." Newspapers throughout the South printed this forecast. The forecast for Cotton in 1927 indicated a big advance, calling final high for September, 1927. Cotton advanced to 24½c a pound in September, 1927. One client in Alabama wrote, "You had the Cotton forecast 100% accurate."

September, 1927—The New York Morning Telegraph concluded an article with the following: "Mr. Gann may not bet a success as a novelist but.he is unique. I am convinced that there is no man alive who could compete with him on his own ground." (Meaning Wall Street).

Most Remarkable Forecast

1928—In November W. D. Gann issued an Annual Forecast predicting the end of the great bull market in stocks for September 3, 1929, and the greatest panic in history to follow. We quote from this forecast, "September —One of the sharpest declines of the year is indicated. There will be loss of confidence by investors, and the public will try to get out after it is too late. Storms will damage crops and the general business outlook will become cloudy. War news will upset the market and unfavorable developments in foreign countries. A 'Black Friday' is indicated and a panicky decline in stocks with only small rallies. The short side will prove the most profitable. You should sell short and pyramid on the way down." Many newspapers commented on the accuracy of this forecast.

The newspapers in Bombay, India, commented on Mr. Gann's accuracy in forecasting the decline in Cotton prices.

Wall Street Stock Selector

In the spring of 1930, Mr. Gann wrote, "Wall Street Stock Selector," which was published in June, 1930. In this book he had a chapter headed, "Investors' Panic," which described conditions just as they occurred during 1931, 1932 and 1933. We quote from the book, pages 203-04:

'The coming investors' panic will be the greatest in history, because there are at least 15 to 25 million investors in the United States who hold stocks in the leading corporations, and when once they get scared, which they will after years of decline, then the selling will be so terrific that no buying power can withstand it. Stocks are so well distributed in the hands of the public that since the 1929 panic many people think that the market is panic-proof, but this seeming strength is really the weakest feature of the market."

The predictions in this book were remarkably fulfilled by panicky declines in stocks during 1930 to 1932.

In April, 1930, when this book was written the Dow Jones 30 Industrial Averages were selling at 297½. They declined to 40½ on July 8, 1932.

"Thousands of people have bought this book and profited by reading and studying it. The book has been favorably commented on by such papers as the Financial Times of London, England, Wall Street Journal, New York Daily Investment News, Coast Investors, and many other newspapers and magazines throughout the world.

Member of Commodity Exchanges

1931—In March W. D. Gann was elected to membership on the New York Rubber Exchange, The New Orleans Cotton Exchange and later became a member of the Commodity Exchange of New York.

In 1941 was elected a member of the Chicago Board of Trade.

He was in good standing when he sold his membership.

1932 Stock Forecast

"On February 10, 1932, Mr. Gann said that Stocks were bottom for a big rally. His 1932 Stock Forecast, issued October 21, 1931, called March 8 for last top for another big decline. During the latter part of June, 1932, and early July he strongly advised buying stocks, stating that final bottom had been reached, as shown by his market letter issued July 8, the day that most stocks reached final bottom. We quote from page 6 of the 1932 Fore-

4

cast: "The latter part of June, July, August and September are the most active and bullish months of the year, when sharp advances will be recorded. First extreme high is indicated around September 20 to 21, when stocks should make extreme high for the year. Then follow a decline, reaching bottom around October 4 to 5."

"Between July 8 and September 8 many stocks advanced 20 to 60 points. The market reached high of a secondary rally on September 23 from which a big decline followed, making low in the latter part of November and early December, as indicated in the Forecast."

"On March 1, 1933, by the use of his Master Time Factor Mr. Gann forecast bottom for stocks and commodities and advised buying for a big advance, as shown by the market letters issued March 1 and 3 given below. This is another proof of the great value of Mr. Gann's discovery of a Master Time Factor."

1932, December—The New York Daily Investment News printed an article written by W. D. Gann entitled, "New Era of Prosperity will be Born in 1933 Student of Cycles Declares in Forecast." This prediction was fulfilled by the Roosevelt Boom.

1933, March—W. D. Gann bought an airplane to tour the country to make crop surveys and study business conditions. His 1933 Stock and Cotton Forecast were fulfilled with remarkable accuracy. The 1933 Stock Forecast called for top July 17 and a sharp decline to July 21st. The Dow Jones Industrial Averages reached high July 17th and a wide open break followed. The Averages declined 25 points in 4 days.

W. D. Gann's Trading Record

Mr. Gann made large profits speculating for his own account in Stocks, Cotton and other commodities during 1933. Below we publish a record taken from brokers' statements, showing the trades made by Mr. Gann for 3 years. This is proof that he can and does make money by following his own rules and methods.

1933—From August 1 to December 31, total number of trades 135 of which 112 showed profits and 23 losses. Percentage of accuracy on total number of trades, 83%. Percentage of profit to losses, 89.9%.

Total number of Trades for the year 1933; 479 of which 422 were profits and 57 losses. Percentages of accuracy, 88.1%. Percentage of profits on capital used 4,000%, or 40 to 1.

1934—January 1 to December 31, total number of Trades, 362. COTTON, 147 trades of which 135 shows profits and 12 losses. GRAINS, 170 trades of which 161 shows profits and 9 losses. RUBBER, 23 trades of which 21 showed profits and 2 losses. SILVER, 7 trades. All showed profits; no losses. SILK, 4 trades, 3 showed profits, 1 loss. STOCKS, 11 trades; 10 profits and 1 loss. Total for the year, 362 trades of which 337 showed profits and 25 showed losses. Percentage of accuracy on total number of trades, 93.09%. Percentage of profits to losses, 93.10%. Percentage of profits on Capital used, 800%, or 8 for 1.

1935—Total trades in Cotton, Grain and Rubber, 98, of which 83 showed profits and 15 showed losses. Percentage of accuracy in total trades, 85%. Percentage of profit to losses, 82½. Percentage of profit on capital used, 336%.

Stocks, total trades 34, of which 29 showed profits and 5 showed losses.

Percentage of accuracy on total number of trades, 85.5%. Percentage of profits to losses, 83%. Percentage of profits on capital used, 100%.

During 1935 W. D. Gann visited all of the Latin American countries to study crop conditions and business conditions.

1935, March 31—The Buenos Aires Herald carried an article about W. D. Gann's record of accurate forecast. W. D. Gann was in Buenos Aires at the time this article was written.

Writes New Books

1936—"New Stock Trend Detector" was written by W. D. Gann. This book was a further advance over "Truth of the Stock Tape" and "Wall Street Stock Selector" and contained an actual trading record for 10 years in Chrysler Motors according to the rules set down in these books.

1936, July—Bought special built all-metal airplane, "The Silver Star," for making crop surveys.

1937—Wrote and published a book, "How to Make Profits Trading in Puts and Calls." Scientific Stock Forecasting again proved equal to the test of predicting a bear year, sharp declines coming in March and September. A maximum decline of 80 points was called for and the actual decline from the March high to the November low was 82 and a fraction points.

These books were favorably reviewed by the Wall Street Journal, The New York Daily Investment News and various other newspapers.

In the 1936 Grain Forecast predicted crop failure and higher prices.

1936, November—Issued the Annual Forecast for 1937 and predicted a panic in stocks. The decline was very severe and lasted into March, 1938, with the Dow-Jones Averages declining 97 points.

1937, November—The Milwaukee Journal gave Mr. Gann credit for predicting the 1929 and 1937 crashes in the Stock Market and the accuracy of his timing. Mr. Gann made large profits selling stocks during 1937 and the certified public accountant has seen the statement of these profits.

1939, July—Bought a new Fairchild airplane to use for business purposes in making crop surveys. He predicted the beginning of World War II and made large profits buying grains.

1941, September 14th—Mr. Gann forecast the top for Soy Beans and sold short, making large profits on the decline. Prices declined to October 17, 1941, being down 48c in 30 days' time.

New Commodity Book

In the fall of 1941 W. D. Gann wrote "How to Make Profits Trading in Commodities." This book has been pronounced the best book ever written on commodities and has been reviewed by many newspapers.

1946—Predicted a big advance in stocks and cotton and the big decline which followed.

Figured the exact date, October 15, 1946, for the big decline in cotton. Prices declined nearly 16c per pound in three weeks and he sold short all the way down.

Trading Record

October 1, 1946, to December 30th—One account started with a capital of $4,500 showed a gross profit of $18,981.30. Total losses $1,165. Net profit $17,816.30 or approximately 400% on the capital used.

Another account started with a capital of $6,000. Gross profits $19,-972.75. Total losses $634.75. Net profits $19,338.00. A percentage of over 320% on the capital used. Other accounts which he handled showed profits as great as these.

W. D. Gann has always made a success trading in very active fast-moving markets and has made a great record for predicting the extreme high and extreme low on commodities and stocks. These accurate predictions are based on his discovery of THE MASTER TIME CYCLE which repeats at certain intervals.

1949—Wrote "45 YEARS IN WALL STREET," giving new rules for stock trading. The International Mark Twain Society awarded Mr. Gann an Honorary Membership in the Society based on the merits of his book, "45 YEARS IN WALL STREET." This book was favorably received by investors and traders throughout the country and is still selling. It has been favorably reviewed by newspapers and magazines.

1951, June 6th—On his 73rd birthday completed writing a new edition of "How to Make Profits Trading in Commodities," giving new rules bringing this book up to date and giving the benefit of his years of experience.

76th Year Trading Record and New Discoveries

Mr. Gann is active and keeps up to date. During his 76th year he made a new discovery and completed two MASTER CALCULATORS for saving time and getting accurate indications on the trend of stocks and commodities. In the spring of 1954 he completed a MASTER THREE-DIMENSION CHART which proves the relative position of TIME, PRICE and VOLUME which produces VELOCITY or SPEED and shows when the trend is changing to a very fast active advancing market or a slow upward movement.

The relative position of PRICE TO TIME TELLS the TIME CYCLES when prices decline very fast or move very slow. History repeats in the stock or commodity markets but you must learn the rules and the GREAT TIME CYCLES in order to take advantage of rapid advances and declines and make profits.

Many people have the idea that W. D. Gann is old and in his dotage and that he cannot still make money trading in the market.

From September 30, 1953, to October 26, 1953, he made 26 trades in Grains, 25 showed profits and one trade showed a small loss of $40. During this same period he made six trades in Eggs, five showed profits and one trade showed a small loss.

We have stated before that W. D. Gann has nearly always been right when there was big advances and big declines in Commodities and Stocks and in markets of this kind you can make LARGE PROFITS ON SMALL RISKS by following the rules which he has discovered and which he follows himself.

1954, April 27 to May 7—W. D. Gann made 17 trades in Coffee, Soy Beans, Rye and Eggs. Sixteen of these trades showed profits and one trade in eggs showed a small loss.

April 27, 1954, he sold July Soy Beans short at 412 and on May 5 bought in these beans at 485½, making a profit of 26½c per bushel in eight calendar days. He placed a stop loss order on the trade at 416, limiting the risk to 4c per bushel, and made 26½c per bushel or a gain of 6½ times the risk. He sold more Soy Beans at 400½, 395½, 390½, 392½ and bought them in or covered shorts at 384, 387 and 388¼. After he covered the shorts July Soy Beans rallied to 395¾ on May 6 and he again sold short at 392½ on May 7. The above record of trades shows that W. D. Gann is still active and he is nearly 76 years of age and follows his own rules and makes profits. With some of the money he made trading in Coffee and Soy Beans he bought a fast express cruising boat and named the boat "The Coffee Bean."

7

You can make money following the same rules that Mr. Gann followed and the rules are not hard to learn.

1954 Coffee Trades

Coffee prices advanced the most rapid in the spring of 1954 and reached the highest prices in history.

1954, April 2nd—Coffee prices reached the highest in history at the opening. The last advance started October 13, 1953, when December coffee was low at 56.70. April 2, 1954, December Coffee high 95.20. Up 38½c per pound in less than six months and up 30c per pound since January 19, 1954.

W. D. Gann's MASTER TIME CYCLE and MASTER THREE-DIMENSION CHART indicated that December Coffee would be high on April 2nd at 95.20. When it reached this price he gave an order to sell short. The market broke very rapidly and he sold December Coffee at 94.31, and on April 14, 1954, bought December Coffee at 84.05 which was the extreme low for the decline at that time. He made 1,036 points profit in 12 calendar days. Based on the risk or stop-loss order he made 1,000% on the risk and the gain in percentage on the capital used was 140%.

April 15th sold December Coffee at 87.75. April 21st bought December Coffee at 85.50. A profit of 225 points in seven days. These were not all of the profitable trades that he made in Coffee. He traded in July and September Coffee also.

This is proof that his mathematical rules work accurately in extreme wild markets and when his rules indicated high for Coffee April 2nd, W. D. Gann had the faith in his knowledge and the nerve to sell Coffee and make quick profits. This record answers the question that he can and does make profits at the age of 76 by following his rules. You can learn these rules and make profits in Rye, Soy Beans, Wheat, Cotton, Coffee, Cocoa and other commodities. You must learn to follow the rules strictly, eliminate hope and fear and protect your capital and profits with stop-loss orders and success is assured.

We will not sell the course of instructions or teach the mathematical formula for market predictions just to get money, which we do not need or have to have; we will only sell the courses to people who meet our requirements, and if we feel after a thorough investigation that a man or woman cannot make a success investing or trading we will refuse to teach them the courses.

WHAT PEOPLE WHO HAVE USED W. D. GANN'S SERVICE AND COURSES SAY OVER A LONG PERIOD OF YEARS

New York, October, 1931

You predicted the end of this terrible condition as being October 3rd, 1931. It happened one hour later . . .

Someone ought to tell the world about you and your knowledge over a nationwide hookup and offer them proof in form of your "Tunnel Through the Air." I am sure we would have better preparations for another October 3rd, 1931, in the future.—G.F.

New York, October, 1931

Dear Friend Gann:

Again I must congratulate you on your marvelous predictions. I have followed your

work closely for the past 23 years. I well remember that in the early part of 1909 you forecast the exact date in August when stocks would reach extreme high and came within about ⅛ of the exact high level for the Wall Street Journal railroad average. Twenty years later I saw your prediction fulfilled in September, 1929, when you said that stocks would make top and that the worst panic in history would follow, all of which has proved too true.

But the most amazingly accurate long-range prediction you have ever made was in your book, "The Tunnel Thru the Air," which you wrote in the early part of 1927. I have watched prediction after prediction fulfilled and have been especially interested in your forecast on the stock market for October 3rd, 1931. I had watched stocks go down and down as if no bottom was in sight and when last Saturday, October 3rd, stocks reached the lowest level in years, I said to myself, my friend Gann has called the turn and it's time for me to take my market basket to Wall Street and fill it with bargains. Monday, October 5th, arrived and stocks smashed to the lowest of the year. Today, at the close, I see that they are up 10 to 15 points from Monday's lowest. You missed the bottom by two days, counting Sunday. Well, that's pretty close when we consider you made the calculations $4\frac{1}{2}$ years ago.

You have certainly demonstrated that when a man understands the practical rules and laws in the Bible, the future becomes an open book. May you live long and prosper, is my sincere wish for you.

Very truly your,

W. E. G.

(Telegram)
Santa Barbara, Cal.
February, 1931

Vanadium yielded about $40,000.00 in two weeks.   J. H.

Following this telegram this same man wrote as follows:

I take genuine pleasure in sending you herewith New York draft for balance due on contract. As I said to Mr. E. this morning, "I have felt, ever since sitting at your feet, that I had obtained a full $4,000 worth of Comfortable Assurance alone, to say nothing of having had a net profit on my very first deal, alone, of just ten times that amount."

Our little Santa Barbara class will all make good; it takes some a bit longer than others, but as far as I am concerned, I just KNOW that I never need have financial worry, for you have given me a key-ring full of pass-keys which will unlock profits with a certainty. I would not take all that I have paid you for just one of those little pocket charts, which will do a lot of profitable trading, all by myself.   J. H. B.

What one satisfied user writes to a prospect:

Cleveland, Ohio
December, 1933

I am in receipt of your letter of the 28th in reference to Mr. W. D. Gann and his mechanical trend indicator.

I have known Mr. Gann for a number of years and have followed and studied his services during this time. Some time ago, I took all the services that he offers, which was an outlay of considerable cash; however, I have found that the investment has proven most satisfactory and the cost is going to be a small item. Several of the

courses were taken under his personal supervision, but I did have a lot of his work through correspondence. If you are not in position to take the services personally, I believe you can get your money's worth by correspondence. His services by correspondence are so detailed that it would be impossible for you to lose the thought he is trying to convey.

Mr. Gann is a man of considerable means and one of the most brilliant men I have ever contacted. He has made his entire fortune out of the market through the methods he will teach you and his market experience has been over a period of thirty years.

I hope I have given you the information requested; however, if you should like for me to answer further questions, it will be a pleasure to hear from you.

Yours very truly,

W. K. G.

Portland, Oregon
April, 1931

I have taken all the principal services, spending as high as four or five thousand dollars per year for these, and I think Mr. Gann has something that is so far in advance of anything else I have seen or worked with that there is no comparison.

W. P. H., Jr.

New Bern, N. C.
August, 1937

In reply to yours of the 19th.

I have known Mr. W. D. Gann for many years. I have been in his office on Wall Street, have seen him trade with his method and take the money out of the market. With it he has made a fortune in speculation. And he does not need the money he gets for his method or market service any more than Mr. Ford does for sale of cars.

His method has been used by me since 1927, successfully. In my opinion, it is the only one with which one can make money in the market and keep it. If you will follow his method and the rules he lays down, you will also make a success and I can assure you without it you will make a failure.

This statement is made after having read every book I could find on the subject, including the lives of all the big operators of the past and subscribed to every financial paper published and most of the market services.

Yours very truly,

C. K.

CERTIFIED PUBLIC ACCOUNTANT'S
REPORT

January, 1933

The 400-share lot transactions were begun on June 4, 1931, and were completed on

December 28, 1932. This showed a net profit of $90,570, after deduction of $5,121 for commissions and taxes.

The $3,000 capital was used exclusively on the 100-share lot transactions and was withdrawn on February 27, 1931. All trading thereafter was done on accumulated profits.

I hereby certify that the schedules submitted correctly indicate the profits that could have been made by this Method.

Might I be allowed to place in this report my private opinion, that the Method, as you demonstrated it, is absolutely foolproof. It requires simply the original capital as provided for by the Method, which is plainly stated in the rules, and thereafter to follow the simple instructions explicitly without any human-made deviations from the rules. If the user of this Method will only remember this one simple suggestion of mine, there is no question nor any doubt but that it will make money for the user.

It is amazing to consider what has been accomplished with so small a capital in such a short period of time by simply following mathematical rules, so easy to memorize that a grammar school boy or girl could follow them.

I am making this digression in my report to you because I bought the Method in 1930 and am using it with good results myself. I have bought and examined the new and improved Method and consider it about 100% better than your Method was in 1930. You are at liberty to use this and I will be very glad to recommend the system.

Respectfully submitted,

S. J. M.
Certified Public Accountant

August 5, 1933

Covering the period from April 1st to July 31st, 1933, you made a total of 344 trades in stocks, cotton, rubber and grain. 310 of these trades showed profits and 34 showed losses. Your percentage of accuracy was 89% on the total number of trades. The capital wih which you operated was increased 26½ times. On each $1,000.00 capital with which you started, you made a profit of $26,500.00 net. This was after paying all taxes, interest and commissions and deductions of all losses.

Yours very truly,

S. J. M.
Certified Public Accountant

New York, N. Y.
May, 1933

I have examined the brokers' statements and trades made by W. D. Gann during the month of April, 1933. They show profits as follows:

Cotton Account	$ 8,136.29
Rubber Account	1,387.01
Grain Account	758.30
	$10,281.60

During that time there was only one loss of $39.25, and the above profits are net after payment of brokers' commissions. There were other trades in cotton, rubber and stocks at the end of the month, that had not been closed out, which showed profits.

When the trading on the above account was started, the greatest risk taken was $800, or in other words, if the stop loss orders had been caught, the loss would have been $800.

C. L. G.

New York, N. Y.
January, 1946

I knew of no one with a deeper understanding of the basic causes of trends in the stock and commodity markets than W. D. Gann and through the years have developed a high regard for his ability to successfully forecast long range movements. He is a practical economist of the first rank. Some of his forecasts for a year ahead, have been so precisely accurate as to attract the attention of leading newspapers that have featured them in large space stories.

Mr. Gann now spends a large part of his time in Florida supervising his extensive realty interests, and the business is ably conducted by John L. Gann, assisted by Miss Gilson, both of whom have had many years of training under the direction of Mr. W. D. Gann, and both of whom are thoroughly qualified in knowledge and character to advise and guide investors in stocks, bonds and commodities.

Yours very truly,

W. M. P.

Miami, Fla.
January, 1946

Gentleman:

I take pleasure in stating that I have known W. D. Gann, John L. Gann and C. L. Gilson of W. D. Gann & Son, Inc., for more than ten years and that they all are persons of integrity, high moral character and proven ability. John L. Gann was a captain in the late war and returned with citations of merit. None of these parties are related to me by blood or marriage.

I have been receiving the W. D. Gann financial service for about eighteen years and it has been very valuable to me. I consider it the best service available. It was one of the very few that warned in no uncertain terms against and ahead of the market crash in 1929.

As to my background, I am a substantial

stockholder and director in:

Pepsi-Cola Bottling Co., of Atlanta, Atlanta, Ga.

Southern Discount Co., 220 Healy Bldg., Atlanta, Ga.

Consolidated Distributors, Inc., Atlanta, Ga.; Macon, Ga.; Jacksonville, Fla., and Tampa, Fla.

Very truly yours,

C. K.

Los Angeles, Cal.
January, 1946

Dear Sirs:

I have transacted business with the firm W. D. Gann, Inc., for approximately 24 years and it is indeed a pleasure to be able to deal with a firm for almost a quarter of a century with complete satisfaction.

I consider each of its members, W. D. Gann, Mr. John L. Gann and Miss C. L. Gilson to be honest, reliable, and trustworthy.

My experience has been satisfactory to the extent that I am still a client of theirs and hope to continue so in the years to come.

Yours very truly,

M. F.

San Francisco, Cal.
February, 1949

Today, I completed my 1948 Federal Income Tax Return, which shows my total dividends amounting to over $4,050.—the result of careful investments and wise speculations during the past decade, which I attribute to Mr. Gann's forecasts, letters and supplements.

W. T. P.

Miami, Fla.
November, 1951

Dear Sirs:

In 1926 I read a book, Truth Of The Stock Tape, written by W. D. Gann, three years before. I was deeply impressed by it. The next year I met Mr. Gann and since then, I have read with pleasure and profit, all the books written by Mr. Gann on the stock and commodity markets. What I learned from these books has paid me off in cash.

I have known Mr. Gann, intimately, 24 years. I never knew of a man who was such a fiend for research work and this would includes Mr. Thomas Edison. Mr. Gann believes, and so did Mr. Edison, to do what was thought impossible, just takes more time and work, than any one else has tried. Men like these go on and prove it.

Very truly yours,

C. K.

New York, N. Y.
November, 1951

I have studied Mr. Gann's books, courses and rules on stocks and commodities for more than a year.

It is a pleasure to recommend Mr. Gann's work to you and to urge study by those interested in the stock and commodity markets.

The courses of instruction are of great value to those with only a casual interest in the markets as well as to the specialist who needs to know.

MATHEMATICAL PREDICTION FORMULA

The four factors: TIME, PRICE, VOLUME and SPEED have been supplemented by a fifth factor, MASS PRESSURE.

TIME

Time is the essential element. Time cycles which he has developed cover the great time cycle and its important harmonics. Time cycles for stocks, commodities or business can be calculated and projected 100 years or more in advance, subject to minor corrections and variations.

He has proven a TRUE TREND LINE as well as a relatively TRUE TREND LINE when prices are advancing, and a relatively TRUE TREND LINE when prices are declining. He has developed rules and indexes which show whether high or low prices will culminate on the true trend line or the relatively true trend line.

A time variable and price variable has been worked out to exact mathematical points.

PRICE

Mr. Gann has developed rules which show the relation between time and price and what happens when prices complete a cycle before time expires.

There is a rule for determining when prices are in balance with time and when prices are out of balance with time. Prices are sometimes behind time and sometimes ahead of time.

TRANSITION PERIODS IN TIME AND PRICE

Rules have been developed showing how long prices and time remain in the transition period. All of the rules prove that TIME is the essential factor and that prices conform to time when a TIME CYCLE is complete.

VOLUME

Volume is the driving power which moves prices up or down, regardless of whether buying or selling is based on supply and demand or not. The increase in volume increases the velocity of prices in an advancing or declining market.

SPEED

Speed or velocity is a movement in price during a unit of time.

MASS PRESSURE

The fifth factor, mass pressure, shows when

the public becomes over-optimistic and buys on hope, and after a certain cycle of time, the public becomes pessimistic and sells because they fear prices are going lower. The mass pressure curve can be calculated 100 years or more in the future, as it is subject to only slight variations and minor corrections at fixed time intervals.

Mr. Gann has formulated and arranged MASTER CHARTS AND TABLES which save time and give greater accuracy with less work. With his mathematical formula and rules, the trend of stocks, commodities, business and crops can be predicted with remarkable accuracy. These discoveries and developments are of great value to investors, traders and business men in all walks of life. I hope his great work will be carried on for the benefit of mankind.

W. G. T.

Thompson, N. D.
November, 1951

In the summer of 1948, I bought Mr Gann's book, "How To Make Profits Trading in Commodities" and "The New Stock Trend Detector" and the "Truth of the Stock Tape." I was so impressed with the practical and valuable rules in these books that I decided to take his courses of instructions covering Stocks and Commodities. I began studying in December, 1948. The rules are all based on Mathematics and are practical and provable. If anyone will stick to the rules and leave out guesswork, they can make large profits trading in stocks and commodities.

After three years' experience, the rules have stood the test of Time, based on actual Market Movements.

Having taken various advisory services on the markets and reading books published by others on the subject, I am fully convinced that this is the best and most complete course available at any price. I highly recommend Mr. Gann's work to others and feel that if they study his rules and follow them, they cannot fail to make profits.

I hope that the work can be carried on for the benefit of business men, investors and traders.

A. O. K.

TO: Mr. C. R. L.
Dear Mr. L.:

I want to say a few words about Mr. W. D. Gann's course in Commodities. I feel that you and I as well as many others are fortunate in having a man like Mr. Gann to teach us in what it would take us years to learn by ourselves . . . It takes a man like Mr. Gann highly trained in mathematics to find the secrets that he can give to us.

I took the course in Commodities because I feel that it is less controlled than stocks and bonds . . . it is also faster and more interesting . . . you can delve in something

slow like oats, or get something that will give you a run like soy beans. Wheat moves steady and about the right speed. From taking Mr. Gann's course I was able to sell December wheat short at 218—30,000 bushels and now it is around 200—$5,400 in about six weeks.

There is only one thing I had trouble with with his course . . . I could not believe it would work and being a skeptic I sometimes did not follow his teaching only to find that I should have . . . that cost me sometimes. I would advise you to take the course in Commodities and for six months after you get home cub trade . . . that is, trade in the minimum amounts that you can with the most backing until you get the feel and confidence in the teachings of Mr. Gann. Those little graphs in his book they work . . . I lost about three deals until I went back and studied and remembered what he said and then checked and saw that I could have made a lot of money except I was not confident until I saw it work on black and white.

I want to also take the Stock and Bond course as soon as I feel that I have mastered what he has given me . . . (he will give you enough to keep you busy for some time). Then when I get both courses I want to have short visits and talks with Mr. Gann to have him sharpen me up.

If you do not take his course the best advice I can give you is to stay away from stocks and bonds and commodities . . . it is like going into the jungle without a gun . . . he will make you safe and smart.

G. W. I. B.

ABOUT LOSSES. We have shown the record of W. D. Gann's profitable trades throughout the years. He wishes to show both sides and does not wish to mislead any one. He states that if he had never had losses himself he would never have learned how to prevent losses and teach others to protect their capital and profits and protect themselves from serious losses.

W. D. Gann states that in the early years of his trading he had many losses and at times had losses of as much as $10,000.00, $30,000.00, and at one time he lost $60,000.00. At another time he lost $50,000.00 following so-called inside information. This taught him a valuable lesson never to believe anything that he heard about what the market was going to do but to follow mathematical deductions which he could prove and knew would work.

In 1913 W. D. Gann lost all of the money he had in a brokerage failure; again in 1919 he lost another fortune which he had accumulated in a brokerage failure. He has been in two bank failures but regardless of all of these losses and misfortunes he has always been able to rely upon mathematical science and come back and make money again.

This is why he states that knowledge of the market is more important than money and with the proper knowledge and rules you will be able to protect yourself and prevent losses which W. D. Gann suffered when he was getting his experience and before he had learned all of the rules.

A great man once said, "One good piece of advice paid for is worth more than two that you receive free."

Do not depend on tips or so-called inside information, learn mathematical rules and SEE and KNOW for yourself and you will make profits.

No man ever became great or good except through many and great mistakes."— (Gladstone)

It is impossible to expect that you will never have any losses because small losses are about the only expenses in carrying on this profession of speculating and investing. The main thing for you to learn is to protect your capital and take small losses and when you get right to follow up with *stop-loss orders* and let your profits run and one big profit which can be easily made will overbalance three or more small losses and leave you away ahead. Again we repeat, follow all of the rules and not part of them, and you will make a success.

WHY TIME CYCLES PREDICT TREND OF COMMODITIES, STOCKS AND BUSINESS

After fifty-two years of experience and research going back hundreds of years, I have proved to my entire satisfaction that history repeats and that when we know the past, we can determine the future of prices. I have put TIME CYCLES to the test in my personal trading, and I have issued Annual Forecasts on Stocks and Commodities for more than 50 years which have proved accurate.

TIME CYCLES repeat because human nature does not change. That is why wars occur at regular CYCLES. Old men do not want wars, neither do they want to go into war after they have been through one. Young men fight the wars because they read history and want to be heroes. Leaders of nations appeal to the young men who have no experience, and induce them to fight. The same desire in men that urges them to risk their lives in war causes them to take a chance in business and in speculation. They take too many chances and get too optimistic after a long period of success in business and after prolonged advances in Stocks and Commodities.

Old men in business, after a prolonged period of prosperity, become too hopeful and get over-extended. It is easy to borrow money after a long period of business prosperity. People who borrow money on hope have to LIQUIDATE when FEAR overtakes them and conditions are at the worst. That is why CYCLES in business and the Stock and Commodity Markets have always repeated and always will.

Nature's laws are unchangeable and no man or set of men can change them. The New Dealers have not proved that they can stop inflation. They claim they can prevent DEPRESSION and PANICS, but no one has succeeded in doing it in the past and the next few years will prove that our Government leaders cannot stop a DEPRESSION by WASTE and SPENDING. The New Dealers have sown to the wind and must reap the whirlwind. During the past 20 years they have spent and wasted all the wealth that our country has accumulated during the past 175 years. Our Federal, State and private debts are the largest in history, and these conditions make the next few years the most critical in our history. The man who knows TIME CYCLES can predict the future, protect his capital and make money, while those who guess will lose. This is the time of opportunity to start to study mathematical, scientific rules for making accurate deductions to determine the trend of Stocks, Business, and Commodities.

April 5, 1954

W. D. GANN

OPPORTUNITIES FOR PROFITS

The greatest opportunities for profits occur at the end of great time cycles when advances or declines are very rapid and you can make large profits in a short period of time and then stay out of the market and wait for another opportunity.

Preparation for Retiring

Business men, lawyers, doctors, engineers, accountants often wish to retire but they want something to do to keep them active and do not want to spend money out of their accumulated capital. By taking a coure of instructions after you retire you will have a new interest in life and can make an income from the market and enjoy greater pleasures.

Course for People in Trade Lines

We train men or women who are buyers or purchasing agents for large concerns and put in a complete set of charts and records and prepare the men or women who do the buying to get quick trend indications in a short period of time by the use of Master Charts, Master Calculators and the Master Three-Dimension Chart.

We teach the things that you need to learn and use in connection with your business.

If you believe in mathematics, which is the only exact science, practical and provable, and no matter what language men speak they all agree on mathematical rules. You can take this course knowing that it is the best because it is based on mathematics and has stood the test of time.

Our business is to teach you the mathematical rules so that you can determine the trend and know when to buy and sell for yourself.

"The Great Art or Learning is to understand but little at a time." (By Locke).

"All knowledge is hurtful to him who has not the science of honesty and good nature." (By Montagne).

W. D. Gann's greatest discoveries on Time Cycles have come from the Bible.

W. D. Gann is a Christian, a member of the Masonic Order and a Shriner. Special consideration and terms will be arranged for members of the Masonic Order to wish to take a course.

W. D. Gann Mathematiical Formula for Market Predictions

THE MASTER MATHEMATICAL PRICE, TIME AND TREND CALCULATOR

W. D. GANN'S latest and greatest invention for predicting the trend on stocks and commodities.

WHAT IT DOES. This Calculator is made of plastic and can be laid over a chart and it is easier to see through it than through glass.

This Master Calculator shows what these time figures are and what they mean.

1. It shows major and minor time periods.
2. Locates a TRUE TREND LINE and a RELATIVELY TRUE TREND LINE for an advancing and a declining market.
3. The main trend and the proportion in minor time periods in days, weeks, months and years.
4. The Price Resistant Levels are shown and a Price and Time Balance.
5. The different divisions for Time and Price.
6. The Master Time Cycles and their relation to price levels and the indication where one time cycle ends and a new cycle begins.
7. The Number Seven is mentioned more times in the Bible than any other number. The Master Calculator proves the importance of 7 in time periods, also 3, 9 and 12 which are referred to in the Bible. This Calculator accurately measures Price Time and Space for future indications of Time Trends.

8. The Master Calculator locates the Corner Stone, the Key Stone and the Cap Stone for price and time Trend. It proves the Master Number and Master Time Cycle and shows why and how they work on price.

9. The Master Calculator proves 9 divisions of time from one center or time factor and shows at a glance whether the price of stocks or commodities are in a weak or strong position.

The Value of Master Calculator to You

It is absolutely mathematically accurate and prevents you from making mistakes on price or time trend. It eliminates human judgment and guesswork and saves at least 75% of the time required to calculate trend indications. This is of great value to people who are busy and whose time is valuable.

One job of research work covering a period of 150 years required one man three weeks to complete. The Master Calculator covered the whole calculation in three hours' time and did not make one error. The man who did the research work averaged one error for every three years.

W. D. GANN has devoted over 52 years to research work on stocks and commodities and has spent a fortune to complete this revolutionary discovery.

The value of this Master Calculator to you cannot be measured in dollars. You have the use of it for your entire lifetime.

You receive with the Master Calculator complete written rules and instructions on how to use it.

We now have two (2) Master Calculators . . . Numbers 9 and 12. With these you can calculate quickly and accurately all future TIME CYCLES, PRICE and TIME RESISTANCE LEVELS. The new discovery used in connection with this Calculator forecast the big advance in Soy Beans from August 20, 1953, to March, 1954; also predicted that Coffee would advance to the highest prices in history in 1954. These Calculators gave these indications, based on the Master Time Cycle, as related to price.

One man who bought the Master Calculator says: "It is the greatest invention since the wheel. It saves me time and makes profits."

A cotton trader says: "I first took your course in 1927, and it has been of great value to me; but your new Master Calculator is the greatest discovery you have ever made, and the most valuable. It indicated top for March cotton at 4020 on September 8, 1952, and called for low at 3210 on January 12, 1953. March cotton sold at 3212 on January 12. That is plenty close for me."

The price of the Master Mathematical Calculator depends upon what courses you take in connection with it. It can be used on any commodity or on stock averages or individual stocks.

The Master Calculator can only be used with the Master Courses. It is not sold separate from the courses and cannot be used with the Mechanical Method.

We are making a special price to students who have taken the Master Courses on Stocks and Commodities. Please write if you are interested in the Master Calculator as we are having a supply made up and will reserve one for you.

COURSES OF INSTRUCTION BY CORRESPONDENCE OR PRIVATE INSTRUCTIONS

We have to develop different courses to fit the needs of different people. Busy men like Doctors, Lawyers and Engineers need a course that requires very little time to keep up every day to get market trend indications. People who have more time and who want to make speculation and investing in business need a different course. Large Business Institutions, of course, require a complete course covering everything. People in trade lines who have to purchase raw commodities need to be able to forecast the trend for several months in advance. We have special courses for people in these lines of business.

Course No. 1—SPECULATION A PROFITABLE PROFESSION. This is a new and up-to-date course completed in May, 1954. The course was gotten up principally to help people with small means to get a market education and start with a small capital which they can do and make a success if they follow the rules. This course for stocks is illustrated with 15 charts and you will receive one new chart, the *Dollar Trend*, which is much more accurate than the Dow-Jones Averages. This course on stocks is priced at $200.00 and it is not sold just to make a profit but to help the beginners get a start.

Course No. 2—THE MASTER FORECASTING COURSE ON STOCKS. This is a complete course and with this course you receive weekly and monthly high and low charts on individual stocks as well as the new chart, the *Dollar Trend*. The price of this course is $2,500.00.

COMMODITY COURSES: *Course No. 1*—SPECULATION A PROFITABLE PROFESSION. This course covers Soy Beans, Corn, Rye and Wheat. Examples are given which prove the rules and the charts show how the rules work. You receive complete set of rules and instructions and everything is made plain so that a beginner can understand it and make progress. The price of this course by correspondence is $200.00. With personal instruction $300.00.

Course No. 2—NEW TIME TREND INDICATOR. This is a more complete course than Course No. 1, but with this course you receive Course No. 1. This course covers all of the same commodities as covered in Course No. 1. The price of this course is $600.00 by correspondence or $800.00 with personal instructions. Suppose you buy Course No. 1 and pay $200.00 and later decide that you want Course No. 2: The $200.00 which you have paid can be applied on Course No. 2, and you would just pay $400.00 more for a correspondence course.

Course No. 1—COVERING COTTON, COFFEE, COCOA OR ANY OTHER COMMODITY, is $200.00 for each commodity.

Course No. 3—MASTER FORECASTING COURSE ON GRAINS, COTTON, COFFEE, LARD AND EGGS. With this course you receive a complete set of weekly and monthly high and low charts, also some daily charts. You receive two *Master Calculators* and other *Master Charts* and up-to-date *Timing Devices*. The price of this complete course by correspondence is $1,500. With personal instructions, $2,000.00.

GREAT MASTER COURSE—Covers 10 to 12 commodities, together with all the *Master Charts*, written rules and instructions and monthly high and low charts going back from 10 to 100 years. The price of this complete course with personal instructions is $5,000.00. The *Master Time Factor*, *Great Time Cycles*, *Master Charts* Nos. 9 and 12 all go with this course.

With all Master Courses we send you a mass-pressure chart calculated for one year in the future. This is free.

W. D. GANN FOUNDATION, INC.
P. O. Box 399, Shenandoah Station
Miami, Florida
W. D. Gann Address: 820 S. W. 26th Road, Miami, Florida

Certified Public Accountant report verifying W. D. Gann's record is printed below:

JOSEPH ZITTRER
CERTIFIED PUBLIC ACCOUNTANT
388 MINORCA AVENUE
CORAL GABLES, FLORIDA
TELEPHONE 8-5278

Mr. W. D. Gann   May 19, 1954
820 S. W. 26th Road
Miami, Fla.

Dear Mr. Gann:

I have read the typewritten proof of the booklet which you intend publishing in the near future. While reading same I had before me your file containing many of the original testimonial letters, newspaper clippings, brokers statements and other data referred to in your booklet.

While practical considerations forbid detailed research into a remarkable history which spans more than half a century, I have delved sufficiently into the evidence submitted to convince me of the authenticity of the historical information contained in your booklet.

Very truly yours,
JOS. ZITTRER
Certified Public Accountant

JZ:f

MASTER 360° CHART

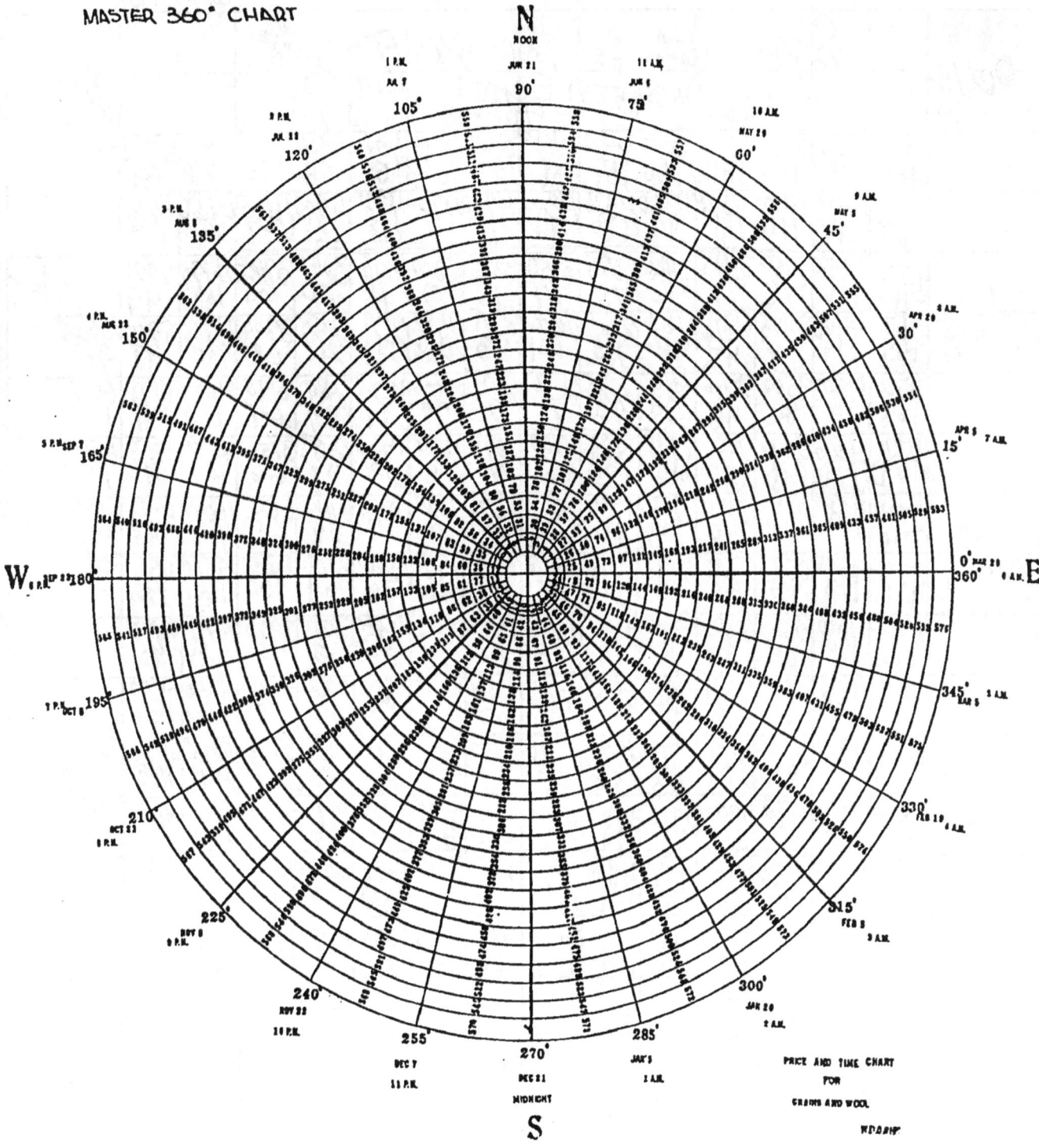

N
NOON

1 P.M.
AA 7
105°

JUN 21
90°

11 A.M.
JUN 6
75°

3 P.M.
JUL 11
120°

10 A.M.
MAY 20
60°

3 P.M.
AUG 8
135°

9 A.M.
MAY 5
45°

4 P.M.
AUG 23
150°

8 A.M.
APR 20
30°

5 P.M. SEP 7
165°

APR 5
15°   7 A.M.

W   SEP 23 180°

0° MAR 20
360°   6 A.M.   E

6 P.M. OCT 8 195°

345°
MAR 5
5 A.M.

210
OCT 23
8 P.M.

330°
FEB 19 4 A.M.

225
NOV 8
9 P.M.

315°
FEB 5
3 A.M.

240
NOV 22
10 P.M.

300°
JAN 20
2 A.M.

255
DEC 7
11 P.M.

270°
DEC 21
MIDNIGHT

285°
JAN 5
1 A.M.

PRICE AND TIME CHART
FOR
GRAINS AND WOOL

W.D.GANN

S

May 28, 1932

Eggs October low 510 May 28 1932

Net high 585 Sept 10 9 Aug 3.

Oct 15 135

5600 164	5575 163	5550 162	5525 161	5500 160	5475 159	5450 158	5425 157	5400 156	5375 155	5350 154	5325 153	5300 152	5275 151
5775 165	4425 116	4400 115	4375 114	4350 113	4325 112	4300 111	4275 110	4250 109	4225 108	4200 107	4175 106	4150 105	5250 150
5750 166	4450 118	3450 77	3425 76	3400 75	3375 74	3350 73	3325 72	3300 71	3275 70	3250 69	3225	4175 105	5225 149
5675 167	4475 119	3475 79	3450 47	3760 46	3625 45	3600 44	3575 43	3550 42	3525 41	3500 40	3700 68	4100 104	5200 148
5700 168	4600 172	3500 80	3775 48		43	3775	3700	3975 19	3450 39	3175 67	4075 103	5175 147	6575 199
5725 (169)	4575 (171)	3525 (8)	3760 (10)	(9)	(8)	3800 6	3650	3725 18	3475 38	3150 66	4050 102	5150 146	6550 198
5750 170	4550	3550 82	3760 50	20	1750 10	3750	1625 5	1425 17	3425 37	3125 65	4025 101	5175 145	6575 197/1932
Nov 29	5775 171	4575 173	3575 83	51	77	1775	1500	4000	1900 16	2400 36	3100 64	4000 100	5700 144	6500 196	3668
150	5800 172	4600 174	3600 84	78	12	1800	1675 13	1850 14	1875	2075 36	3475 63	5075 99	6475 143	195
5825 173	4625	3625 65	53	30	31	2300 32	2375 33	34	2850 62	3950 98	5050 142	6450 194
5850 174	4650	3650 86	54	55	56	57	58	59	60	61	3925 97	5075 141	6475 193	337 1/2
Dec 31	5875 175	4675 176	3675 87	3700 88	3725 89	3750 90	3775 91	3800 92	3825 93	3850 94	3875 95	3900 96	5000 140	6400 192	May 0
202 1/2	5900 176	4700 175	4725 124	4750 130	4775 131	4800 132	4825 133	4850 134	4875 135	4900 136	4925 137	4950 138	4975 139	6375 191
5925 177	5950 178	5975 179	6000 180	6125 161	6150 182	6175 183	6200 184	6225 185	6250 186	6275 187	6300 188	6375 189	6350 190

227 Jan 12

JAN 12

July 4

270 Feb 26

March 11

315 Dec 12

Cosmological Economics

The Masters Of Technical Analysis Series

The Masters of Technical Analysis Series brings together a collection of the most important classical and modern works on technical analysis and financial market forecasting. These classic works from the Golden Age of Technical Analysis were carefully selected by the late Dr. Jerome Baumring of the Investment Centre Bookstore in the 1980's, as representing the most valuable and important works in technical analysis ever written. They were included as the foundational source texts for his program in advanced financial market analysis and forecasting, and serve as the ideal foundation for any analyst seeking a thorough education in market theory and technical trading.

The Golden Age of technical analysis was a period from the early 1900's through the 1960's where the foundational theories of modern financial analysis were initially developed. The ideas and technologies developed during this fruitful period have formed the basis for most modern technical market theory, which is considered to be mostly a repetition or reworking of these past ideas and techniques developed by the Old Masters of the Golden Age. In these historical works can be found the timeless trading wisdom which has laid the foundation for all modern investment theory and literature. These techniques are as useful in today's markets as they were in the past, providing rare and valuable insights, tools and strategies that give the modern trader an edge over traders and investors that are unaware of these time honored tools.

Each quality reprint of these classical texts has been reproduced as an exact facsimile of the original text, maintaining the original layout, typeset, charts, and style of the author and time period, helping to preserve and communicate a sense of the feeling of the original work that a reproduction in modern format does not capture. Many of these rare works and courses were originally printed in only very small private editions or as correspondence courses, so that the originals were easily lost or destroyed over time. Our reproductions of these important source works have been printed on acid free paper and bound in a quality hardcover format that will compliment any trading library and help to preserve this important resource for generations to come.

The series is also currently being digitized and archived for permanent digital preservation by the Institute of Cosmological Economics, creating a searchable reference library of market wisdom accessible globally and available in new digital formats to keep the knowledge fresh and accessible through new devices and technology as we advance further into the information revolution. To see our full catalog of hardcover reprints, new publications, and digital editions please visit our website at www.CosmoEconomics.com.

- ❖ **Samuel Benner, An Ohio Farmer** - Benner's Prophecies - *Of Future Ups and Downs in Prices* - (1879)
- ❖ **Geo. W. Cole, La Marquette** - Graphs & Their Application to Speculation - (1936)
- ❖ **Frank Tubbs** - Tubbs' Stock Market Correspondence Course - (1944)
- ❖ **R. N. Elliot** - Collected Works of R. N. Elliot - *The Wave Principle. Nature's Law: The Secret of the Universe. "The Wave Principle": A Series of Articles Published in 1939.* - (1946)
- ❖ **Joseph A. Wyler** - Wyler Series on Stock Market Speculation - *Vol.1, The Application Of Scientific Principles To Stock Speculation. Vol.2, Trading And Trending* - (1960)
- ❖ **Edward Dewey** - How to Make a Cycles Analysis - *Correspondence Course in Advanced Cycle Analysis*- (1955)
- ❖ **Nikolai D. Kondratieff** - Long Waves In Economic Life - (1935)
- ❖ **Pickell & Daniel** - Pickell-Daniel Extension Course of Market Analysis - (1937)
- ❖ **Franklin Paul Jackson** - The I-S Method - *Individual Stock - Intermediate Swing* - (1972)
- ❖ **Richard Schabacker** - Technical Analysis & Stock Market Profits - (1930)
- ❖ **Richard Schabacker** - Stock Market Profits - (1934)
- ❖ **M. V. Woods** - Seven Studies In Stock Market Trading - (1943)
- ❖ **William Dunnigan** - Collected Works of William Dunnigan - *Gains in Grains. New Blueprints for Gains in Stocks & Grains; Barometers for Forecasting Stocks. One-Way Formula for Trading In Stocks & Commodities* - (1957)
- ❖ **Henry Ludwell Moore** - Collected Works of Henry Ludwell Moore - *Economic Cycles Their Law & Cause. Generating Economic Cycles. Forecasting The Yield of Cotton* - (1923)
- ❖ **Edwin S. Quinn** - Action - Reaction Signals - (1950)
- ❖ **Emil Schultheis** - Basic Trend Barometer - *A Long Term Stock Trend Study* - (1946)
- ❖ **Payson Todd** - The "Todd Theory" of Market Measurement & Price Projection - (1953)
- ❖ **Dr. Alexander Goulden** - Behind The Veil - (2010)
- ❖ **C. S. Johnson, C. P. A.** - A New Technique of Stock Market Forecasting - (1931)
- ❖ **William D. Gann** - The Collected Writings of W. D. Gann, Volume I - *Marketing Brochures, Interviews, Annual Forecasts & Trading Records* - (1909-1954)
- ❖ **William D. Gann** - The Collected Writings of W. D. Gann, Volume II - *The Master Time Factor: No. 3 Master Forecasting Method & Stock Market Forecasting Courses* - (1921-1954)
- ❖ **William D. Gann** - Collected Writings of W. D. Gann, Volume III - *Master Mathematical Formula & Calculators* - (1955)
- ❖ **William D. Gann** - Collected Writings of W. D. Gann, Volume IV - *The Complete Commodity Courses* - (1940)
- ❖ **William D. Gann** - Collected Writings of W. D. Gann, Volume V - *Introductory Stock Market Courses, Mechanical Methods, & Trend Indicators Courses* - (1935-1950)
- ❖ **William D. Gann** - Complete Collected Writings of W. D. Gann - In 6 Volumes - (1955)
- ❖ **Timothy Walker** - How To Trade Like W. D. Gann - *An Exploration of the Mechanical Trading Lesson on U. S. Steel* - (2014)
- ❖ **James P. Morton** - When to Sell to Assure Profits - (1926)
- ❖ **Daniele Prandelli** - The Polarity Factor System - *An Integrated Forecasting & Trading Strategy Inspired By W. D. Gann's Master Time Factor* - (2012)
- ❖ **Daniele Prandelli** - The Law Of Cause And Effect - *Creating A Planetary Price/Time Map Of Market Action Through Sympathetic Resonance* - (2010)
- ❖ **Perspectives, National Graphic Co.** - The Great Bull Market & Collapse - (1932)
- ❖ **Richard Martin** - An Introduction to Trend - Action - *A Scientific Method of Forecasting* - (1943)

- ❖ **George Bayer** - Money Investing In Stocks, Trading In Commodities, Or The Time Factors In The Stock Market - *The Art of Scientifically Detecting Direction & Distance of Swings* - (1937)
- ❖ **George Bayer** - The Egg of Columbus - (1942)
- ❖ **George Bayer** - Stock & Commodity Traders Hand-Book of Trend Determination - *Secrets of Forecasting Values, Especially Commodities, Including Stocks* - (1940)
- ❖ **George Bayer** - Gold Nuggets for Stock & Commodity Traders - (1941)
- ❖ **George Bayer** - Preview of Markets - *VOL. I, NOS. 1-10* - (1939)
- ❖ **George Bayer** - George Wollsten - Expert Stock & Grain Trader - (1946)
- ❖ **George Bayer** - The Collected Works of George Bayer - *9 Books In 2 Hardcover Volumes* - (1939)
- ❖ **Cliff Stewart** - Magic of Making Money in The Stock Market - (1951)
- ❖ **Dickson F. Watts** - Speculation as a Fine Art - *& Thoughts On Life* - (1865)
- ❖ **Henry Ansley** - I Like the Depression - (1932)
- ❖ **Henry Hall** - How Money is Made in Security Investment - *Or A Fortune At Fifty-Five* - (1908)
- ❖ **Dr. Jerome Baumring & Julius J. Nirenstein** - Gann Harmony: The Law of Vibration: The Complete Course Manuals & Lecture Notes - *The Complete Gann 1-9 Course Manuals. Compiled By Dr. Jerome Baumring With Notes On W. D. Gann's Hidden Material: The Complete Gann 1-9 Lecture Notes* - (1989)
- ❖ **Dr. Jerome Baumring** - Gann Harmony: The Law of Vibration. The Complete Course Manuals - *Course Manuals For Gann 1 Through Gann 9* - (1989)
- ❖ **Julius J. Nirenstein & Dr. Jerome Baumring** - Notes on W. D. Gann's Hidden Material: The Complete Lecture Notes - *Lecture Notes for Gann 1 through Gann 9* - (1989)
- ❖ **Alfred Friedman** - Lecture Notes from Baumring's Investment Centre Series - (1987)
- ❖ **B. Edlin** - Minor Swings of the Stock Market and their indications - (1924)
- ❖ **Henry Howard Harper** - The Psychology of Speculation - *The Human Element In Market Transactions* - (1926)
- ❖ **S. A. Nelson** - The ABC of Options & Arbitrage - (1904)
- ❖ **Daniel T. Ferrera** - The Gann Pyramid - *Square of Nine Essentials* - (2001)
- ❖ **Daniel T. Ferrera** - The Mysteries of Gann Analysis Unveiled! - *A Detailed Presentation of W. D. Gann's Technical Trading Principles* - (2001)
- ❖ **Daniel T. Ferrera** - Wheels Within Wheels – *The Art of Forecasting Financial Market Cycles* - (2002)
- ❖ **Daniel T. Ferrera** - W. D. Gann's Mass Pressure Forecasting Charts - (2004)
- ❖ **Daniel T. Ferrera** - The Keys to Successful Speculation - (2004)
- ❖ **Daniel T. Ferrera** - Spirals of Growth and Decay - *Exposing the Underlying Structure of Financial Markets* (2005)
- ❖ **Daniel T. Ferrera** – Gann for the Active Trader - *New Methods For Today's Markets* (2006)
- ❖ **Daniel T Ferrera** – Economic & Stock Market Forecasting – *W.D. Gann's Science of Cyclical Periodicity Sequencing* (2013)
- ❖ **Daniel T. Ferrera** - The Path of Least Resistance - *The Underlying Wisdom & Philosophy of W. D. Gann Elegantly Encoded in the Master Charts* - (2014)
- ❖ **Warren Hickernell** - What Makes Stock Market Prices - (1932)
- ❖ **William C. Moore (Market Expert)** - Wall Street - *Its Mysteries Revealed, Its Secrets Exposed.* - (1932)